Introduction to International Relations

Theory and Practice

Second Edition

JOYCE P. KAUFMAN
WHITTIER COLLEGE

ROWMAN & LITTLEFIELD
Lanham • Boulder • New York • London

Executive Editor: Susan McEachern
Assistant Editor: Rebeccah Shumaker
Senior Marketing Manager: Kim Lyons

Published by Rowman & Littlefield
A wholly owned subsidiary of The Rowman & Littlefield Publishing Group, Inc.
4501 Forbes Boulevard, Suite 200, Lanham, Maryland 20706
www.rowman.com

Unit A, Whitacre Mews, 26-34 Stannary Street, London SE11 4AB, United Kingdom

British Library Cataloguing in Publication Information Available

Library of Congress Cataloging-in-Publication Data

Names: Kaufman, Joyce P., author.
Title: Introduction to international relations : theory and practice / Joyce
  P. Kaufman, Whittier College.
Description: Second edition. | Lanham, Maryland : Rowman & Littlefield,
  [2018] | Includes bibliographical references and index.
Identifiers: LCCN 2017045210 (print) | LCCN 2017058157 (ebook) | ISBN
  9781538105382 (electronic) | ISBN 9781538105368 (cloth : alk. paper) |
  ISBN 9781538105375 (pbk. : alk. paper)
Subjects: LCSH: International relations—Philosophy.
Classification: LCC JZ1305 (ebook) | LCC JZ1305 .K37849 2018 (print) | DDC
  327—dc23
LC record available at https://lccn.loc.gov/2017045210

Contents

Preface to the Second Edition

As I was revising this book in the summer of 2017, the world was fraught with anxiety and uncertainty. Tensions between the United States and North Korea were rising amid a tweet storm by President Trump about "fire and fury" and U.S. weapons being "locked and loaded" in response to North Korea's missile tests. That escalation of the war of words and the potential for a major crisis as a result flies in the face of everything I know about the way in which foreign policy is supposed to be made and the role of negotiation and diplomacy in trying to deescalate a situation. But it is also clear that these are not "normal" times in terms of the political environment of the United States and the international community. This suggests to me the continuing importance of studying international relations and foreign policy, especially now in a period of turmoil.

I started the preface to the first edition of this text this way: "Understanding international relations (IR) is an important part of an undergraduate student's education, whether as a staple of a political science program, an introductory course in an international relations/international studies track, a class on globalization, or simply as a guide to better understand the world in which he or she lives. Yet, increasingly, international relations texts are chock full of details about theories and ideas that are abstract and seen as removed from reality rather than helping the student apply the theories to the 'real world.'" I continue to believe that this is true, perhaps more so now than previously, especially if we are to be able to think critically about what is going on around us and try to understand the impact of policy decisions in the short but also longer term.

This edition of the text is organized much as the first edition, around levels of analysis and the major theories and actors that govern the field of international relations. However, I have also updated the book to include a section on the role of the media as a nonstate actor that has taken an increasingly important part in the current political discourse. I included another section on cyberterrorism as a new threat to international security. And I have updated all three cases in chapter 6 as well as including a fourth case on China and its role as a regional hegemon, including what that might mean to the balance of power in Asia if not internationally. I think that the result is an updated study of the current international environment.

Even with the additions, my goal has remained to keep the text succinct and clear and to highlight the main points. It is up to any faculty member who uses this text to augment it with any sources that he or she thinks are appropriate. It is also important to note that while everything in this revised version of the text was current as of the end of August 2017, things can change quickly as events unfold. I often use newspaper articles clipped the day of class to bring in current events and as a way of reminding students that what they are studying has "real world" applications.

As I was updating this edition, I was helped immeasurably by Russell De La Rosa (Whittier College, 2017). As an undergraduate at Whittier College, Russell was in both my Introduction to International Relations class (PLSC 220) and my Seminar in International Relations (PLSC 420). As a student who had to use the first edition of this book as his basic text in PLSC 220, which was also the foundation for much of what I did in the seminar, Russell's insights were very helpful, as was his research in updating aspects of the volume. And our weekly conversations about the book, about questions that he had and about parts of the book that were not clear to him as a student, helped to clarify many of the ideas for me as I was revising. I hope that the result is a stronger volume that will be more helpful to students. Since this book is written for undergraduates, having his input was very helpful, and I owe Russell a great deal for the care and consideration he put into this task.

I also owe my thanks to the reviewers who responded to the questionnaire about the book. As faculty members who also use the book in their own classes, I appreciated their thoughts and feedback and think that the book is more complete because of their suggestions. My own foundations in international relations came from two former professors, my undergraduate adviser at NYU, Robert Burrowes, and my graduate adviser at the University of Maryland, Jonathan Wilkenfeld. I owe each of them a huge debt for helping direct and mentor me throughout my career, and I value the friendship with each of them that continues to this day.

As usual, I did most of my writing during the summer while I was at our home in the Eastern Sierra. My ability to get away and work on this text was made possible in no small measure by the hard work of the staff of the Center for Engagement with Communities (CEC) at Whittier College who were able to keep things moving forward even with my absence. Associate Director Gina Di Pierro; program coordinators Kenneth Jimenez, Diana Yoon, and Katya Murillo; and program manager (and special "councilor") Patricia Pint all knew what they had to do and took charge, thereby ensuring that the summer programs ran smoothly, as did the preparations for the fall. Special thanks go to my administrative assistant, Marilyn Chavez, who not only does a superb job of managing the office but also of making sure that there was a regular flow of information to me so that I was apprised of the important things going on, but who also kept the minutia off my plate. I could not do what I do without their hard work and dedication.

My tennis and golf friends in the Eastern Sierra helped provide a much-needed balance between thinking and writing and play. I would not be as productive if I did not have that balance, for which I am very grateful.

My deepest thanks also to my editor at Rowman & Littlefield, Susan McEachern. By coincidence, my husband, Robert Marks, and I have worked with Susan on our various book projects for many years, and she has become far more than an editor, but a good friend. This project would not have moved forward without her prodding and her insistence that it is time for a second edition. Also at Rowman & Littlefield, thanks to assistant editor Rebeccah Shumaker, who responded to all my questions promptly, no matter how insignificant. And thanks to production editor Alden Perkins, with whom I have worked before, and copy editor Matt Evans. All responded to questions and comments promptly, which made the various stages moving to publication much easier. The excellent feedback and input of all involved notwithstanding, any errors or omissions are my responsibility.

Finally, no preface would be complete without thanking the person who really started me on the path to understanding the importance and role of short, concise texts and of writing in my "teaching voice." My husband and colleague Robert Marks has been a role model in many ways for how to teach and write for undergraduates, as well as everything else he is to me. Those roles are too numerous to elaborate on here—but he knows what they are.

Even though Stanton was not with us this summer, he was with me in spirit. He is deeply missed.

Joyce P. Kaufman

1

Introduction

International Relations in a Globalized World

On September 11, 2001, why did nineteen men affiliated with the terrorist group al-Qaeda hijack four planes and attack the twin towers of the World Trade Center in New York and the Pentagon outside Washington, D.C., and attempt to crash the fourth one perhaps into the White House or the Capitol? Who were these men, and what were their motives? What did they hope to gain from this attack, and did they achieve their ends?

Almost ten years later, in May 2011, U.S. Navy special forces (SEALs) attacked a compound in Abbottabad, Pakistan, killing Osama bin Laden. Abbottabad is home to a large Pakistani military base and a military academy of the Pakistani army. Pakistan, a supposed ally of the United States in the fight against al-Qaeda, was not informed of the raid in advance. Furthermore, following the raid, serious questions emerged about what the Pakistani military knew—or did not know—about who lived in that compound. If Pakistan was aware of bin Laden's whereabouts in the country, shouldn't they have notified the United States, an ally? How could bin Laden, a wanted criminal, have lived within a mile of Pakistani military forces for so long undetected? Should the United States have notified its alleged ally prior to the raid? And did President Obama make the correct decision in authorizing the raid and then bin Laden's burial at sea immediately after? Who else was involved in these decisions?

Here is another set of questions to ponder that might strike a little closer to home. How does Wal-Mart, one of the largest corporations in the world, influence policy not only in the United States but in the countries in which it has factories? What is the trade-off between allowing you, the consumer, to purchase goods at a relatively low price if that possibly comes at the cost of exploiting the laborers who produce those goods? Or, looking at it another way, is the labor really exploited when working for Wal-Mart in a factory in Bangladesh is the difference between a worker being able to put food on the table and starving? How can a company, which exists outside the bounds of government, have so much power?

These are a few examples of the questions that we ponder and study in the field of international relations.

WHY INTERNATIONAL RELATIONS IS IMPORTANT

International relations (IR) as a field of study deals with decisions that are made within a country that have implications for relationships outside the borders of that country. But it also asks a number of other important questions: Who makes those decisions? Why? How are they made? Who is affected by them? And what are the likely responses to those decisions? But what makes the study of international relations especially complex is the range of actors who could be involved with answering any and all aspects of these questions.

One of the really important questions to ask as you begin this study is, what does IR have to do with me personally? These seem like really big questions that are removed from most of us. But the reality is that they are not. Every time a country decides to go to war, it has implications for what happens not only to the people in that country but also in other countries as well. For example, when President George W. Bush authorized the invasion of Afghanistan in October 2001 in retaliation for the September 11 attacks, he committed the U.S. military. That meant ensuring that there were enough U.S. military forces available to fight that war. But it also meant supplying the military for that invasion, which resulted in more money being required for the Defense Department. Tax money spent for the military cannot be spent for other things, such as education; this is known as "guns versus butter." Furthermore, little did anyone know at that time that, as of this writing in 2017, that war would continue, making it the longest war the United States has been involved in, and so those same choices and trade-offs have continued for almost two decades, with no end in sight. So, directly or indirectly, that decision affected and will continue to affect you.

Other countries are also affected by terrorist attacks and therefore have a vested interest in confronting al-Qaeda and, more recently, a group like ISIS.[1] It is therefore necessary to round up other countries to work with the United States in Afghanistan so that the United States does not have to bear the burden alone. That is the role of *alliances*, specifically bringing in other countries to work together in pursuit of common goals. So other countries, and the people within them, were affected by the decision made by President Bush. And, clearly, so were the people of Afghanistan.

Let's look at another case. The economic instability in Europe in 2011 and 2012 and the decision of the euro zone to bail out Greece and Spain might seem irrelevant to you, but in a world in which countries are interdependent, economic instability in Europe can affect the U.S. economic system. Entities in the United States own European debt just as China owns U.S. debt. The possibility that there could be a default on that debt in Europe could panic the people in the United States who own the debt, which in turn could lead to more economic uncertainty in this country. Similarly, there are some in the United States who are concerned about how much U.S. debt China owns. Does that mean that China "owns" parts of the United States?

What about the "Brexit" vote, the decision that the people of the United Kingdom made in June 2016 to leave the European Union (EU)? That seems like a decision that affects the twenty-eight countries of the EU, so why is it important to those of us in the United States and why should we care? The EU is the world's largest trading bloc, and the United States is its main trading partner. Thus, any disruption to the economic situation of the EU will have a direct impact on the economy of the United States and, indirectly, on each of us. The Brexit vote came at a time when the Obama administration was trying to negotiate a major Transatlantic Trade and Investment Partnership (TTIP) with the EU that would, in theory, bolster trade and economic relations between the United States and the EU even more. What is not clear is what the impact of Brexit will be on this negotiation. Similarly, the start of the Trump administration in the United States with its "America First" policy and its promise to revisit all major trade agreements raises questions about the U.S. commitment to a multilateral trade agreement at this time. The bottom line here is that after years of ongoing negotiations to move toward an agreement, a number of events, both domestic and international, have interrupted the flow of those negotiations. Hence, how can countries ever negotiate in good faith if the domestic political situation could totally disrupt years of progress?

These questions are all a function of an interdependent globalized world that, in some ways, brings countries closer together. But they also illustrate the dangers of that close relationship, where uncertainty or change in government in one country or region can have a marked impact on another.

This intersection of politics and economics is becoming more prominent in our globalized world and is necessary to help us understand how and why changes occur in the distribution of states' wealth, power, and relationships. That particular subfield of international relations is known as *international political economy*, and while not a particular focus of this introduction to the field of international relations, it is an area that it is important to understand if you are to get the "big picture."

The bottom line is that international relations studies a range of difficult issues that generate complex questions, and if we are ever going to attempt to answer them, we need to find a way to simplify the reality so that we can focus on one aspect of the problem at a time. For example, in the case of September 11, if we want to know more about the hijackers, we can focus on the men who acted together as part of a terrorist group that sought to inflict damage on the United States. Or, put into IR terms, we are looking at the impact that a nonstate actor (al-Qaeda) had on an important nation-state (the United States) in order to influence U.S. policy in some way.

Or we can look at it another way that would also provide some explanation for the actions of 9/11. In this case we can start by identifying the nineteen men as individual actors who were part of a larger group and agreed to engage in a suicide mission. If we were to take that approach, our focus would be on the men as the actors and on what motivated them to act as they did. This would be a smaller or more microlevel response.

Or we can approach it in yet another way: We can ask why Osama bin Laden, as the leader of al-Qaeda, wanted to inflict damage on the United States, which he saw as the ideological enemy of all that he believed in. In that case, our focus would be on an individual leader who made decisions that had an impact on many other people. This is an even smaller or more micro level—that of a single individual.

No one of these approaches is a right or wrong way to begin to understand the complexity of the 9/11 attacks. But if we take them apart, we can focus on different aspects of the attacks that allow us to begin to answer some of these questions. When we put them together, we can get a more complete picture of the various actors involved (bin Laden, al-Qaeda, the nineteen hijackers), what the motives of each of them were, the decisions that each made, and the outcome of their decisions.

Conversely, we can look at the same event from the perspective of the United States, the country that was attacked. We can focus on the options available to then-president George W. Bush as the primary decision maker and on what he ultimately decided to do (the micro or *individual* level). We can concentrate on Congress and the support that Congress gave to President Bush when he asked for authorization to use military force (*government* level). We can focus on the role of the American public as it (as a whole) tried to understand what happened and why (the level of *American society*). And we can look at the United States acting as if it were a single entity, which weighed options and then responded. That response committed the United States to a course of action. The focus on the United States as a whole is the largest and most macrolevel response, that of a country (or *nation-state*, in IR terms). Again, as in the above case, each of these approaches allows us to focus on some aspect of the U.S. response to the attack; taken together, they give us a more complete picture of who made the decisions, how they were made, and what they meant for the United States.

By breaking one event, in this case the 9/11 attack, into these smaller pieces, it is possible to answer questions about the event that might seem way too large to answer as a whole. In other words, we are breaking a complex event into its component pieces while holding the other parts aside so that we can arrive at some answers that will help us understand the event as a whole.

Similarly, we can look at different aspects of the events to determine the primary actor or actors who made the decisions. This can range from an individual (e.g., bin Laden or Bush) to the government (Congress and/or the executive branch of the United States), the public as a whole, or even the nation. This levels-of-analysis approach, then, allows us to pick the pieces apart in order to analyze them one at a time.

And we can do this with virtually all of the examples given above, or almost any other example you can think of. For example, in the case of the attack on the bin Laden compound, we can focus on an individual—President Obama as the primary decision maker, and his national security team—to try to understand the processes that led to the decisions not only to attack but also to leave Pakistan uninformed. This will help us understand the inputs or factors that led to the decision that was ultimately made. We can focus on the nation-state level and the interaction between the United States and Pakistan as a way to understand more about this alliance and its weaknesses. And we can focus on the perceptions of the American public as they reacted to the news of bin Laden's death.

In the Wal-Mart case noted above, we can study and try to understand the impact of this corporation from the point of view of the American consumer (individual or culture/society), the workers who produce the goods (individual), or the corporation itself and its relationship to the nations in which it is based (nation-state). Or we can look at the role that Wal-Mart plays in influencing or affecting the economies of the various countries in which it has a role (global or international level). Focusing on each of these levels of actors/analysis gives a different picture of the question; when taken together, they allow us to understand the whole.

We can look at the Brexit vote and ask what the outcome of that vote means for the policies of the UK (the individual prime minister, in this case, then–prime minister David Cameron, resigned as a result of the vote, to be replaced by Theresa May), what it means for the people of the UK (society), and what it means for the other members of the EU and for their trading partners, such as the United States (nation-state). Or we can look at a change in the government, for example, the election of President Trump following eight years of Obama (individual and government), and ask how that will alter the perceptions other countries have of the United States and how those perceptions will be translated into policy decisions at the nation-state level.

This short overview should help you understand how we approach some of these big questions in IR—and how we can answer them by identifying the various actors and thereby simplifying the analysis. We will describe the levels of analysis in more detail later, but you should now see why this approach is so important.

Why Study IR?

Traditionally, international relations is the most macro level of all the subfields of political science, as the international system and the actors that make up that system are the basic units of analysis. Rather than looking at the specific political processes within nation-states (such as the study of American government) or across different political systems (which is comparative politics), IR looks at the ways in which decisions made within a country affect that country's relationships with other countries or nation-states. The focus remains on the interaction between countries or among countries and other actors in the international system, including nonstate actors such as multinational corporations (MNCs), international organizations (IOs), and nongovernmental organizations (NGOs). It also looks at the impact of these macrolevel decisions on the various actors who exist within the nation-state and how they in turn affect these major decisions. Hence, IR looks at who makes the decisions (from the role of the government to the individual decision maker) and how those decisions then affect the people, society, culture, or even individuals within the nation-state or other nation-states. In short, IR looks at "big picture" questions.

We live in a world today in which nation-states are not only interrelated and interdependent, but in which nonstate actors have also emerged as major players, as noted in the example above. Clearly, terrorist groups such as al-Qaeda and more recently ISIS have affected the behavior of states, not only as a response to actions that the group has actually perpetrated, but in anticipation of what the group *might* do. If you have gotten on a plane recently and at the airport had to take your shoes off for security and put your resealable plastic bag with shampoo and toothpaste in it through the X-ray machine, you have seen the increased security designed to prevent a terrorist action. In other words, policy is made not just based on what did happen but what *might* happen.

The presence of nonstate actors has tossed on their head many of the questions that have guided traditional IR. Nowhere is this seen more dramatically than in the case of ISIS, a terrorist group that crosses a number of state borders, is clearly tied to an ideology and culture, has taken actions against a number of nation-states, and has in turn evoked a response from those nation-states. Yet who are these countries fighting? Is it possible to "declare war," traditionally the purview of the nation-state, on a nonstate actor? If so, doesn't that require violating the sanctity of a nation-state in order to attack a group that exists within its borders?

In addition to terrorist groups, other nonstate actors play a critical role in affecting or influencing the decisions made by various actors in the international system. Multinational corporations have become major players in the international system, and because they straddle the boundaries of many countries, they have some influence on them as well as on the international system as a whole. Again, going back to the example used above, where and how does the levels-of-analysis approach account for the role of an MNC such as Wal-Mart? Understanding this, and the impact that a major MNC like Wal-Mart has on the policies of various countries with which it does or has business, will help us see more clearly the impact of globalization.

A series of Pulitzer Prize–winning articles published in the *Los Angeles Times* in November 2003 clearly describe the impact that MNCs such as Wal-Mart can have on a nation-state, society, culture, and even individuals as consumers—but also on the people who produce the goods that Wal-Mart sells.[2] Rather than taking a position or making a judgment, articles such as these point out the power that an MNC can have and the dangers that come with corporations that seem to exist outside the boundaries of traditional and established international law. The main point is that in a world in which economic power equals political power, corporations like Wal-Mart, ExxonMobil, Shell Oil, and Toyota all have power. Yet, in many ways, they exist outside the reach of any single nation-state, and it can be difficult to hold them accountable. Questions and issues surrounding the role of MNCs, which are an integral part of international relations today, are discussed in more detail in chapter 5.

International organizations are also important actors. In addition to the United Nations, regional organizations such as the European Union take on power internationally that is far greater than the power that any single member country would wield. But the integration and desire to create a single foreign, defense, and/or monetary policy for the group that comes with organizations such as the EU also brings with it a challenge to the very notion of sovereignty that is central to the essence of any nation-state. It was the perception of that challenge to British sovereignty by decisions made by the EU that provoked the Brexit vote.

Understanding how to reconcile the apparently contradictory conflicts of integration and sovereignty is another aspect of international relations. But it is even more important to understand the role that international organizations in general play in a globalized world. We will discuss all these concepts in more detail later in this book.

Many of these examples point out one of the flaws of the traditional levels-of-analysis approach to international relations. Specifically, the field of international relations is premised on the idea that the nation-state is the primary actor, meaning that it is state centered or *state-centric*. But the contemporary international system has seen the emergence of a host of nonstate actors, all of which play a role in what happens in international relations. Yet they exist outside the traditional levels of analysis that guide most international relations theory. Therefore, one of the dilemmas facing those of us who study IR is how to account for those nonstate actors; more specifically, what framework can we use that incorporates them as major players in the international system? Doing so will allow us to answer an expanded range of questions about what is going on in the world today.

Just as there has been a growth of nonstate actors that have called into question some of the basic approaches to IR, the newer theoretical frameworks seek to account for the role of these actors and the changing nature of the international system. For example, *constructivists* argue for the need to take variables such as identity and other socially constructed realities into account in order to better explain the decisions made in the contemporary international system. *Feminist IR theorists* also discount the centrality of the traditional patriarchal/hierarchal assumptions about decision making in order to focus on the role played by women and other actors in the decisions that are made (albeit often an indirect one), but without whose presence the decisions would not be implemented successfully. For example, could a country go to war to protect the "mother country" without the symbolism of women? In thinking about broad IR decisions, feminist writers in the field also tell us about the need to study those within the country who are most affected by the decisions that are made. Women and children are the ones most removed from foreign policy decision making, and yet they are often directly affected by the results of those decisions.

Raised above are a number of prominent and real questions that have been prompted by recent events, and yet, technically, international relations has no set framework for responding to these questions. Or, when it does, the framework is often limited and inadequate. This does not in any way suggest that the traditional approaches can or should be rejected. Rather, starting with and trying to understand the complexity of the world as it currently exists will give you some relevant and current examples to grapple with as you try to define a framework appropriate for dealing with these questions.

While the levels-of-analysis framework provides the guiding structure for this short volume, grappling with the need for the emergence of a new theoretical framework or even a paradigm shift that addresses the role of nonstate actors and a globalized world in which nation-states and nonstate actors interact regularly is not a trivial exercise. Just as IR scholar and realist theorist Hans Morgenthau[3] proposed in 1948 to recast our understanding of international relations so that it is focused on power, so too we now need to rethink the larger international system and broaden our understanding of how to address nonstate actors and the role that they play in a globalized world. Doing so will illustrate the importance of having a theoretical framework that is appropriate for the realities of the twenty-first century.

IR as a Field of Study

The main point made thus far is that by simplifying an otherwise complex situation, we can start finding answers to these often difficult and challenging questions. That is why the study of international relations is such an important part of understanding our world today. It provides a theoretical framework that allows us to simplify the complexity by breaking the component pieces apart, identifying the relevant actors, understanding their approaches, and drawing conclusions that help us answer these questions. And it also helps us understand what assumptions we need to make about the behavior of individuals, groups, and nations in order to answer those questions.

As you will see, there are advantages to the theoretical approaches outlined in the field of IR, but also disadvantages. The field itself really emerged after World War I, when sovereign nation-states eclipsed monarchies and empires as the primary actors.[4] Thus, the field tends to be very state-centric, assuming that the traditional nation-state is—and will be—the primary actor. But as the examples of ISIS and Wal-Mart show, nonstate actors have emerged as major players in the international system in the twentieth and certainly the twenty-first century. To some extent, the emergence of nonstate actors has changed the field. The traditional model has little room for other than nation-states, the societies that make up those states, and the people and governments who lead them. Does that mean that we need to throw out the old models? Absolutely not! They can still help guide our approaches both to asking questions and answering them. But now we need to do so with an awareness of the limitations of those same theoretical approaches and models.

While international relations theory still relies heavily on the basic theoretical paradigms (realism, liberalism, and constructivism, for example, to be explored in more detail in the next chapter), there has been a proliferation of other theoretical approaches. These all have some merit, although they might appear to be a bit esoteric to someone who is trying to understand basic questions, such as why there is so much war and conflict, or why there was a global economic crisis. In fact, one of the hardest parts of studying international relations is drawing the distinction between learning the way things are supposed to operate in theory and using that theory to understand how they actually do operate. For example, why do countries behave as they do? Why do some societies rise up against a leader, as was the case in Tunisia, Libya, and Egypt early in 2011, and what prompted them to do so after years of relative silence? Why have the "Arab Spring" revolts that were settled peacefully in those countries led to a protracted and bloody civil war in Syria? Thus, the real dilemma for the student trying to understand international relations comes in trying to apply all that theory to real-world questions.

In order to be able to do this—that is, to apply the theory to an understanding of real-world issues or problems—it is necessary to have not only a basic grounding in the theory but also an approach that will help guide us through the complexity of the real world. That is what this book will help define.

The Levels-of-Analysis Framework

Levels of analysis will become the overarching framework as we begin to understand international relations. Levels of analysis "presumes that decisions are made at different and distinct levels, that is, from a fairly micro-level, such as the role of an individual decision maker (who is usually male), to society and culture, and then becoming more macro-level, moving to the nation and finally the international system."[5] Another underlying assumption is that each level exists fairly independently, with little interaction between or across levels.[6] While that allows us to arrive at a model that helps us with our analysis of a particular situation, the reality often belies that assumption. Events that take place at one given level of analysis have the potential to impact other levels. For example, a president or prime minister can move a nation to war, which in turn has an impact on the society and the individuals within it. And while the levels of analysis can provide an important guiding framework, the limitations of the approach must also be noted; we have alluded to them already and will discuss them in more detail in the next chapter.

Briefly, though, because of its emphasis on the nation-state, the framework does not really have a place for nonstate actors or even supranational organizations such as the United Nations. Rather, it assumes that all actors within the international system are nation-states, with a defined leader/decision maker who heads a government, and that decisions are tied to the values and goals of the culture and the society. Collectively, all of these make up the nation-state. As seen above, the Wal-Mart and al-Qaeda/ISIS examples point out quickly the flaws in this approach. Even with its limitations, though, levels of analysis provides a clean, unifying model for approaching international relations and is a useful tool—as long as we remain clear about its weaknesses.

The levels-of-analysis framework allows us to ask who or what we will be focusing on as we try to get answers to some of our questions. In many ways, the approach is somewhat circular. The questions we ask will determine the appropriate level of analysis that will be our focal point. But it does allow us to focus on one level at a time while holding the others constant, thereby allowing us to simplify the approach we are taking.

Broad Theoretical Perspectives

From a theoretical perspective, *realism* (both classical and neostructural/structural) is the bread and butter of basic IR theory. It puts the state firmly at the center of our analysis, and it then puts states' actions into terms of power and balance of power. This is fairly easy to understand intuitively, and there are numerous examples of applications of the theory. Furthermore, this approach is grounded in history. But again, it is very state centered, which raises questions when we try to apply it to the world today.

Since the end of the Cold War especially, a plethora of new theoretical approaches have either emerged or gained prominence in order to explain what is and what has been taking place in the international system. *Liberalism* and *constructivism* are two such approaches, both of which focus on different levels of analysis in order to better describe and explain the behavior of the international system. Where constructivist theorists focus on social structures both within and outside states and the impact that these have on states' behaviors, liberal theorists make other assumptions about what drives a state's behavior that are more normative (or what "should be") in approach. Note that in this case, *liberal* does not refer to an ideological perspective (versus *conservative*) but to a particular theoretical approach.

Growing from the desire to integrate women—their roles in the international system and the impact on women of political decisions made at various levels—another approach was born; feminist international relations theory not only provides a critique of the existing theoretical approaches but also offers an alternative that looks at international relations through gender-sensitive lenses.[7] As you will see, feminist theory is featured prominently throughout this book. I am not trying to proselytize; rather, my own research has highlighted the importance of looking at some of the basic questions in the field with gender-sensitive lenses in order to get at more complete answers to the questions. In fact, feminist IR theorists argue that unless you look at all the actors who are involved with or are affected by a decision, it is impossible to get the complete picture. This is a very different way to approach the study of international relations. While I try not to privilege one theoretical approach over another, I do believe that the feminist perspective is valuable for posing different questions and positing answers regarding international relations and therefore deserves to be included in our study of IR theories.

It is important to note that, although the theories included here are often depicted as competing with one another to offer the "best" explanation for why countries behave as they do, an alternative model would be to look at them as offering complementary explanations depending on the questions asked and the level of focus. Thus, it is not necessary to assume that one must take a particular theory as the single guiding framework. Rather, it is possible and sometimes beneficial to move between and among theories and levels of analysis, depending on the question or focus of the inquiry.

As we continue our discussion of IR theories, it is also important to remember that in this field, a theory cannot be tested as it is in the sciences. We cannot hold one part of the world constant while we test another, as we would do in a laboratory. Rather, in the field of IR our laboratory is the world, and we do our best to approximate the variables so that we can describe, explain, and predict. Some political scientists even in IR use mathematical models as a way to improve our explanatory power. But the main point is that the world we deal with is complex and full of uncertainties, and our job is to try to describe and explain events that occurred and why. Theory can help us do that.

An example can best illustrate what is meant by all of this. The first Persian Gulf War in 1991 was an example of a coalition of the willing, which involved a group of countries coming together to use military force against Saddam Hussein. Iraq had invaded Kuwait, an ally of the United States, and the first President Bush (George H. W. Bush) worked with the United Nations and a group of countries to apply political pressure, and later the use of military force, to get Iraq to withdraw from Kuwait. From a *realist* perspective, this is an example of a group of countries uniting to use their collective power (military and political) to counter the actions of a single state, Iraq. From that perspective, power triumphed and helps us explain the event.

But this same case can be examined from other theoretical perspectives. For example, *liberal* theorists might argue that this is a case of countries working together to achieve a common goal. They worked first within the framework of the United Nations to try to bring about a peaceful settlement of the issue through negotiation. When that failed, countries cooperated to achieve a particular end, which was to get Iraq to withdraw from Kuwait. From that theoretical point of view, the important thing to consider is the idea of cooperation, rather than conflict or power as we saw in the realist approach. Here the emphasis is on how countries could and did work together to achieve a common goal, rather than the assertion of military power.

The *constructivists* would focus more on the individual leaders, as well as the social and cultural constructs of the states and societies involved. So a constructivist might ask what Saddam Hussein wanted to accomplish given his role, the countries with which he interacted, and the political structure of Iraq—and then, given all that, try to understand the responses of the coalition partners. Or, from the other side, a constructivist might ask how President Bush's perceptions helped him determine what responses to take in this case. The constructivists do not ignore the central role of the state but rather put the state and the leaders into the broader social and political constructs that led to the particular processes and decisions that we are studying.

The *feminists* would ask who made the various decisions, from Hussein's decision to invade Kuwait to the responses of the United States and other countries to employ military force, but they would also ask who was most affected by those decisions. What role did the people of Iraq or Kuwait or the United States play, and how did the decisions made by their respective leaders affect them and their society?

Each of these theoretical examples also relies on a different set of assumptions and focuses on a different level of analysis. When viewed separately, they allow us to explain some portion of the event in great detail; taken together, they can give us a more complete picture of the entire event.

Clearly, it is important that students of IR understand the role of theory and how theory and the basic paradigms that exist in the field guide our understanding of international relations. Similarly, it is important to understand circumstances under which the existing theories don't explain events adequately, let alone predict what might happen in the future. The role of the major theories will be woven throughout each of the chapters in this book and will provide an important unifying theme throughout the narrative. Each of the major theories offers some explanation as to why countries behave as they do. In addition, all rely heavily on the notion of levels of analysis to help frame the approach.

This concise text takes as its starting point a discussion of the theoretical frameworks that are the foundation of current international relations. The book draws on and explicates the traditional international relations theories, but it also makes a place for understanding the areas that lie outside of or cannot be explained by those approaches. Although levels of analysis will be the primary unifying force, one of the strengths of the book is addressing the weaknesses of this approach in understanding the contemporary international system—that is, a globalized world. Integrated throughout the text are applications of the theories so that students like you can understand that learning the theories will actually help you better understand the "real world." That in turn will help you make informed decisions about issues pertaining to current international events.

INTERNATIONAL RELATIONS IN A GLOBALIZED WORLD

In this chapter, we begin with a very broad overview of what studying international relations means in a world that is globalized. In contrast to the world of nation-states, upon which most of IR was premised, globalization offers challenges that come with understanding a world in which those states and even nonstate actors are interconnected. But before we can begin to address globalization, we need to define the fundamental actor in the international system: the nation-state. (This idea will be developed in even more detail in chapter 3, where the focus is on the nation-state level of analysis.)

The Concept of the Nation-State

This concept is two-pronged: the *nation*, which is a group of people with similar background, culture, ethnicity, and language who share common values, and the *state*, which is an entity with a defined border under the rule of a government that is accepted by the people. The concept of the nation-state originated in Europe and can be traced to the Treaty of Westphalia (or Peace of Westphalia), which ended the Thirty Years' War in 1648.[8] Along with the emergence of the nation-state, the Treaty of Westphalia also specified a governmental order *within* each of the new states, as well as the relationship among them. Paramount among the concepts that emerged is that of *sovereignty*, which means that within a given territory, the government is the single legitimate authority, and no external power has the right to intervene in actions that take place within national borders. Within the past few decades, since the Cold War ended, some governments seem to have abrogated their right to protect their own peoples—for example, either committing or permitting acts of genocide and ethnic cleansing to take place. These actions have called into question the concept of sovereignty, as other countries' governments have debated when or whether it is appropriate to intervene to protect basic human rights, even if it means violating a state's sovereignty. We are going to explore these concepts in more detail in a later chapter, but until then, it is important to get the fundamentals.

Forces of Integration, Disintegration, and Self-Determination

Until the end of the Cold War, which fostered the era of globalization,[9] most of international relations was based on and/or tied to relationships between and among nation-states and the assumption that each state is a sovereign entity. However, that changed after 1991, when the prevailing patterns of international relations shifted. No longer were relations between and among countries tied to the United States and the Soviet Union—"West" versus "East." In fact, without the dynamics of the two superpowers, relations between and among countries became far more fluid. Rather than a world of discrete nation-states competing with one another for power, which was the old order, the globalized world that we see today is characterized by the integration of nation-states into larger regional blocs, such as the European Union, that are developing common policies not only on economic issues but increasingly on issues of foreign policy and security. While this does not suggest that the era of sovereign nation-states is over, it does suggest that countries believe that they can benefit from cooperating rather than competing with one another. In terms of IR theory, this might suggest acknowledging the primacy of liberal thought at the expense of realism.

Similarly, while some countries have been working together to pursue common policies, others have been dividing into component parts as the various "nations" within the states seek self-determination—the desire to be recognized as a nation and to be able to govern themselves. Thus, we see the peaceful breakup of Czechoslovakia into two component pieces (the Czech Republic and Slovakia) and the bloody disintegration of Yugoslavia into six republics, each of which has become an independent country. In contrast, the Palestinians are a stateless people who seek to create their own state with defined borders and a government that is sovereign. The Kurds, a distinct ethnic group who possess their own language, traditions, and lifestyle and account for substantial communities in Iraq, Turkey, Syria, and Iran, seek to create a formal country of "Kurdistan" that will guarantee them their sovereignty free from the strictures of another state. More recently, we have seen the country of Sudan divided into two parts—Sudan and South Sudan—following a referendum after a peace treaty ended a decades-long civil war. However, that peace has not lasted, and the country continues to face civil and ethnic violence. The implosion of the Soviet Union in 1991 led to the creation of fifteen countries, all of which had been "constituent republics" of the larger group (see map 1.1). While the initial breakup was relatively peaceful, conflicts remain, leading to bloody wars and terrorist attacks regarding the status of Chechnya and subsequently the status of other areas of the Caucasus. Thus, as recent history has shown, it is not that easy to create a new nation-state. In other words, being a nation does not necessarily mean that there is justification for a state or that the outside world will recognize that state, nor that the formal creation of a state will result in peace.

Many would argue that none of these changes—forces of integration and disintegration, desire for self-determination, and so on—would have been possible were it not for the end of the Cold War. In fact, the Cold War, which dominated international relations from the end of World War II until the unification of Germany (1990) and the breakup of the Soviet Union (1991), can be seen as critical to providing a stabilizing framework for nations' interactions. The ongoing threat of nuclear war and the fears that came with

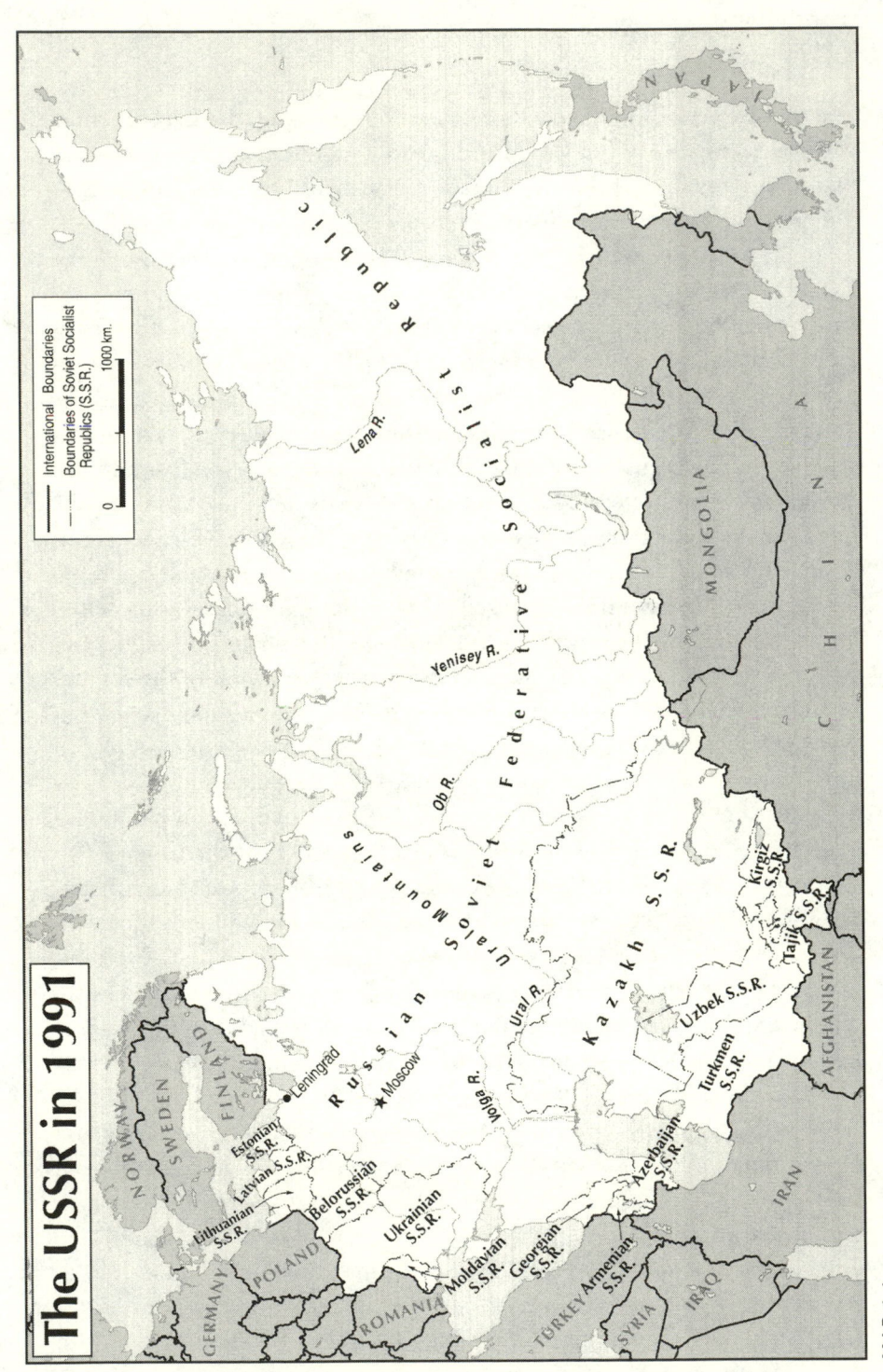

MAP 1.1

The USSR in 1991

it helped keep countries in check. Many governments were afraid to appear too aggressive out of concern that if they did so, either the United States or the Soviet Union would intervene, which would inevitably provoke a military response by the other country. In order to avoid any direct military confrontation, the United States and the Soviet Union interacted through what became known as proxy wars, where battles were fought indirectly through their allies. This meant that the United States would sometimes take the side of repressive regimes rather than allowing a communist government (which would appear to be loyal to the Soviet Union) to take control of a country. For example, when the left-leaning Sandinista government took control of Nicaragua in 1984, deposing the U.S.-backed Somoza family, hostility toward the United States caused the new government to turn to the Soviet Union and Cuba for support. This set the stage for a U.S.-backed counterrevolution, with the United States arming the opposition forces, or the Contras. Thus, although the United States and the Soviet Union did not directly confront one another, they were involved through their respective allies.

During the Cold War, it was also important that the respective allies remain firmly within the Eastern or Western bloc. For example, when the government of Czechoslovakia, one of the Eastern bloc countries, got out of hand in 1968, the Soviet Union came in and forcibly suppressed the nascent rebellion. The Soviet Union did not want any dissension or rebellion that could upset the delicate balance of power that existed. What happened in 1968 stands in contrast to what happened in 1993, following the end of the Soviet Union, when Czechoslovakia peacefully divided.

This introductory overview is designed to stress a few main points as we begin the study of IR: that the nation-state has always been seen as the fundamental actor in international relations; that the concept of nation-state has a number of component parts, many of which can now be questioned; that the nature of the international system is and has been changing, and no doubt will continue to; and that the old world of "balance of power," whether as it existed traditionally or as seen through the Cold War, has now ended and has been replaced by a globalized world in which nonstate actors (actors other than the traditional nation-states) are playing an increasingly major role.

What does all this mean for understanding international relations? In order to understand the changes to the international system, it will be important to understand the fundamental building blocks: the nation-state, the concept of sovereignty, and the notion of power, to name but a few. But it also means that we really need to step back and look at the world today and at what it means to be living in a world that is globalized. The very nature of globalization, with the interconnections among countries that help define the concept, has changed the nature and understanding of international relations.

GLOBALIZATION

We are beginning our study of international relations by asking a number of very macrolevel questions, which means that we are looking at the questions that affect the international system as a whole. In order to do this, we need to know what assumptions we are making and to define some basic terms and concepts. In this section, we will focus on issues of political stability and economic equality, what they mean, and why they are important when we consider the international system.

We are going to start with the international system as it exists today. To look at the international system in the twenty-first century is to look at a world that is interdependent—that is, what happens in one state directly affects what happens in others. Why is this the case and when and why did this happen?

What Is Globalization?

We are going to begin by asking a very basic and important question: What do we mean by *globalization*? This is a term that we hear all the time, and it is one that can generate a great many negative feelings. For example, periodically meetings of the Group of Seven (G7) industrialized countries and meetings of the World Trade Organization (WTO) have been disrupted by protestors. These protestors wanted to point out what they saw as inequities in the global economic system and especially the role of those major economic powers that are seen as the ones who make the rules. But can protests really change what has become a global reality? Can anyone stop or reverse the process of globalization? A more realistic set of questions might be, What do we mean by the current international economic system? How did it get here? And can it change?

Globalization as Historical Phenomenon

In order to answer these questions, we need to look at the concept of globalization not as a current phenomenon but as a historical one. For example,

Thomas Friedman, columnist for the *New York Times*, describes three periods of globalization. In his estimation, the first lasted from 1492 (the voyage of Columbus) until around 1800. According to him, this phase of globalization "shrank the world from a size large to a size medium. . . . [It] was about countries and muscles." As he describes it,

> the key agent of change, the dynamic force driving the process of global integration, was how much brawn—how much muscle, how much horsepower, wind power, or, later, steam power—your country had and how creatively you could deploy it. In this era, countries and governments (often inspired by religion or imperialism or a combination of both) led the way in breaking down walls and knitting the world together, driving global integration.[10]

Again, according to Friedman, the primary questions asked during this phase were, "Where does my country fit into global competition and opportunities? How can I go global and collaborate with others through my country?"[11]

Friedman looks at the second era of globalization as lasting from around 1800 to 2000, interrupted by major events such as the two world wars and the Great Depression, during which the world shrank still further. In this era of globalization, "the key agent of change, the dynamic force driving global integration, was multinational companies. These multinationals went global for markets and labor, spearheaded first by the expansion of the Dutch and English joint-stock companies and the Industrial Revolution."[12] Friedman also notes that it was during this period that we really see the birth of a global economy. What he is also telling us is that the international system changed in nature to include countries and companies working in collaboration. With this, we start seeing the impact of nonstate actors. All this was made possible by changes in technology that helped encourage more rapid movement of goods and information, as well as increasing the means of production.

He then identifies what he calls the third era of globalization, which he sees as beginning in 2000, and he says it

> is shrinking the world from a size small to a size tiny and flattening the playing field at the same time. . . . And while the dynamic force in Globalization 1.0 was countries globalizing and the dynamic force in Globalization 2.0 was companies globalizing, the dynamic force in Globalization 3.0—the force that gives it its unique character—is the newfound power for *individuals* to collaborate and compete globally. (emphasis added)[13]

Hence, Friedman tells us that the world/international system in general and the economic system in particular is changing, that it is getting smaller, that individuals and multinational corporations now make more of a difference, and that all this has happened relatively recently.

Historian Robert Marks, in his book *Origins of the Modern World*, similarly identifies a number of cycles of globalization that exist in a historical context. However, he looks at the first globalization as part of a system of trade among the then nations—or, more accurately, empires—going back to the 1200s. He notes the three primary trade routes that linked the major subsystems that existed at that time: East Asia, which linked China and parts of Southeast Asia to India; the Middle East–Mongolian subsystem, which linked Eurasia from the eastern Mediterranean to Central Asia and India; and the European subsystem, which linked Europe to the Middle East and the Indian Ocean. According to Marks, these subsystems "overlapped, with North and West Africa connected with the European and Middle East subsystems, and East Africa with the Indian Ocean subsystem."[14] Again, what is important about this is that it suggests that there was a very well-developed trade system that linked most of Africa, Europe, and Asia as far back as the thirteenth century. And according to Marks, one of the important things to note when looking at and trying to understand the development of the international system from the perspective of globalization is that, like political scientists, "until quite recently, historians have practiced their craft taking current nation-states as their unit of analysis, rather than adopting a more global approach."[15] Thus, he argues, the international system actually pre-dates modern nation-states, and we need to look at and understand components of the international system and globalization from this very broad historical perspective.

He also takes this approach out of the realm of the realist thinkers, and he claims that the thirteenth-century world system "functioned without a central controlling or dominating force. To those who conceive of the modern world system as growing under the domination of a single state or group of states, the idea that a system could work without a controlling center is somewhat novel." He looks at a world that is *polycentric*—that is, "it contained several regional systems, each with its own densely populated and wealthy 'core,' surrounded by a periphery that provided agricultural and industrial raw materials to the core, and most of which were loosely connected to one another through trade networks" (see map 1.2). And in his estimation, the world retained this polycentric character until around 1800, with the expansion of European colonization.[16]

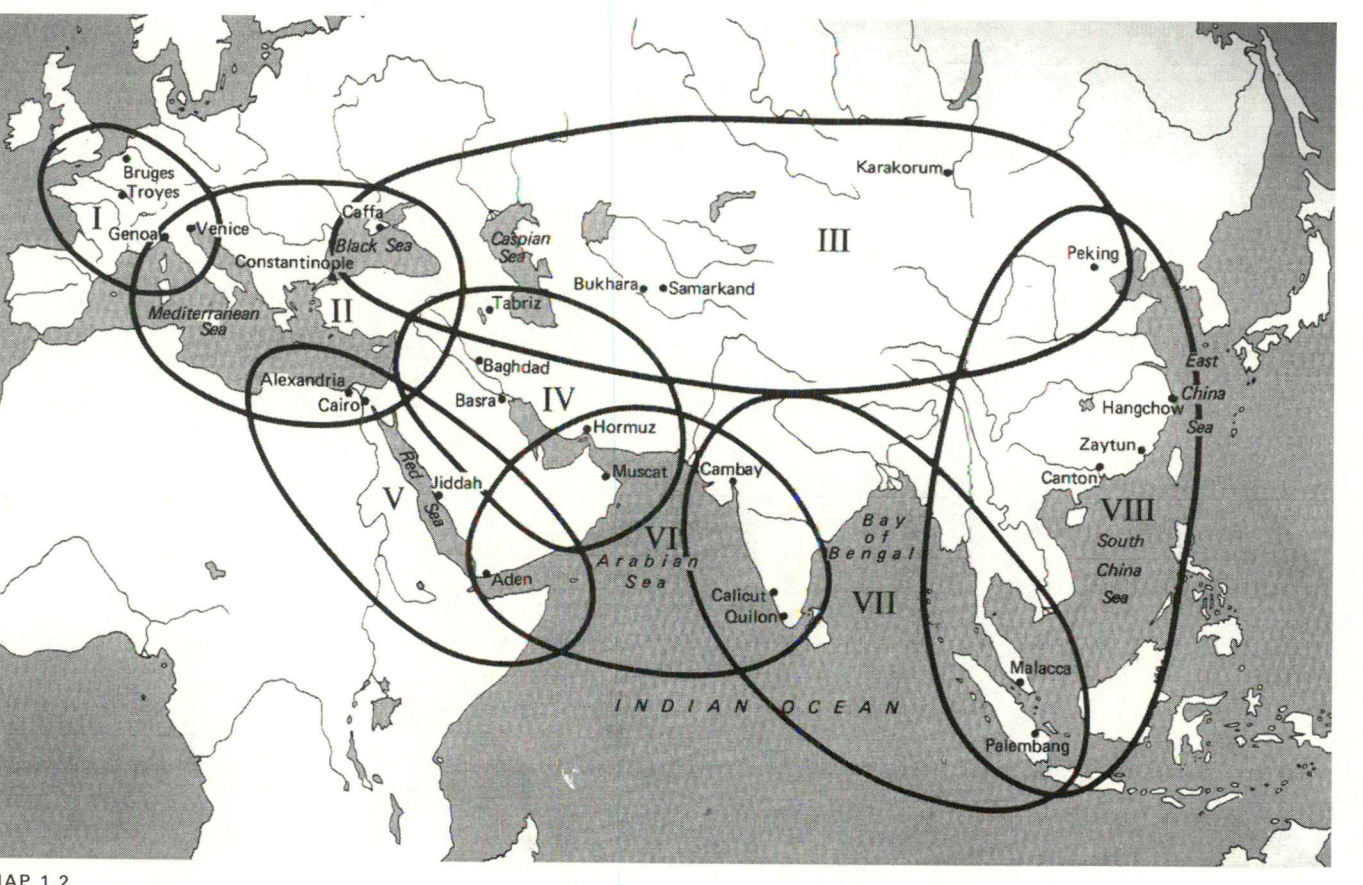

MAP 1.2

The Eight Circuits of the Thirteenth-Century World System

If we look at the current international system, Marks traces it to the nineteenth and twentieth centuries, with the solidification of the modern concept of the nation-state system. He claims that the advent of *nationalism*, or the desire for national peoples to have a state, was congruent with the growth of industrialization, which allowed states to grow and expand their territory. But he also notes that along with this expansion came a growing gap between the richest and the poorer nations within the international system. *Thus, globalization and the increased trade that came with it should help diminish this gap or division between countries. In reality, however, this has not been the case.*

In theory, then, the modern concept of globalization is tied to the notion that nation-states are interdependent and that progress in one will help others. Here we see the idea of the "rising tide lifting all boats," to use a cliché. But Marks and others warn us that this has not been the case and that the current round of globalization has actually exacerbated the differences between and among nations rather than closing them. He ties much of this to the concept of development, which should equal industrial growth. So, as long as a country remained tied to traditional agriculture or resisted industrialization, as was the case with many countries in Africa or even China and India until relatively recently, they would continue to fall at the "poor" end of the international economic system.[17]

But it is also important to remember that many of these countries in Africa and Asia had been colonies of the major European powers. Even after they gained their independence, they remained tied to the colonial powers or were dependent on them for many reasons. This reinforced the patterns of trade tied to the export of raw materials from the colony to the mother country and the import of manufactured goods from the colonial power to the colony. This in turn led to the emergence of the so-called dependency theory, which posited that the poorer countries of the developing world (also known as the third world) would remain tied to and dependent upon the major developed countries and therefore could not develop or prosper on their own.[18] The subfield of international political economy (IPE) has much more to say about this.[19]

Hence one of the goals of the movement toward development among many of these countries in Africa and Asia was to break the cycle of dependency. But that cycle is not easy to break, and it comes at a cost. Often (and we see this with China and India) the push toward development and industrialization comes at the expense of the environment, as countries see this as a necessary trade-off. These are often countries that tend to have agriculture-based economies, and even as they do move forward and develop, the majority of the population still lives on the land and depends upon it for food and sustenance. Peasant or rural economies depend upon a relatively large population—more children are needed to work the land—and so population growth continues without the economic base to sustain it, thereby perpetuating the pattern. Furthermore, the developed countries often have a vested interest in keeping the economic growth of the developing countries in check, lest it upset the entire and often delicate economic balance.

But what we are also seeing in a globalized world is how the impact of natural resources, such as oil, uranium, diamonds, and other precious substances, can alter that balance. For example, with the growing importance of and need for oil, some of the less-developed countries started to become more prominent, both politically and economically. Thus, otherwise poor countries, such as Venezuela and Nigeria, have been able to exert relative power in the international system because of their possession of oil. This too has altered the balance of power within the international system and changed the perspective of "developed" and "developing."

When we look at the international system today, we see the emergence of a global free market that has allowed for the growth and prominence of countries like China, India, and Brazil, as well as the increasing role of countries such as Nigeria, Venezuela, and some of the countries of the Middle East, such as Iran. No one country can control the international economic system, anymore than it can now control the international political system. The end of the Cold War and the subsequent emergence of more states and also more conflict have shown us that. While this also suggests that the theory is correct and that more countries are becoming economically strong, what the theories underlying globalization do not account for is the unequal distribution of wealth *within* any of those countries. So, while some people within countries such as India or Nigeria are growing wealthy, others remain in a cycle of poverty that is virtually impossible to break. It is this aspect of globalization that has elicited protests.

As might be expected, those who take a more feminist approach to international relations have a different take on globalization and what it means. According to political scientist J. Ann Tickner, feminists call our attention to the fact that while women's positions vary according to race, class, and geographical location, women are disproportionately situated at the bottom of the socioeconomic scale in all societies; drawing on gender analysis, they point to the devaluation of women's work and the dichotomy between productive and reproductive labor as explanations of the relatively disadvantaged position of women and the growing feminization of poverty. . . . Globalization involves more than economic forces; it has also led to the spread of Western-centered definitions of human rights and democracy. Feminist scholars are questioning whether these definitions are gender biased.[20]

Thus, feminist theorists encourage us to explore all aspects of questions in IR, even areas that we might assume to be beneficial to all, such as human rights and democracy. For example, in her work, Tickner asks whether democracies really are friendly toward women, as feminists see the traditionally Western model of democracy and nation-states tied to a system that is patriarchal and traditional, which favored and privileged men's interests over women's. But she makes another important point that "since women have traditionally had less access to formal political institutions, the focus on state institutions by scholars of democratization may miss ways in which women are participating in politics—outside formal political channels at the grassroots level."[21] In other words, Tickner directs us to look at the changes that have taken place at the level of the international system as a whole to see the impact they have had on women in general, and she admonishes us to look *within* the state to determine whether the spread of values such as democracy or even human rights has worked against women or has minimized the role that they play as actors in the international system.

The work of Friedman, Marks, and Tickner, among others, all suggests that the advent of globalization forces us to look at the international system in a new and different way. That means moving beyond the traditional theories and levels of analysis, as well as looking at the role played by primary actors other than the nation-state.

Conflict in a Globalized World

As alluded to earlier, the Cold War seemed to keep ethnic and civil conflicts in check because of the danger that even a small relatively localized conflict could spread to become a major confrontation between the United States and the Soviet Union. Since that time, conflicts seem to have proliferated, many because of fighting over scarce resources.[22] This does not mean that they are now contained or confined to a single area; in fact, if anything, the globalized nature of the world today brings with it the risk that *more* countries are involved in a conflict, rather than fewer, as more seem to have a vested interest in the outcome. The civil war in Syria, which has been going on since 2011, is an example of this. While this war had its origins in the uprisings known as the "Arab Spring," unlike the cases of Tunisia, Libya, and Egypt, which ended relatively quickly with what is colloquially known as "regime change," President Bashar al-Assad and his supporters dug in, refusing to give up. That war has now expanded, and Russia is the primary backer of Assad while the United States along with Turkey and Kurdish forces are supporting the rebel forces. ISIS is now part of the equation, with the fighting regularly spilling over the borders of Syria. As of June 2017, an estimated four hundred thousand Syrians have been killed, more than five million Syrians have fled the country, and approximately 6.3 million are internally displaced.[23] As of this writing, there is no end in sight to this conflict. Where globalization becomes especially relevant here is that one of the results of this war has been a refugee crisis, as people flee the war in search of peace and some security. One result has been an influx of refugees into parts of Europe, leading to strains on those countries as they attempt to accommodate the humanitarian crisis. Germany has been the most welcoming country, albeit putting Chancellor Angela Merkel's leadership at risk. Other countries, such as Hungary, have sealed their borders claiming that they cannot take any more refugees. And fears of refugees and immigrants, who are perceived as taking the jobs of citizens, contributed to the results of the Brexit vote. The lesson here is that conflict is more difficult to contain in a globalized world—not necessarily that the conflict will spread but that the conflict can contribute to humanitarian crises which, in turn, tax national systems and also contribute to fears which then fuel nationalism and xenophobia.

WHAT DOES GLOBALIZATION MEAN FOR THE STUDY OF IR?

In beginning our study of international relations by looking at globalization and the changes it has brought to the international system, we are moving beyond the traditional paradigms and approaches to the study of the field. What we are suggesting here is that in order to really understand

international relations in the twenty-first century, we need to begin by understanding what the international system looks like *today* if we are to understand all its component parts and how they have changed. That does not
mean that we can ignore the traditional framework upon which the study
of international relations is based. Quite the contrary. The theories, actors,
and framework that have guided the study of international relations since
it emerged as a discipline remain the building blocks for understanding the
international system. Only by understanding those as our starting points
can the contrasts with the world today really have meaning.

However, understanding IR in a globalized world also means going beyond the traditional state-centered approach that the field has often had.
We need to be able to see the limits of that approach and to expand our
understanding and definitions in order to incorporate the roles of nonstate actors. But it is also important to remember that it is not possible to
critique the traditional theoretical perspectives or to offer new ones unless
or until we have a good solid grounding in the fundamentals. Through the
remainder of this book, our goal will be to provide those fundamentals so
that we can, in turn, understand the weaknesses in current theory and look
for alternative explanations and approaches.

With that introduction, we will now turn to the theories and framework
that we will use to approach the field of international relations. After we
have looked at these—theories, actors, and framework—we will return to
our starting point of globalization and macrolevel questions in order to pull
all the pieces together.

FURTHER READINGS
These additional readings are worth exploring and elaborate on some of the
points raised in this chapter. This list is not meant to be exhaustive but only
illustrative.

Cleeland, Nancy, et al. "The Wal-Mart Effect." *Los Angeles Times*, November 23, 24,
    and 25, 2003. http://www.latimes.com/la-walmart-sg-storygallery.html.
Singer, J. David. "The Levels-of-Analysis Problem in International Relations." *World
    Politics* 14, no. 1 (October 1961): 77–92.
Tickner, J. Ann. "You Just Don't Understand." *International Studies Quarterly* 41, no.
    4 (December 1997): 612.
"Treaty of Westphalia." http://avalon.law.yale.edu/17th_century/westphal.asp.

NOTES

1. ISIS, the Islamic State of Iraq and Syria, is also known as ISIL, the Islamic State of Iraq and the Levant, and by its Arabic-language acronym, Daesh. For the sake of simplicity, we will refer to it as ISIS.

2. See Nancy Cleeland et al., "The Wal-Mart Effect," *Los Angeles Times*, November 23, 24, and 25, 2003.

3. See Hans J. Morgenthau, *Politics Among Nations: The Struggle for Power and Peace*, originally published in 1948. Many more recent and abridged editions have come out since that time.

4. As you will see later, the concept of the sovereign nation-state actually grew from the Treaty of Westphalia (also known as the Peace of Westphalia), which ended the Thirty Years' War in 1648. But it was after World War I that the map of Europe as we generally know it now was redrawn, with the emergence of new sovereign states. That process continued after World War II, as many then colonies were granted independence.

5. Joyce P. Kaufman and Kristen P. Williams, *Women, the State, and War: A Comparative Perspective on Citizenship and Nationalism* (Lanham, MD: Lexington Books, 2007), 12–13.

6. J. David Singer, "The Levels-of-Analysis Problem in International Relations," *World Politics* 14, no. 1 (October 1961): 77–92.

7. J. Ann Tickner, "You Just Don't Understand," *International Studies Quarterly* 41, no. 4 (December 1997): 612.

8. "Treaty of Westphalia," http://avalon.law.yale.edu/17th_century/westphal.asp.

9. Some have argued that globalization is not a new concept but that it actually dates back to the age of exploration in the fifteenth century or even earlier, a point that is explored in this chapter. See, for example, Thomas Friedman, *The World Is Flat: A Brief History of the Twenty-First Century* (New York: Farrar, Straus & Giroux, 2005), and Robert B. Marks, *The Origins of the Modern World*, 3rd ed. (Lanham, MD: Rowman & Littlefield, 2015).

10. Friedman, *The World Is Flat*, 9.

11. Friedman, *The World Is Flat*, 9.

12. Friedman, *The World Is Flat*, 9.

13. Friedman, *The World Is Flat*, 10.

14. Marks, *Origins of the Modern World*, 33–34.

15. Marks, *Origins of the Modern World*, 35.

16. Marks, *Origins of the Modern World*, 35–36.

17. See Marks, *Origins of the Modern World*, especially "Introduction: The Rise of the West" and chapter 6, "The Great Departure," for more development of this idea.

18. For a concise definition of dependency theory, see J. Ann Tickner, *Gendering World Politics* (New York: Columbia University Press, 2001), 68. See also Marks, *Origins of the Modern World*.

19. For more basic information on international political economy, see, for example, part 3, "International Political Economy and Globalization," in Art Jervis, *International Politics: Enduring Concepts and Contemporary Issues*, 10th ed. (Boston: Longman, 2011), 259–365, and Renée Marlin-Bennett, "International Political Economy: Overview and Conceptualization," *Encyclopedia of International Studies*, http://www.oxfordreference.com/view/10.1093/acref/9780191842665.001.0001/acref-9780191842665-e-0233?rskey=MGE2FP&result=265. The Marlin-Bennett piece has a very extensive bibliography.

20. Tickner, *Gendering World Politics*, 7.

21. Tickner, *Gendering World Politics*, 7.

22. See Donald Snow, *Cases in International Relations: Principles and Applications*, 7th ed. (Lanham, MD: Rowman & Littlefield, 2018), especially chapter 3, "Territorial Disputes: This Land (Palestine and Kurdistan) Is *Whose* Land?"

23. CNN, "Syrian Civil War: Fast Facts," June 13, 2017, http://www.cnn.com/2013/08/27/world/meast/syria-civil-war-fast-facts.

2

Theoretical Overview

This chapter outlines the basic theoretical approaches that are the foundations of international relations and are critical to understanding the field. As a starting point, we will begin with realist/power politics, as articulated by Hans J. Morgenthau. This has been one of the founding tenets of international relations since the end of World War II. (His seminal text, *Politics Among Nations*, was initially published in 1948.) Since then, the international political landscape has changed; new organizations tied to the notion of collective security assumed idealistically that security could best be assured not by having nations increase their power but by working cooperatively toward common goals and ends that would benefit all. Thus, a competing or (perhaps more appropriately) alternative theory of international relations was born, which challenged the basic principles of realism. This new approach focused more on cooperation between and among nations rather than competition for power, and it embodied many of the ideals earlier espoused by Woodrow Wilson. Referred to as "liberal theory," it incorporates economic ideas as well as political ones, and it has grown in prominence and importance since the end of the Cold War. Hence, the changes in the international system have contributed to a proliferation of other theories, all of which were designed to explain on a macro level, or more often on a micro level, some aspect of international relations.

In this chapter, we present a brief introduction to these various theoretical models (i.e., realism and structural realism, liberalism, constructivism,

Marxism and its offshoots, and feminist approaches), with concrete examples of how each can be applied to understanding the international system and world events. Note that this is not meant to be a comprehensive study, as there are a number of approaches that we will not address in this short overview, nor do we go into a lot of detail on the basic theories that we do explore. If you are interested in learning more, there are many readings you can delve into. Rather, what we want to do here is offer an introduction to the major approaches so that you can determine which of these makes the most sense to you and when and how you can apply each approach. This starting point will lead into the body of the remainder of the text.

WHAT IS THEORY AND WHY IS IT IMPORTANT?

Before we can delve into IR theories, however, it is important to set out a few basic assumptions and to situate international relations within the broader field of political science. As noted in chapter 1, IR is the most macro level of all the subfields of political science. In contrast to the other subfields, such as American politics or comparative politics, international relations deals with the entire international system, which generally is made up of nation-states but also nonstate actors. Most nation-states have a political structure of some type, a culture and social organization that help define their values, and individuals who influence the decisions that are made and who are, in turn, affected by those decisions. Within each nation-state there are countless other groups that play a role in the decision-making process and interact with the political system in some way. This structure does not even begin to take into account the ways in which these broad entities, the nation-state or country, interact with and influence one another, although these too are legitimate questions for exploration within the area of international relations.

Given this proliferation of actors and variables that can affect these actors and the international system as a whole, how can we begin to understand this complexity? That is the role of theory, which exists to provide the framework that can help guide our understanding of various events that occur within this complex system.

Theory and International Relations: Some Basic Assumptions

Every field of study has its theories or basic paradigms, as does international relations. These theories provide the framework that allows us to begin to simplify reality so that we can better address the complexities of the world. *Theory* is a linked set of propositions or ideas that simplify a complex reality so that we can *describe* events that have happened, *explain* why they happened, and *predict* what might happen in the future. In the field of international relations, it is very difficult to predict with certainty, as there are so many variables that can affect the outcome of events. Unlike the "hard" sciences, where it is possible to work in a lab and control the environment, in the social sciences in general, and in IR in particular, it is virtually impossible to control any single variable, let alone the interaction among these variables—although political scientists who employ various modeling techniques do try. This means that the theoretical perspectives are dynamic and evolve as situations change, as do the variables. Nonetheless, the main theories that have emerged allow us to identify general patterns that help us understand what has happened and why (i.e., describe and explain), and in so doing give us some indicators of what might happen in the future under similar sets of circumstances (predict). So theories are important guides that allow us to navigate the complexity of the world.

Using these theories or paradigms can help us know how to ask and how to answer some of the fundamental questions in the field. As a macrolevel field, IR tends to ask macrolevel questions—for example, what is war and why do countries go to war? Why did a particular country act as it did or respond to events in a particular way? How can one country influence another to engage in a particular pattern of behavior or stop it from behaving in a particular way? Why do some states appear to be cooperative and others appear to be warlike? These are but some of the general questions that we see often in the field of IR and that any number of theories and theorists have tried to answer. But how can we answer such questions in a world in which we can't identify all the variables or hold things constant?

Political scientist Christine Sylvester provides some important clues when she writes, "In an international system filled with tensions, IR analysts are keenly interested in questions of *continuity* and *discontinuity*. States persist as key political entities, as does a world capitalist *system* of commodity production and exchange" (emphasis added). She continues, "Conventional wisdom has it that this is a world of states, nonstate actors and market transactions. It is a world in which neither men nor women figure *per se*, the emphasis being on impersonal actors, structures, and system processes."[1]

Sylvester seems to be telling us that in the traditional approaches to IR, people don't matter; IR is a field of actors, structures, and processes. But underlying this is another reality that Sylvester touches on later in her book, which gives us a more complete understanding of international relations— and that is *who* makes the decisions for these actors that result in the actions that we can see. Are states monolithic entities that operate on their own? Or, put another way, what roles do individuals really play in steering the direction of a state?

This leads us to another component of our basic framework: the assumptions we have to make about nation-states and their behavior in order to arrive at generalizations (theories) about them. Whether they are accurate or not, making certain assumptions allows us to generalize, which in turn enables us to identify patterns as well as to draw conclusions based, in part, on studying cases that don't fit the patterns. These generalizations and patterns, and determining where there are deviations from these patterns and why, contribute to further information about and knowledge of the behavior of the international system.

To begin, we assume that states will behave as *monolithic* actors (that is, they will behave as if they were one single entity rather than being made up of many individuals and groups) and that they will act in a *rational* manner (that is, they will make decisions based on a process that weighs costs and benefits to arrive at a decision that allows them to further their self-interest). States might choose to act in a certain way in order to maximize their power (the realist theoretical perspective) or because they feel that they will better achieve their interests by cooperating with other states (the liberal approach). But this also suggests that states have a way to identify what is in their *national interest* and that they will then act accordingly. Again, one can easily question this assumption, as any state has a number of competing interests, all of which can be argued to be in the best interest of the state. Nonetheless, for realists especially, it is important to assume that national interest can be identified and that states will pursue policies that help them achieve that interest.

The Concept of National Interest

What is *national interest* and how do countries actually achieve it? This is one of the critical concepts in IR and one that is addressed in virtually every textbook on the subject. For example, according to political scientist Charles

Kegley, "The primary obligation of every state—the goal to which all other national objectives should be subordinated—is to promote its *national interest* and to acquire power for this purpose" (emphasis in original).[2] Realist thinkers define national interest in terms of *power*, in the belief that only by acquiring power can a country achieve its primary goals. But some political scientists define national interest more broadly than simply the acquisition of power, such as protecting what the state sees as its core interests, which are those that involve the protection and continuation of the state and its people. For example, Barry Hughes sees core interests as those that "flow from the desire [of the state] to preserve its essence: territorial boundaries, population, government, and sovereignty."[3] From his perspective, core interest is more than simply security defined in traditional military terms, but it also means assuring a country's economic vitality, its values, and other components that are central to the essence of the state. One can argue that these are also essential to a country's security, but they fall outside the traditional definition, a point that we will return to later. So a country will pursue the policies that it deems to be in its national interest while also furthering its core interests related to its survival.

A point made in a recent book by Richard Haass is that a country might choose to pursue what it believes to be in its national interest even if that defies the wishes or norms of the international system. The example that he gives is Pakistan, which pursued its nuclear ambitions in the face of international sanctions and alienation. In his words, "There is scant evidence that sanctions can ever be made strong enough to dissuade a country from pursuing what it believes to be *a vital national interest*" (emphasis added).[4] We can also see that type of behavior with North Korea, which continues to build and test nuclear-capable missiles despite international warnings and sanctions. What this tells us is that a country's perception of its own national and core interests can determine its behavior, even if doing so appears to result in international condemnation and even questions about the rationality of the decision.

Tied directly to core interests/values and a country's national interest in general is the traditional notion of *security*, since one of the core values of any country is ensuring the safety and protection of the population. But this also leads to the dangers of the "security dilemma," which is a situation in which one state improves its military capabilities as a way of trying to ensure its own security. However, in doing this, the military buildup is seen by other states as an act of aggression and therefore a direct threat. Thus, each state tries to increase its own level of protection and hence its security to meet the perceived threat coming from another state, which contributes directly to the insecurity of others. The result is often an arms race, and no greater sense of security.

Generally, security is thought of in military terms. However, feminist theorists have challenged this preconception by expanding the definition to make a distinction between security defined in terms of the military and militarism and "human security," which refers to a broader set of issues necessary for human survival (core issues)—for example, protection of the environment, eradication of diseases, freedom from hunger, access to potable water, and so on. In looking at these security issues, "feminists focus on how world politics can contribute to the *insecurity* of individuals, particularly marginalized and disempowered populations" (emphasis added).[5] Put another way, "IR feminists frequently make different assumptions about the world, ask different questions, and use different methodologies to answer them."[6]

Feminist IR theorists would argue that only by broadening the approach to international relations as a field of study is it possible to get a complete picture of and accurate answers to many of the basic questions asked. As feminist theorist Gillian Youngs describes it, "In arguing that women and gender are essential to the field of International Relations, feminist scholars have had to address the *core* concepts and issues of the field: war, militarism and security; sovereignty and the state; and globalization" (emphasis in original).[7] In other words, while feminist theorists address the critical concepts, they inject a different perspective that should give us a more complete understanding of the issues studied.

This is not to suggest that one theory or approach is better or worse than another, or that one is right and another is wrong. What we do want to make clear, though, is that there are any number of approaches that can be used to understand international relations and that it is important to be clear about the questions we want to ask and then to draw on the appropriate approach to answering those questions.

INTRODUCTION TO LEVELS OF ANALYSIS: A FRAMEWORK FOR UNDERSTANDING INTERNATIONAL RELATIONS

We noted above that international relations deals with the international system, which we can think of as being made up of nation-states but also nonstate actors, each of which has a distinct political structure of some type, a culture and social organization that help define its values, and individuals who influence the decisions that are made and who in turn are affected by those decisions. In effect, what we are referring to here are the *levels of analysis*. It is important to know more about what this concept means, as it is one of the primary building blocks for understanding international relations.

We can think of levels of analysis as forming a pyramid. At the base is the *international system as a whole*, which is made up of nation-states, nonstate actors, and international/multinational organizations. If we look within the international system, we can focus on the *individual nation-state*, the major component of the international system. Each nation-state, in turn, has a *government* and a *society*, which has its own *culture*, and then the *individuals* who make the decisions (see figure 2.1).

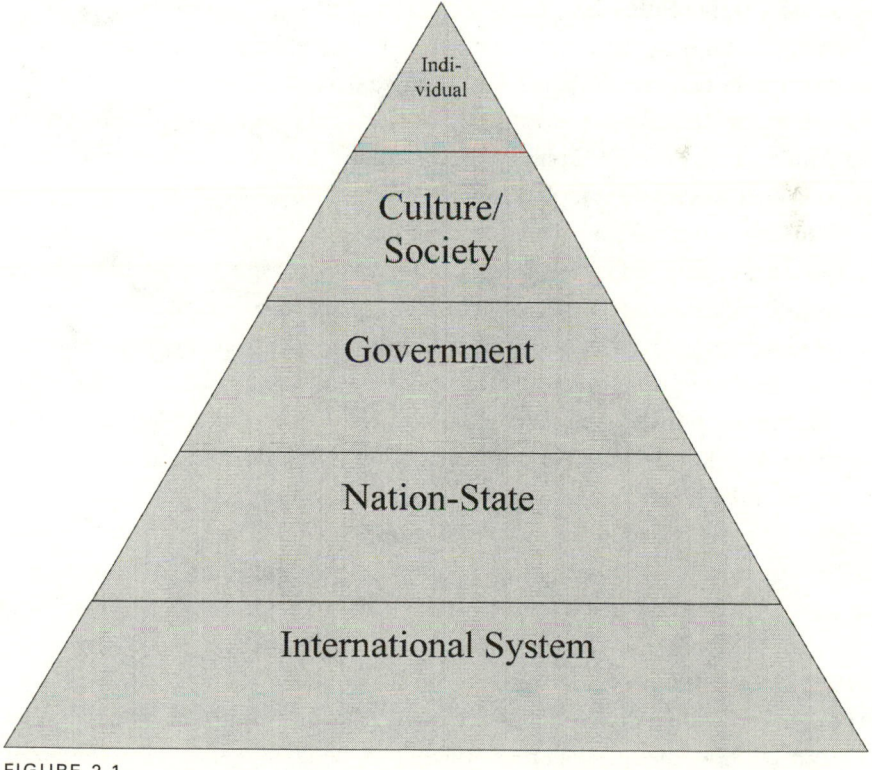

FIGURE 2.1
Levels of Analysis

Put another way, we can start with the individual decision maker who emerges from the society and the culture of the nation and who should reflect those norms and values. Similarly, the government makes decisions for the nation-state and is tied directly to the society and culture. (In democratic societies, the government is elected, at least in part, by the members of the society.) Taken together, these are the primary component parts of the nation-state. Nation-states combine to create the international system. In fact, according to realist thinking, nation-states are the essence of the international system.

The logical question to ask here is, why does this structure matter? It matters because it is important when asking a question about international relations to understand what level the question is really addressing so that it can be answered correctly.

For example, the Cuban missile crisis of October 1962 was one of the defining events of the Cold War. We can look at that incident and ask why President John F. Kennedy made the decisions that he did which ultimately resulted in a peaceful end to the crisis. When asked that way, the focus of the question is the level of the individual decision maker, and it can be answered by reading about the processes Kennedy followed in order to make his decisions. What was he thinking? Whom did he turn to for advice?

But we can also ask how the American people reacted to what was going on at this time of heightened tension. To answer this question, we would have to look at the society and culture, which we can gauge through polls, newspaper accounts, and so on. Asking what role the formal governmental structure played gives us another insight into the crisis and how it was addressed. Was the Congress involved, and if so, in what ways? Or were decisions made by a small group of advisers to Kennedy, and what does that tell us about the role of government in crisis decision making and how decisions were made?

We can ask even more macrolevel questions, such as how did the missile crisis change U.S. and Soviet relations during the Cold War? This is a question that can be answered by focusing on the nation-state level. At that level, we are looking at the United States and the Soviet Union as two major players in the international system and focusing on their reactions to one another given their tense relationship during the Cold War. And, finally, we can ask how the missile crisis affected the global balance of power. This question can best be answered at the macro level by looking at the patterns of behavior of nation-states, what took place in the United Nations, and other macrolevel indicators.

The point here is that using levels of analysis as a framework makes it possible to ask specific questions and get the answers that are appropriate to the particular questions being asked. Each of the questions asked above is a valid one and can be answered. Using the levels of analysis allows us to focus on one level at a time, holding the others constant, in order to simplify the reality. This is the best way we can approximate what scientists do in a laboratory. It also allows us to look at a specific event and, using the basic framework for theory, *describe* what happened, *explain* why things happened as they did, and then *draw lessons* about what that might mean for similar events in the future. (Note that we are not saying that we can predict, but we can make educated guesses.) When the answers are taken together, it is possible to get a more complete picture of the event—what happened, how, and why.

The notion of using levels of analysis as a framework for approaching international relations goes back to the early 1960s and the work of political scientist J. David Singer. His article "The Level-of-Analysis Problem in International Relations"[8] draws on the even earlier work of Kenneth Waltz, who in his seminal book, *Man, the State, and War*, suggests that in order to really understand international relations in general and to address specific questions, such as why wars occur and whether there can ever be peace, it is necessary to understand human behavior (individual level), states (nation-state level), and how they are constructed (society, culture, and government levels), and finally to then address the international level.[9]

What Singer does in his article is to remind those of us who study international relations that until this point we have "roamed up and down the ladder of organizational complexity with remarkable abandon," which in turn has contributed to a failure "to appreciate the value of a stable point of focus."[10] After reminding us of the importance of a model or theory (to describe, explain, and predict), Singer illustrates the ways in which approaching international relations by using levels of analysis can provide a critical focal point for analysis. Furthermore, he alerts us to the fact that while the "big picture" might be lost by focusing on one level at the expense of another, what is gained is a picture that is richer in detail.

Singer describes for us the importance of being able to distinguish between levels, thereby aiding us in answering important questions. "So the problem is really not one of deciding which level is most valuable to the discipline as a whole and then demanding that it be adhered to from now unto eternity. Rather, it is one of realizing that there *is* this preliminary conceptual issue and that it must be temporarily resolved prior to any given research undertaking" (emphasis in original).[11] Thus, it is important to identify the appropriate level to be addressed early in the research process. But Singer also warns us of the dangers that can come with shifting between or among levels. "We may utilize one level here and another there, but we cannot afford to shift our orientation in the midst of a study."[12] When the answers are taken together and a number of levels analyzed, it is possible to get a more complete picture of the event—what happened, how, and why.

The "System" in the International System

In order to start applying these ideas and to be able to focus the theories most effectively, we also need to define what we mean by the concept of the *international system*. Here we can draw on the work of political scientist David Easton, who wrote in the 1960s about the concept of a "political system."[13] He drew on the ideas of systems theory to view political life as a "system of behavior" that has certain characteristics that can be defined, analyzed, and therefore understood. This approach makes certain assumptions that may or may not be accurate. However, it provides a good starting point for our understanding of international relations.

As Easton described it, political life can be seen as a pattern of behavior that exists within an environment that exerts influence on it and that it, in turn, influences. Components within this system are dynamic, and as each moves or acts, it affects the actions and behaviors of the other actors that also exist within the system. Since one of the primary functions of any system is to endure, the system as a whole will constantly be adjusting to changes within the environment. Another assumption is that these patterns of behavior have a certain regularity that can be identified and can therefore be described and explained. It is the role of theory to help us do these things.

But, we might ask, is there really such a thing as an *international system*? Clearly, there are political relationships that exist within the international community that can be identified, such as the United Nations (UN) or the North Atlantic Treaty Organization (NATO), both of which are made up of nation-states. But do these organizations exhibit regular patterns of behavior?

Do they ensure that nation-states will do so? The only way we can answer these questions and continue to build our theories of international relations is to make assumptions about the ways in which those entities or actors in the international system behave. We can then learn more by comparing the reality that we study with our assumptions to see how well the theory describes reality.

So, we can *assume* that there is an international system that can be identified, that it is made up of actors that exhibit some regular and identifiable patterns of behavior, that the nation-states that are the bases of international relations will act rationally (maximize gains and minimize losses), and that they act as monolithic entities. Without those assumptions, it would be impossible to understand or address the international system/international relations, let alone answer the complex questions that emerge in this field of study. And this brings us back to theory.

Theory provides the framework that allows us to begin to address the complexity of the world by providing us with a way to simplify it. But it is also important to remember that theory does not emerge in a vacuum but must be tied to reality in some way, nor can it be so grounded in abstraction as to be virtually useless. Rather, good theory draws on concrete examples to arrive at generalizations that can help us explain real-world events. Ideally, a theory should be able to be tested in order to see whether it can be proved or disproved and whether it holds up under a range of circumstances. It was in the attempt to do these things that the basic theories of international relations evolved.

Power

One of the assumptions of IR theories, especially within realist thinking, is that nation-states will be motivated in no small part by a desire to increase their power. Hence, power is one of the most critical concepts in international relations. Simply put, power is the ability of one actor to influence the behavior of another in order to achieve a desired end. If we were to graph this very simply, it would look like this:

Country A wants Country B to do X.

Country A can then use its power to "persuade" (or encourage, motivate, or even coerce) Country B to take a particular action. This example assumes that Country A is the more powerful or has power over B and that it can persuade Country B to take the desired action. It also assumes that Country A has determined what the desired outcome (X) is and how and why it needs Country B in order to achieve that outcome. But it is also important to remember that power is not necessarily unidirectional (Country A imposing its will on Country B), nor is it symmetrical. Or, looking at it another way, if Country A wants Country B to do X, Country B says that it will, but it wants something in exchange. In that case, there might be a negotiation that results in each country asking something of the other, and in that way, both can get what they want.

Another important point to remember when we introduce the concept of power is that it is a relative term. One country has power over another (A over B), meaning that it is relational; one has "power over" in relative terms. Although the feminist theorists have problems with this understanding of power, as noted below, it represents one of the easiest and most straightforward ways to think about this concept, and so we will continue with this basic approach. Given this relationship and understanding of power, a third country might be more powerful than both, in that it might have a greater number of weapons or resources than either of the two. These are the *capabilities* or materials and resources that a country has relative to others. And it is not only having the resources that makes a country powerful, but the willingness to use them, or its *credibility*. We will come back to these points in more detail below.

Countries have a range of policy options available to them that can be placed along a continuum from positive (rewards) to negative (punishment), which can be used in order to get a desired outcome. In all cases, Country A decides which particular course of action to pursue by weighing the relative costs and benefits. Country B can then decide how to respond, based on what Country A is asking but also on what it is offering. Like Country A, Country B will engage in an evaluation of what it wants and needs, what it can get in exchange, and what is in its best interest. Thus, we are looking at a dynamic process.

A government, acting rationally, should choose the option that promises to give it the desired outcome at the least possible cost. In most cases, while a country might decide to offer or grant a reward to a country unilaterally, it generally will look to other countries to support it when the option chosen is negative. Threatening or imposing economic sanctions, for example, is a far more credible threat when more than one country agrees to abide by those sanctions. In deciding which option to pursue, the other thing any country must remember is that it must be credible; that is, it must have the resources and the will to follow through on the policy decision made.

Political scientist Joseph Nye identifies power as either *hard power* or *soft power*.[14] According to him, "Hard power rests on inducements (carrots) or threats (sticks)," whereas "soft power rests on the ability to set a political agenda in a way that shapes the preferences of others."[15] Generally, hard power is associated with military and/or economic strength, while soft power is tied to values. Nye later built on that starting point and included the concept of *smart power*, which he defines as "the ability to combine hard and soft power resources into effective strategies." And then he elaborates on this idea by adding, "Unlike soft power, smart power is an evaluative as well as a descriptive concept. Soft power can be good or bad from a normative perspective, depending on how it is used. Smart power has the evaluation built into the definition."[16] According to Nye, then, smart power is something that is available to all states, large or small, and is a function of the policies a country develops and the ways in which a country chooses to use its resources.

Another author, Walter Russell Mead, divides power into four types: sharp (military), sticky (economic), sweet (culture and ideals), and hegemonic. Sharp, sticky, and sweet together contribute to hegemonic power, as they come together and create a whole that is bigger than the sum of the parts.[17] Clearly, power can be defined in any number of ways. A country is deemed powerful if it can use its power and the capabilities that make up that power (whether real or perceived) to influence the outcome of events. But this also assumes that County A knows what it wants to achieve, has an understanding of its own power relative to the needs and power of Country B, and can determine how best to use that power in order to achieve what it wants. That assessment governs many of the interactions in international relations.

It is important to note here that not all of the patterns between and among countries are conflictual. It should be clear from figure 2.2 that sometimes the best way for a country to get what it wants is to find ways to cooperate and negotiate with other countries. Offering rewards, such as foreign aid or other inducements (i.e., "carrots") can sometimes be a more effective policy tool than threatening or imposing economic sanctions (i.e., "sticks"). But it is also

Continuum of Actions

Positive (Cooperative)			Negative (Conflictual)	
Granting → Offering →		Threats →	Imposition of →	Armed
rewards rewards			punishment	conflict

Foreign aid	Economic sanctions
Military technology	Boycotts
Military support	Recalling diplomats
Diplomatic recognition	Threaten force
Form alliances	Use of force

FIGURE 2.2
Continuum of Actions

important to remember that the particular policy chosen should grow out of an understanding of the situation, the desired goals, and the relative power of each of the countries involved.

In thinking about power and the international system, it is important to think about which countries have power and what gives them their power. As noted above, power is a relative concept, so when we talk about which countries are powerful, we mean relative to other countries with which a country interacts.

There would be little dispute that the United States is a powerful country because of its economic and military strength. Similarly, China has clearly become a powerful country, not only because of its growing economic role internationally and its military strength, but also because of its size and its population; people are a *capability* that can enhance a country's power. So are a country's size and geography and topography. But if you were asked to make a list of other powerful countries, what would that list look like? What countries are powerful?

How about a country like Sudan—is it powerful? Generally, we would say that because of its lack of resources and relatively low level of economic development, it is not powerful. But it was able to perpetrate genocide in Darfur in defiance of the wishes of most other countries in the international system, including the United States. Does that mean it has power? If so, what is the basis for that power? What about a country like Nigeria? It is politically unstable, but it has oil. Does that make it powerful? Venezuela is a similar case—is it powerful?

In other words, we can argue and make lists of what countries are powerful, as long as we have established criteria for defining *power* and as long as we see power as relative rather than in absolute terms.

When we talk about power, which clearly is one of the central concepts in understanding international relations, each of the theoretical perspectives has its own way of viewing the concept and even of understanding how critical it is. For example, power is central to realist thinking, as we have noted. Liberal thinking and constructivist thinking focus less on power and more on other components of nation-state relationships, including cooperation and the structures that can hold them together rather than leading to competition. In contrast, feminist IR theorists inject some warnings into the discussion of power that are worth considering here. Specifically, they question the assumption that "power" equates to "power over" or "the ability to get someone to do what you want."[18] Feminist theorists are concerned that this approach to power "emphasizes separation and competition: Those who have power use it (or its threat) to keep others from securing enough to threaten them."[19] In effect, they argue that defining power in this way obscures critical aspects of relationships and does not take values into account. In contrast, they suggest that we need to think about a different definition of power that is less coercive and more about interdependence and relationships, less about zero-sum approaches and more about achieving a desired outcome through cooperation rather than conflict. In other words, it requires rethinking our definitions of basic concepts such as *security* and *power*. However, as Tickner and other feminist scholars note, "Imagining security divested of its statist connotations is problematic; the institutions of state power are not withering away."[20]

When we think of many of the basic concepts in IR, such as power, they tend to fall into the *public realm* (that is, they are considered part of the state, the government, and decision making), which tends to exclude women who exist in the *private realm* (that is, the home and the family). However, feminist theorists remind us, first of all, that more women are moving from the private realm to the public, thereby making women more visible. (We can see this with women such as Hillary Clinton and Condoleezza Rice, both of whom were U.S. secretaries of state, and one, Hillary Clinton, was the first woman to run for president from a major U.S. party.) But sometimes that might mean working at a grassroots or community level, where women can often have a direct impact, rather than at the national or international level. In general, though, this suggests that women are finding ways to have their voices heard and to play more of a role in political decision making. This was not something that was considered when the field of IR came into its own, and it was certainly not part of the thinking of the realist theorists.

There are many other concepts and definitions that will come into play as we continue our study of international relations, and we will review them as needed. But with the main concepts outlined, we will now turn to an introduction of the basic theories.

INTRODUCTION TO BASIC IR THEORIES

As noted above, the major role of theory is to provide a framework that will allow us to simplify a complex reality so that we can describe the events that took place in the past, try to explain them in causal terms ("this happened because that happened"), and, in doing so, try to predict or at least anticipate what might happen in the future. Each of the major theoretical approaches attempts to do this. Remember that no one theory can explain all events or sets of circumstances. Thus, which theory is the most appropriate to use is partly a function of the question(s) asked, understanding the context for the particular event, and the assumptions we choose to use. Some IR scholars believe that one theory is inherently better at answering questions than another. But others take the viewpoint that the question(s) we ask should determine the theoretical approach we use to find the answer. The main point is that theory should provide a framework or a guide to help us understand the world.

Realism and Neo-/Structural Realism

As noted above, the major role of theory is to serve as a framework or a guide. In the words of one political scientist, "The realist tradition is certainly regarded by an overwhelming majority of scholars to be the definitive tradition in the field of international relations."[21] Because of the importance of realist theory in defining international relations, we will begin with that, and we will give a lot of attention to it. As you will see, many of the other modern theories grew up, at least in part, as reactions to realist theory. This means that realist theory should be our starting point.

The realist school puts the concept of *power* at the center of all the behaviors of the nation-state; the assumption is that nations act as they do in order to maximize their power so that they can better achieve their own goals. As described by Hans Morgenthau, the father of realist theory, "the main signpost that helps political realism to find its way through the landscape of international politics is the concept of *interest defined in terms of power*" (emphasis added).[22]

Although it is most associated with the work of Hans Morgenthau, realist thought can be found throughout history. Early versions of this description of the competition for power can be attributed to Thucydides, whose *History of the Peloponnesian War* is seen as one of the first examples of realist thinking. The "Melian Dialogue" between the Athenians (the stronger group) and the Melians (the weaker) describes a situation that took place during the Peloponnesian War as the great city-states of the time were vying for power. There are important lessons to be learned from this history, written almost twenty-five hundred years ago. In fact, in a recent book, Graham Allison updates this idea by focusing on the United States and China in the twenty-first century and a number of other cases in order to draw lessons for current international politics.[23]

The Melian Dialogue describes not only issues of power but also the role of alliances as a strategy that states can use to maximize their power or to provide additional security. These are concepts that are central to the current understanding and application of realist thinking, and the same basic ideas can be and have been applied in modern times.

Thomas Hobbes, who wrote in the seventeenth century, also talked about the "state of nature," which is an anarchic world in which everyone pursues his or her own self-interest. Hobbes was heavily influenced by his time—he wrote his famous work *Leviathan* (published in 1651) while he was in exile—and he is best known for his discussion of the state of nature.[24] Like the realist thinkers, Hobbes begins with his understanding of basic human nature, which he believed required a strong government to keep people in check. For Hobbes, without that government, people would constantly be vying for power.

For modern realist political thinkers,

Hobbes's description of the state of nature has been viewed as analogous to the international system. Just as in the state of nature in which individuals stand

BOX 2.1

THE MELIAN DIALOGUE

Written in approximately 400 BCE, the Melian Dialogue is an example of the belief that in the real world, basic ideals such as justice and freedom will fall to the demands of the powerful. In the dialogue, for example, the Athenians do not worry about whether they are acting in a way that is just or right. Rather, the Athenians argue that "you know as well as we do that right, as the world goes, is only in question between equals in power, *while the strong do what they can and the weak suffer what they must*" (emphasis added). In response, the Melians contend that "we speak as we are obliged, since you enjoin us to let right alone and talk only of interest—that *you should not destroy what is our common protection, the privilege of being allowed in danger to invoke what is fair and right*" (emphasis added).

And foreshadowing the idea of balance of power, in which one country aligns with another in order to balance the power of a superior one, the Melians also state, "You may be sure that we are as well aware as you of the difficulty of contending against your power and fortune, unless the terms be equal. But we trust that the gods may grant us fortune as good as yours, since we are just men fighting against unjust, and that what we want in power will be made up by the alliance of the Lacedaemonians, who are bound, if only for very shame, to come to the aid of their kindred. Our confidence, therefore, after all is not so utterly irrational."

In this case, the Lacedaemonians were a rival of the Athenians whom the Melians hoped to enlist as allies in their fight against the Athenians. However, the Lacedaemonians were engaged in their own battles and did not support the Melians, as the Athenians correctly anticipated ("and as you have staked most on, and trusted most in, the Lacedaemonians, your fortune, and your hopes, so will you be most completely deceived"). Ultimately, the outcome of the conflict was that the Melians were defeated by the Athenians.

Source: Thucydides, "The Melian Conference," in *History of the Peloponnesian War*, chapter 17, https://www.mtholyoke.edu/acad/intrel/melian.htm.

alone, so too in the international system are states driven to maintain their independence. As in the state of nature, the international system is marked by constant tension and the possibility of conflict.[25]

Thus, there is historical precedent for the realist approach to understanding international relations and the idea of countries seeking to maximize their power using whatever means are necessary. In many ways, that understanding fits with the overall approach to the international system at a time when countries were vying for colonies, wealth, military superiority, and therefore power. When countries did enter into alliances, they were transitory and often seemed to create more problems for the countries than they gained in security, which has become the more modern interpretation of an alliance.

BOX 2.2

LEVIATHAN, BY THOMAS HOBBES

Nature has made men so equal, in the faculties of body and mind as that, though there be found one man sometimes manifestly stronger in body; or of quicker mind than another; yet when all is reckoned together, the difference between man, and man is not so considerable, as that one man can thereupon claim to himself any benefit which another may not pretend, as well as he. For as to the strength of body, the weakest has strength enough to kill the strongest, either by secret machination, or by confederacy with others that are in the same danger as himself. . . .

Hereby it is manifest that, during the time men live without a common power to keep them all in awe, they are in that condition which is called war and such a war, as is of every man, against every man. . . .

To this war of every man against every man, this is also consequent: that nothing can be unjust. The notions of right and wrong, justice and injustice have there no place. Where there is no common power, there is no law.

Source: Thomas Hobbes, "Of the Natural Condition of Mankind as Concerning Their Felicity and Misery," in *Leviathan*, part 1, "Of Man," chapter 13 (Indianapolis, IN: Bobbs-Merrill, 1958), 104–9.

Thus, there were few opposing perspectives or understandings of the ways that states (city-states or nation-states) behaved beyond what we now know or think of as the realist tradition.

It was really after World War II, especially with the writings of Hans Morgenthau, that we saw the development of realist theory as we know it today. Realism presumes that the nation-state is the primary actor in the international system, that it will act rationally and as a unitary (monolithic) actor, that states are sovereign entities with sole responsibility to act within their borders, and that they will act to maximize their power. (We will explore the concept of the nation-state, its evolution, and the concepts such as sovereignty that are part of it in more detail in the next chapter.) To Morgenthau, states act in a way that assures their survival or their core interests, which in turn stems from maximizing their power; it is the phrase "interest defined as power" that embodies realist thought.

As Morgenthau assumes that the statesman and the state he[26] represents are virtually identical, it is logical that he would conclude that "statesmen think and act in terms of interest defined as power, and the evidence of history bears that assumption out."[27] Thus, while understanding motives would be helpful, he does not believe that is necessary in order to understand events. In fact, Morgenthau says that what is important to know "is not primarily the motives of the statesman, but his intellectual ability to comprehend the essentials of foreign policy, as well as his political ability to translate what he has comprehended into successful political action."[28] And, according to realist thinking, that necessarily ties to power.

For Morgenthau and other realist thinkers, the principles of this approach are grounded in the belief that all relationships are ultimately rooted in power. To the realists, then, the ongoing struggle for power, whether between individuals or nations, means that conflict is inevitable. It is in this basic approach to and understanding of human nature that other theorists—liberals and constructivists, especially—deviate from the realists. But realism also advocates that alternative political actions must be weighed, with their consequences assessed and evaluated and placed within the specific political and cultural environment. This means that the concept and conditions for the uses of power can and will change and that the change must be recognized by those who make decisions.

> **BOX 2.3**
>
> ## MORGENTHAU'S SIX FUNDAMENTAL PRINCIPLES OF POLITICAL REALISM
>
> 1. "Political realism believes that politics, like society in general, is governed by objective laws that have their roots in human nature."
> 2. "*The concept of interest defined as power.* This concept provides the link between reason trying to understand international politics and the facts to be understood" (emphasis added).
> 3. "Realism assumes that its key concept of interest defined as power is an objective category which is universally valid, but it does not endow that concept with a meaning that is fixed once and for all."
> 4. "Political realism is aware of the moral significance of political action."
> 5. "Political realism refuses to identify the moral aspirations of a particular nation with the moral laws that govern the universe."
> 6. "The difference, then, between political realism and other schools of thought is real, and it is profound."
>
> *Source*: Hans J. Morgenthau, *Politics Among Nations: The Struggle for Power and Peace*, brief ed. (Boston: McGraw-Hill, 1993), 4–16.

Morgenthau and realist theory gave rise to a number of other important political thinkers, such as Kenneth Waltz (who in turn was one of the earlier theorists of neorealist or structural realist refinement, described below) and John Mearsheimer.[29] Realist theory influenced the approach of important policy makers such as George Kennan, who was the architect of the U.S. Cold War foreign policy of containment, and Henry Kissinger, who was secretary of state under President Nixon and helped frame the diplomatic opening between the United States and the People's Republic of China. Many would argue that until the end of the Cold War, virtually all of U.S. foreign policy was based on realist thinking—specifically, the constant assessment of U.S. power vis-à-vis Soviet power—and finding ways to ensure that power was balanced, at the very least.

Neorealism/Structural Realism

Realist thinking gave birth to other theoretical approaches in IR, notably *neorealism* (also called *structural realism*), as well as a number of theoretical perspectives that grew up in reaction to it. The latter group will be explored in more detail later in this chapter.

Neorealist thinking was led by Kenneth Waltz, who attempted to take realist theory one step further by asserting that there are general "laws" that can be identified to explain events in the international system. Waltz and other neorealists put the greatest emphasis on the international system rather than the nation-state as the primary unit of analysis. Neorealism also assumes that power within the international system will shift and that states will seek to balance that distribution of power. Hence, the structure of the international system and the distribution of power within it become determining factors in the ways in which states behave. Many of the principles of alliance theory grow from the approach taken by the structural realists.

Waltz introduces the idea of neorealism or structural realism by critiquing realist theory. He writes, "The new realism, in contrast to the old, begins by proposing a solution to the problem of distinguishing factors internal to international political systems from those that are external. Theory isolates one realm from others in order to deal with it intellectually."[30] He continues to introduce his approach to solving this problem with the modification of realism that he has just identified:

> Neorealism develops the concept of a system's *structure* which at once bounds the domain that students of international politics deal with and enables them to see how the structure of the system, and variations in it, affect the interacting units and the outcomes they produce. International structure emerges from the interaction of states and then constrains them from taking certain actions while propelling them toward others. (emphasis added)[31]

Thus, the essence of neorealism lies in concentrating on the overall structure of the international system, as well as understanding its various parts, in order to arrive at what Waltz claims will be a more cohesive theory of international relations.

Like realist theory, the neorealists also look at balance of power, but they place this idea of balance within the structure of the international system as a whole rather than focusing just on the nation-state. The assumption of balance also contributes to the role that alliances play, as they affect the structure of the international system. One of the major assumptions of the neorealists is that peace is most assured as long as power is roughly balanced within the international system—a situation of *bipolarity*, that is, balance between two major powers.[32] To the realists, the Cold War, despite its tensions, was also a period of stability because of the perception of a balance of power between the United States and the Soviet Union.

In their way of thinking, least stable is a multipolar system, with a number of power centers and the dangers of countries shifting alliances. Thus, to many neorealists, the post–Cold War period is more dangerous and unstable than the Cold War was, with the ongoing power of the United States, but also the European Union, Russia, and more recently the rise of China, as well as any number of other countries also seeking to gain more power and international prestige. It is the jockeying for power and position that makes a multipolar system inherently unstable.

A unipolar system with one major power (*hegemon*) potentially can be stable if the dominant country is strong enough to enforce rules and keep the lesser powers in check. However, realist political scientist John Mearsheimer warns that "great powers" are always vying with one another for power, as each strives to become the hegemon or dominant power. In the current international system, Mearsheimer warns, the dangers come not from global hegemons but from competition among regional hegemons, which could in turn lead to conflict or war.[33] We can see that with the rise of China in Asia and its aggressive behavior in the South and East China Seas. According to this theory, China's actions are a result of its asserting itself as a power within its region. That assertion of power will lead to conflict, although not necessarily to actual warfare, as we can see with the increase in tensions between China and the United States vis-à-vis the South China Sea.

Clearly, realists and neorealists take power as the core concept of their theoretical approach to understanding international relations. Where they diverge is in identifying the principal actors and the underlying assumptions governing their behavior.

Limitations and Critique of Realism and Neorealism

In looking at realism and its offshoots, we can argue that both realism and neorealism offer insights into understanding some aspects of international relations. Both approaches clearly put forward their assumptions and the central role that power plays. Both make it clear that they are not really looking within the nation-state but rather only at the *decisions* made by or the policies of the nation-state and trying to deconstruct the reasons behind those decisions. And both assume prescriptions for foreign policy decisions. One of the other advantages of the realist and neorealist approaches is that they are relatively straightforward and easy to understand.

That said, both approaches have weaknesses or limitations as well. Both of them are premised on the importance of power, but power is a relative concept, not an absolute. In many ways, it is intangible and tied to perceptions as much as it might be tied to any actual measure. Whether pure realism or neorealism, the concept of national interest is assumed to be of great importance, although this too is an intangible that cannot be clearly identified or measured. As a result, as students of international relations we are left to wonder how we know that a state really acted in its own self-interest. For example, was the U.S. decision to go to war with Vietnam in its own interest? What about the U.S. invasion of Iraq in 2003?

Furthermore, there are questions about how applicable realist or neorealist thinking is in a globalized, post–Cold War world in which countries are increasingly interdependent economically. As we saw in chapter 1, a globalized world suggests the need for countries to work together, which speaks to the liberal approach, rather than seeing nation-states compete with one another, as would be suggested by the realist approaches to international relations. Also associated with the application of Realpolitik,[34] many see realist politics as having a negative connotation, as it suggests that states will do anything in order to gain power. However, rather than thinking of it in that way, as either negative or positive, it is more important to think of realist perspectives as offering one explanation as to why states act as they do.

Finally, feminist IR theorists, such as Tickner, would argue that neither the realist nor the neorealist approach takes gender into account, claiming that "virtually no attention has been given to gender as a category of analysis," nor has any attention been paid to "how women are affected by global politics or the workings of the world economy."[35] If realism is tied to certain assumptions of human nature and behavior, are they truly generalizable to all men, let alone women? This is not to suggest that women or women's experiences need to be injected into all aspects of international relations theory. But it does mean that we need to be aware of the ways in which these theories are framed if we are to understand their weaknesses.

These critiques or limitations do not mean that realism and/or neorealism cannot be applied to help us understand some aspects of international events. And in fact, they can and do help us explain some of the actions that states take. The warnings mean that we must be aware of the assumptions, and we must apply these theoretical approaches carefully.

Liberalism as a Theoretical Model

We just looked at realism and neorealist theory, both of which posit a world and an international system in which power is one of the primary driving forces, if not the single force, that determines how states behave and why they act as they do. We are now going to turn to other theoretical models that enhance our understanding of the international system by approaching it, and the actors within it, differently. We will begin with the liberal model, also known as the pluralist approach. The liberal theoretical model should not be confused with the popular labels *liberal* and *conservative* pertaining to political ideology. Ratner, in this case, the concept of liberal thinking grows out of early nineteenth- and twentieth-century approaches to understanding international economics as well as politics. Thus, this theoretical approach blends economics and politics, which is one of the reasons it seems to fit well with our current globalized international system.

Within the field of IR, liberalism really emerged as an important theoretical construct in the 1970s as a critique of realism with its focus on power and conflict. "Liberal scholars pointed to the growth of transnational forces, economic interdependence, regional integration, and cooperation in areas where war appeared unlikely—trends and issues not amenable to realist analysis."[36] Thus, liberal thinking grew up to fill the theoretical void emerging in an increasingly globalized and interdependent world. This approach relies heavily on the confluence of economics and politics in its belief that everyone and all states will benefit from the flourishing of free markets, trade, and the open exchange of ideas. In many ways, liberalism is tied heavily to a belief in the importance of both capitalism and democracy and to the notion that free trade will create interdependence among states that will result in greater benefit for all.

Liberalism starts with different assumptions about the world than does realism, and it believes in pursuing policies that can be termed to be in the common good rather than what is good for the individual state. In fact, early hints of this idea of idealism can be found in the description of the Peloponnesian War, referenced above under "Realism and Neo-/Structural Realism." However, in this case, it was the Melians who called upon the Athenians to practice "what is fair and right," and, in the spirit of cooperation, they asked the Athenians "to allow us [the Melians] to be friends to you and foes to neither party, and to retire from our country after making such a treaty as shall seem fit to us both."[37] Liberalism is also tied directly to twentieth-century ideas of idealism embodied by Woodrow Wilson and to the belief that wars can be avoided if countries work together cooperatively. Because of its broad worldview and its acceptance of interdependence, there are many in international relations who think that the liberal model is more appropriate than realist theory in describing and explaining international relations in a globalized, post–Cold War world.

Like realism, liberalism has many offshoots. In fact, political scientist Michael Doyle, one of the preeminent liberal theorists, describes it this way:

> There is no canonical description of liberalism. What we tend to call *liberal* resembles a family portrait of principles and institutions, recognizable by certain characteristics—for example, individual freedom, political participation, private property, and equality of opportunity—that most liberal states share, although none has perfected them all. (emphasis in original)[38]

Like realism, liberalism builds on the work of earlier philosophers and theorists, including economist Adam Smith, and sees mutually beneficial exchanges, especially economic exchange, as central. But unlike realism, liberalism looks both within the nation-state to understand the impact of domestic politics and also at the system as a whole, in order to understand the growth and role of international organizations, for example. Taken together, they provide a more complete picture or understanding of a state's actions. Thus, liberalism covers more levels of analysis than realism does, while also making its own assumptions about the ways in which states behave and why.

Further, unlike realism, which starts with power as its major concept and assumes that states are motivated by a desire to increase their power, liberalism starts with the premise that the *individual* is the critical actor and that human beings are basically moral and good. Hence, liberalism injects a normative perspective into its basic starting assumptions. Because of this assumption, it follows that evils, such as injustice and war, are the products of corrupt institutions and/or misunderstandings or misperceptions among leaders. Thus, there is no assumption of the inevitability of international events, such as war. Rather, the assumption is that war and conflict can be eliminated or mitigated through cooperation, reform, or collective action initiated by individual leaders. In these assumptions, liberalism also draws on the work of eighteenth-century political philosopher Immanuel Kant, who argued that "a world of good, morally responsible states would be less likely to engage in wars."[39] This also assumes that international cooperation and engagement are possible and that if all states adhere to basic global norms, war can be avoided and peace will result.

This approach to studying international relations also assumes that there will be multiple actors who interact in some way other than competing with one another. While liberal theory recognizes the importance of states, clearly it also sees other actors as important; those within the nation-state (i.e., the individual decision makers, people within the political system), the broader international system, and the various multinational organizations all play a role. Liberal theorists look at a world that they believe is truly global in order to account for actors that go beyond any single set of borders.

At the level of the individual, liberalism assumes that individuals are rational beings who understand and accept basic laws that govern human beings and society, and that in understanding these things, individuals can work to make them better. Thus, war is a product of people not understanding these basic laws or interactions, or not working to do anything to improve these conditions. Furthermore, this approach also assumes that individuals can satisfy their needs in rational ways, often by working together in cooperation so that all benefit. It is out of this approach that the idea of collective security and international organizations had its origins.

Also implicit in this theoretical approach, because of its focus on the individual and the inherent worth and goodness of individuals, is the assumption that democracy will be the best and most effective form of political system because it allows for individual freedom and choice. As noted above, economics is tied heavily to liberal political thinking, and the assumption is that capitalism, especially democratic capitalism, will help lead to peace. The political side of this approach is embodied in what has become known as Wilsonian idealism, the principles put forward by Woodrow Wilson that have become one clear stream of U.S. foreign policy. The desire to encourage countries to pursue democratic forms of government that was advocated by President George W. Bush is a recent example of this type of approach put into practice, but using U.S. military might to accomplish his goals. However, in that case what Bush advocated was something that he called "practical idealism," or the belief that "America's national security is tied directly to the spread of free and open societies everywhere."[40]

Many of these same ideals can be found embedded in the charter of the creation of the UN, and they pervade major security alliances, such as NATO. For example, the preamble to the treaty creating NATO states,

> The parties to this Treaty affirm their faith in the purposes and principles of the Charter of the United Nations and their desire to live in peace with all peoples and governments. They are determined to safeguard the freedom, common heritage and civilization of their peoples, founded on the principles of democracy, individual liberty and the rule of law. . . . They are resolved to unite their efforts for collective defense and for the preservation of peace and security.[41]

Hence, liberalism stands in contrast to realism in its understanding of human nature and human good and how that gets translated into actions. The underlying assumption is that when nations work together, the result will be a more peaceful and cooperative world. This approach gained increased credibility after the Cold War ended for a couple of reasons. Partly it is due to the spread of democracy and capitalism in the countries that had formerly been under the wing of the Soviet Union. Liberal thinkers saw the democratic and capitalist movements that swept the countries of Eastern Europe as vindication that the socialist/communist/Marxist approaches could not be sustained. Rather, when given the chance, the will of the people was to promote a democratic system of government coupled with a capitalist economy. These furthered the integration of the former Soviet states into the international political and economic systems to the benefit of the states and the people within them. Tied to this, then, is the thesis that the integration of these states contributes to globalization, which in turn assumes interdependence that will contribute to peace. This suggests that all will benefit if states work together for the common good. The Cold War world, with its boundaries between East and West, communist and capitalist, precluded such an interaction.

BOX 2.4

WILSONIAN IDEALISM

President Wilson believed in the important role that values played (or should play) in determining the ways in which states act. In his speech in his declaration of the U.S. entrance into World War I, he said:

> The world must be made safe for democracy. Its peace must be planted upon the tested foundations of political liberty. We have no selfish ends to serve. We desire no conquest, no dominion. We seek no indemnities for ourselves, no material compensation for the sacrifices we shall freely make. We are but one of the champions of the rights of mankind. We shall be satisfied when those rights have been made as secure as the faith and the freedoms of nations can make them.[1]

This ideal was further embodied in the Fourteen Points, when Wilson addressed the Congress in January 1918 (during World War I) and said,

> We entered this war because violations of right had occurred which touched us to the quick and made the life of our own people impossible unless they were corrected and the world secure once for all against their recurrence. What we demand in this war, therefore, is nothing peculiar to ourselves. It is that the world be made fit and safe to live in; and particularly that it be made safe for every peace-loving nation which, like our own, wishes to live its own life, determine its own institutions, be assured of justice and fair dealing by the other peoples of the world as against force and selfish aggression. All the peoples of the world are in effect partners in this interest, and for our own part we see very clearly that unless justice be done to others it will not be done to us. The program of the world's peace, therefore, is our program; and that program, the only possible program, as we see it, is this. . . .

> I. Open covenants of peace, openly arrived at, after which there shall be no private international understandings of any kind but diplomacy shall proceed always frankly and in the public view. . . .

> XIV. A general association of nations must be formed under specific covenants for the purpose of affording mutual guarantees of political independence and territorial integrity to great and small states alike.[2]

NOTES

1. U.S. Declaration of War with Germany, April 2, 1917, https://wwi.lib.byu.edu/index.php/Wilson%27s_War_Message_to_Congress.

2. President Woodrow Wilson's Fourteen Points, January 8, 1918, http://avalon.law.yale.edu/20th_century/wilson14.asp.

Neoliberalism

Like realism, liberalism has also given rise to other perspectives, including *neoliberalism*, which is a refinement of the liberal approach. Neoliberalism recognizes the role of actors other than nation-states and places greater emphasis on the role that nonstate actors play in understanding international relations. Like realists, neoliberal thinkers start with the assumption of the state as a unitary actor that will act in its own best interest. However, here the two approaches diverge. Rather than assuming that the inevitable result will be conflict, as the realists do, the neoliberals conclude that cooperation will be in the state's interest. Thus, even in an international system without a single central authority, states will work together cooperatively because it is in their best interest to do so. Using that logic, security can best be achieved through the emergence of agreements, enhanced trade, and other cooperative ventures that will benefit all states involved.

In another variation of liberal/neoliberal thought, *neoliberal institutionalists* also factor in the role that international and intergovernmental organizations play in world politics. They too look at security as an important variable, but they arrive at a different conclusion as to how best to ensure it. In this case, neoliberal institutionalists believe that security and cooperation can best be achieved through the creation of international *institutions*. In this variant, it is the international institutions that are created by individual leaders to represent states that ensure that there will be interaction on a range of issues—political, economic, security, environmental, and so on. The assumption here is that these institutions, which states enter into voluntarily, provide the framework for cooperative and peaceful interaction even in an anarchic international system.

Limitations and Critique of Liberalism

Like realism, liberalism and its variations also have their limitations. As noted above, liberalism and to a lesser extent neoliberalism assume the best of human nature, and they assume that this "good" behavior will ensure cooperative and beneficial relations among nations. This presumes that an individual can, in effect, steer a nation. While it is true that in some cases the individual can have an impact, in most nation-states today, governing or policy making is the product of a group of people who comprise the government. In parliamentary systems, there is also the opposition. So, while there might be some general agreement as to ideology or the direction of the nation, it is determined by more than any single individual.

Moving beyond the role of the individual, the liberal perspective also assumes that nation-states will benefit from cooperation, which in turn will affect the ways in which they behave. Thus, countries will join together to create organizations such as the United Nations as a way to promote cooperation and stability in the international system. Yet a counterargument to that is the point that international organizations really exert only minimal impact on the behavior of nation-states. Or, put another way, nation-states will only remain in these organizations and conform to their policies if it is in their national interest to do so, which takes us back to the realist idea. Thus, there are questions about how effective international institutions, which are the backbone of this approach, really are unless states give them the power to act. An international organization like the UN will only be as effective as countries allow it to be. And then one has to question whether— or how much—power states will surrender to these institutions. Thus, to critics (especially those in the realist school), it is virtually impossible to move beyond the basics of states and power.

The reality is that international organizations cannot force sovereign nation-states to behave in any particular way; rather, nation-states behave in a certain way because they perceive it as beneficial for them to do so—that is, in their national interest. Thus, questions remain about whether countries really will work together unless they perceive that it is in their own interest to do so. Or, put another way, will they really do something simply because they perceive that it is "good"? Liberal thinkers imbue states and individual leaders with making those moral judgments. But does that assumption really reflect reality?

Furthermore, some critics of liberalism say that it focuses on the areas of "low politics," such as human rights or the environment, rather than "high politics," primarily security. In a globalized world, countries have become more aware of the fact that decisions made within one country affect others, which reinforces the liberal perspective. In cases such as the environment that do not respect national borders, liberal theorists would say that *all* countries benefit from cleaning up their environments; it is in their common interest to do so and to cooperate. But the theory does not account for "free riders"—countries that do not take action but benefit from the action of others.

Furthermore, ultimately a country's survival hinges on ensuring its security, which is a core interest and in the category of "high politics." Unless a country is assured of its own survival, the other values become secondary.

Constructivism

Constructivism, also known as *social constructivism*, is one of the newer theoretical approaches, really coming into prominence in the 1990s. According to two political scientists who wrote about this theoretical approach as it fits within introductory IR classes, it "is now the main theoretical challenger to established perspectives [i.e., realism and liberalism] within the discipline of international relations. This approach . . . rose to prominence as an alternative to the dominant paradigms by challenging their positions on the nature of the international system, the nature of actors within it, and indeed, the nature of social/political interaction in general."[42] This, in turn, requires a solid grasp of the other "dominant paradigms" in order to really be able to understand the social constructivist approach and how it differs from the others.

Social constructivism focuses on international issues and questions as they exist within a larger social and political context and the ways in which those relationships help a state frame its policies. It also stresses the importance of ideas and the ways in which states socially construct reality and then act upon their constructions of reality. Alexander Wendt, one of the first political scientists to define and advocate for this approach, describes it as follows: "Social theories which seek to explain identities and interests do exist. . . . *I want to emphasize their focus on the social construction of subjectivity.* . . . I will call them 'constructivist'" (emphasis added). He then notes how many of the theoretical approaches "share a concern with the basic 'sociological' issue bracketed by rationalists—namely, the issue of identity- and interest-formation."[43]

For constructivists, where institutions are relatively stable and set, relationships between states are more fluid. States, like people, may have multiple identities. They will respond to the actions of other actors depending, in part, on how the state views itself, as well as the ways in which it views the other actor, whether that is a state, a nonstate actor, an individual, etc. Clearly, this is dynamic and will change over time depending on the interactions between those states and the ways in which they perceive themselves and the other country. So these perceptions will constantly be redefined as circumstances change. It is this dynamic and the ways in which states alter

BOX 2.5

ALEXANDER WENDT ON SOCIAL CONSTRUCTIVISM

Wendt elaborates on some of these ideas in an article when he writes,

> Constructivism is a structural theory of the international system that makes the following core claims: 1) states are the principal units of analysis for international political theory; 2) the key structures in the state system are intersubjective, rather than material; and 3) state identities and interests are an important part *constructed by their social structures*, rather than given exogenously to the system by human nature or domestic politics. (emphasis added)[1]

Thus, states form ideas about and understandings of the world around them based on the structures with which they interact, and they then act on the perceptions that they form. Wendt also writes, "A fundamental principle of constructivist social theory is that people act toward objects, including other actors, on the basis of the meanings that the objects have for them."[2]

NOTES
1. Alexander Wendt, "Collective Identity Formation and the International State," *American Political Science Review* 88, no. 2 (June 1994): 385.
2. Alexander Wendt, "Anarchy Is What States Make of It: The Social Construction of Power Politics," *International Organization* 46, no. 2 (Spring 1992): 396–97.

their actions in response to differences in context that makes constructivism relatively unique.

For example, one can ask why the possibility of Iran's acquiring nuclear weapons is a threat to the United States. China has nuclear weapons already and, realistically, with its size and military might, should pose more of a threat than Iran. Yet, despite periods of tension between the United States and China, it is Iran that is seen as relatively more threatening and potentially destabilizing. Why?

To look for an answer to that question, constructivist theorists would look first at the relationship between the United States and China, which is built on economic interdependence and areas of mutual cooperation (for example, the two countries worked together to try to counter the possible threat from a nuclear North Korea), despite periods of tension. That stands in contrast to the difficult relationship that the United States and Iran have had since the Iranian Revolution in 1979 and the taking of hostages at the U.S. embassy in Tehran. In looking at these two cases, constructivists would argue that it is important to understand the full extent of the relationship, their identities, and their interactions and to use that as the context for understanding the nature of the threat. In addition, constructivists would argue that China's behavior will be relatively constrained by international norms. China wants to be regarded as an important player internationally and therefore will adhere to basic international guidelines and structures. In contrast, Iran is seen as less rational and less willing to accept those same norms, thereby making it potentially more dangerous and threatening. Thus, where realists would respond to this question by focusing on the destabilizing effects of Iran's nuclear weapons, constructivists would respond differently. Ultimately, their focus would be on the perceptions that the United States has of Iran and of the idea that Iran is acting in a way that is outside the accepted or appropriate mean of behavior in the international system. In other words, Iran's behavior flies in the face of established and/or accepted structural norms.

Like realists, constructivists see states as the principal units/actors in the international system, but what becomes most important about them is their interaction with other actors and structures that also exist within the international system, that is, the context. Thus, constructivists see the actors in the international system as existing within their environment, which influences them and changes them. The behavior of states, therefore, is shaped by a number of factors that are *socially constructed*, such as the attitudes and beliefs of the decision makers, social norms, and identities. Furthermore, it is characterized by the belief that these various actors not only respond to this constructed system but change it through their actions. Therefore, constructivism looks at a system that is inherently dynamic.

Although its focus is on the state, like the liberal perspective, constructivist theory crosses levels of analysis to look *within* the state, but it also suggests that what happens at one level, such as the individual or societal level, directly shapes the actions of the state. So as the interests or values of the components of the state change, ultimately the behavior of the state will change as well.

Therefore, a new leader coming to power with a different worldview can alter significantly the behavior of a state. And like realism, constructivism acknowledges the importance of power as a concept, but it defines the term more broadly than just military or economic power. Rather, this approach sees power as tied to broad concepts and ideas that feed into the notion of "soft power" discussed above. Hence, negotiation and persuasion, rather than threats or acts of political violence, become important tools of foreign policy.

Limitations and Critique of Constructivism

Among the criticisms leveled at this approach is that it really is not a theoretical model, but it exists more as a set of concepts tied to individual ideas and understandings that can change. In fact, one of the basic premises of constructivism is the need to address structural change. Since the very basis of the approach is tied to dynamics, questions arise about how to account for these changes. Is it possible to generalize beyond any single case in order to build a model of behavior? And if change and dynamics are an inherent part of this approach, how can we use it to predict what might happen in the future? While constructivists value the social structures that make up nation-states and the international system, the approach raises questions about what changes these structures and what those changes ultimately mean for the international system.

If one of the goals of theory is to describe, explain, and predict, another critique that can be leveled at the constructivists is that if identities and perceptions can change over time, how can we predict what might happen? Constructivists might recognize the fact that identities and interests are always evolving through the process of interacting with others. But that makes this approach less useful to determining what might happen because of the number of variables. It also makes certain assumptions about the state, including the central role of the state's identities (plural, as there are many). Yet, while acknowledging that these are always in flux, the approach does little to help us understand where these come from or even how they evolve.

Where this approach has made an important contribution to the field, however, is in reinforcing the uncertainties and complexities of understanding international relations, acknowledging the fact that there are dynamics that can and do change, and providing certain guidelines and assumptions that help us in dealing with these many factors.

Other Theoretical Approaches: Marxism

Karl Marx (1818–1883) was a German philosopher and social theorist who saw the world in economic terms that have political implications. His emphasis was on the "dialectic," the often conflicting or contradictory patterns that emerged within societies. Much of his work was premised on the idea of unequal relationships that exist across economic classes, which would eventually lead to conflict both within and, ultimately, across states. Marx believed that the more powerful classes would oppress the less powerful, leading eventually to some form of class warfare as the less powerful rise up against the established order and try to gain power for themselves. At an international level, Marxism sees relations between countries as similarly characterized by class struggle, with the richer oppressing the poorer and the poorer struggling to gain power. This approach also suggests that domestic and economic factors shape the country's external relations, thereby blending both domestic and international attributes in a way that contrasts with most traditional IR theories. Hence, Marxist thought injects economics into our understanding of world affairs, specifically in its suggestion of capitalism as a dominant economic phenomenon and in its certainty that those who are oppressed by capitalism will rise up against it.

The underlying premise has to do with the control and distribution of wealth. While Marx developed his theory specifically to address what he saw going on within countries, it was then adopted as a framework for understanding relationships across countries. It can be seen in the development of socialism and communism, as political and economic systems within countries, and then more broadly to explain the conflict between capitalist and communist systems across countries.

Marxist approaches have to do with the unequal distribution of wealth and power. From the perspective of IR, this approach gave rise to dependency theory (introduced in chapter 1) and the idea that the wealthy countries benefited at the expense of the poorer and less powerful countries that they colonized and exploited. Those less developed countries in Africa, Latin America, and Asia then became dependent upon the very countries that had colonized and exploited them. Or seen another way, the developed countries of the Northern Hemisphere gained their wealth at the expense of the less developed and exploited countries of the Southern Hemisphere, also known as the North-South divide. This thinking helps explain the revolutions of the

BOX 2.6

EXCERPTS FROM THE *MANIFESTO OF THE COMMUNIST PARTY*, BY KARL MARX AND FRIEDRICH ENGELS

The history of all hitherto existing society is the history of class struggles.

Freeman and slave, patrician and plebeian, lord and serf, guild-master and journeyman, in a word, oppressor and oppressed, stood in constant opposition to one another, carried on an uninterrupted, now hidden, now open fight, a fight that each time ended, either in a revolutionary reconstitution of society at large, or in the common ruin of the contending classes. . . .

Our epoch, the epoch of the bourgeoisie, possesses, however, this distinct feature: it has simplified class antagonisms. Society as a whole is more and more splitting up into two great hostile camps, into two great classes directly facing each other—Bourgeoisie and Proletariat. . . .

The immediate aim of the Communists is the same as that of all other proletarian parties: formation of the proletariat into a class, overthrow of the bourgeois supremacy, conquest of political power by the proletariat. . . .

We have seen above, that the first step in the revolution by the working class is to raise the proletariat to the position of ruling class to win the battle of democracy.

The proletariat will use its political supremacy to wrest, by degree, all capital from the bourgeoisie, to centralise all instruments of production in the hands of the State, i.e., of the proletariat organised as the ruling class; and to increase the total productive forces as rapidly as possible. . . .

In short, the Communists everywhere support every revolutionary movement against the existing social and political order of things.

In all these movements, they bring to the front, as the leading question in each, the property question, no matter what its degree of development at the time.

Finally, they labour everywhere for the union and agreement of the democratic parties of all countries.

The Communists disdain to conceal their views and aims. They openly declare that their ends can be attained only by the forcible overthrow of all existing social conditions. Let the ruling classes tremble at a Communistic revolution. The proletarians have nothing to lose but their chains. They have a world to win.

Working Men of All Countries, Unite!

Source: Karl Marx and Friedrich Engels, *Manifesto of the Communist Party*, https://www.marxists.org/archive/marx/works/1848/communist-manifesto.

South as the workers (those without the wealth and power) rose up against the existing order in order to break loose from the system and to establish themselves as the ones with the power. This can be seen to have happened in some cases, such as China under the leadership of Mao Tse-tung, who in effect led a peasant rebellion to overthrow the existing—and corrupt—order. However, in reality, it was not until China started to become a more market-oriented economy that it really started to develop economically.

Looking at it another way, the rhetoric of the inevitability of conflict between the capitalist economies, such as the United States, and the socialist or communist systems led to the Cold War between the United States and the Soviet Union. Rather than a class struggle, this became a political and military as well as an economic conflict that lasted for almost fifty years and defined many aspects of modern international relations.

In addition to dependency theory, Marxism also contributed to the growth of a number of other theoretical approaches that tried to explain international relations through the lenses of economics (especially capitalism) and the distribution of power relationships. All of these can fall broadly into what is generally called the "radical critique" or "radical perspective." Another offshoot of this approach is world systems theory, in which the world is seen as divided not just into rich and poor, developed and less developed, but into a core of strong and well-integrated states; a periphery, or states that depend largely on an unskilled, low-wage labor pool; and a semiperiphery of states that embody elements of both. This approach also assumes that the core group of nations exploits those at the periphery. But it also stresses the rise and fall of those at the core, as technological innovations and capital flows change the dynamics among the group.

From the perspective of IR, though, Marxism and the radical critiques it inspired continue to serve as an alternative to mainstream theories.

Limitations and Critique of Marxist Theory and Its Offshoots

In theory, as noted in chapter 1, globalization should have started to equalize the economic and then power divisions that exist among countries, as interdependence should have led to fairer exchanges among them. In reality, this has not been the case, thereby calling into question some of the premises of this group of theories. As long as countries remained agricultural and tied to the land and as long as the international economic system remained under the control of the developed (wealthy) countries, inequalities continued, and there were "have" and "have not" countries.

Feminist theorists also raise the critique that the economic interpretations and assumptions of the Marxist and other "radical" theorists do not take gender into account as an explanatory factor.[44] While the other theories do not do so either, they also do not presume to speak for the powerless, which these variants do. Thus this becomes a significant omission limiting its explanatory power.

Theory Continued: Feminist Perspectives

Most of the traditional approaches to international relations theory have certain assumptions, tend to seek answers to certain types of questions, and draw on certain methodological tools in order to answer those questions. Just as it is important to understand the levels of analysis and know which theoretical perspective is appropriate to help guide the answer to questions at different levels, by making these assumptions and using these tools, we are ignoring or not taking into account whole areas of international politics. Thus, in order to get a more complete picture, we need to refocus our thinking so that it specifically includes women, and gender becomes a variable that is part of our ongoing understanding of international relations. In other words, we need to look at international relations through gender-sensitive lenses.

It is important to note that not all questions might involve gender, nor is it appropriate to artificially include gender or insert it into our analysis of international relations. However, what the feminist approach reminds us of from the beginning is that we need to be aware of the role of women, the impact of decisions on the people within the nation-state, and the ways in which women and gender affect our theoretical understanding of the international system. If we then choose *not* to include gender in our questions or analysis, at least it becomes a conscious choice and not an oversight. Thus, in our overview of international relations theory, we are going to give some additional attention to this approach because it is so often overlooked in traditional international relations, and yet without consciously addressing women and gender, we cannot get a complete picture.

When we speak of gender and international relations, or "gendering world politics," what we are referring to is the introduction of the concept of "gender," which refers to "socially learned behavior and expectations that distinguish between masculinity and femininity. Whereas biological sex identity is determined by reference to genetic and anatomical characteristics, socially learned gender is an acquired identity."[45]

So what does this have to do with international politics? According to political scientists V. Spike Peterson and Ann Sisson Runyan, "The dominant masculinity in Western culture is associated with qualities of rationality, 'hardheadedness,' ambition, and strength. . . . Similarly, women who appear hard-headed and ambitious are often described as masculine." Also, the traits associated with masculinity "are perceived as positive and admired traits that are in contrast to less desirable feminine qualities."[46] Ann Tickner notes that a widely held belief is that

> military and foreign policy are arenas of policy-making least appropriate for women. Strength, power, autonomy, independence, and rationality, all typically associated with men and masculinity, are characteristics we most value in those to whom we trust the conduct of our foreign policy and national interest. Those women in the peace movements . . . are frequently branded as naïve, weak and unpatriotic.[47]

Therefore, generally when we look at qualities associated with international relations and foreign policy—power, politics, military might, strength—they assume that men are present and women are absent. Furthermore, they also assume that we can explain decisions by looking at the ways in which *men* are engaged in these activities.

By looking at the world through gender-sensitive lenses, we are able to understand how women are also present, even though they are often obscured by the focus on men. "Through a gender-sensitive lens, we see how constructions of masculinity are not independent of, but dependent upon, opposing constructions of femininity."[48] Understanding this can then give us a more complete picture about and understanding of international relations.

The introduction of the feminist perspective has its origin in the 1980s, and it has become more prominent in the last ten-plus years. To give you an idea as to how far we have come, remember that Morgenthau referred to "statesmen" in his book *Politics Among Nations*, and there is no entry for "women" in the index. Kenneth Waltz, who wrote *Man, the State, and War* in 1954, has one entry for women in the index: "Women, role in government." If you look at the entry, it is found within Waltz's discussion of peace and trying to understand human behavior in order to help understand what leads to war. This illustrates clearly the set of assumptions that have swirled around the study of international relations, which in many ways grow out of social beliefs about the nature of men and women: men are warlike, militaristic, and competitive, while women are peace loving and inherently cooperative by nature. All of this obscures or muddles our understanding of international relations. So the real questions become, what roles *do* women and gender play in our understanding of international relations, and how should we draw on them to help us describe/explain/predict? Perhaps more important, where does the feminist perspective fit as a valid theoretical approach to understanding international relations?

What Ann Tickner and other feminist thinkers have done is to force us to consider the presence and roles of women in international relations. They have allowed us to better understand how decisions are shaped by gender and the ways in which political decisions affect men and women. This allows us to look at the roles women have played in various ways that affect the international system and at the contributions they have made. It also allows us to understand that it is no longer acceptable to study scholarly areas, especially those pertaining to important policy decisions, without acknowledging women and gender in some way.

So let us see how feminist theory fits within our understanding of international relations. Tickner begins by saying that we need to step back and really understand the way in which the world is constructed, to move beyond the stereotypes and assumptions and look at how women and gender fit within the field of international relations. But she also warns us that

> feminist theories must go beyond injecting women's experiences into different disciplines and attempt to challenge the core concepts of the disciplines themselves.... Drawing on feminist theories to examine and critique the meaning of these [key concepts, such as power, sovereignty, and security] could help us to reformulate these concepts in ways that might allow us to see new possibilities for solving our current insecurities.[49]

Tickner and other feminist thinkers argue that it is no longer possible to examine the new questions of security that we are now grappling with using the traditional theoretical approaches. The changes that have taken place in the international system since the end of the Cold War especially have led to the growth of new questions about what has been happening and why. And feminist IR thinkers argue that it is time to find theoretical approaches that are more appropriate for answering these new questions.

Tickner provides examples of the types of questions feminists would ask—and then how to answer them. For example, she notes that

> whereas IR theorists focus on the causes and termination of wars, feminists are as concerned with what happens *during* wars as well as their causes and endings. Rather than seeing military capabilities as an assurance against outside threats to the state, militaries are seen as frequently antithetical to individual security, particularly to the security of women and other vulnerable groups. (emphasis added)[50]

Like liberalism and constructivism, feminist approaches generally focus within the state, looking at the role of the individual within the social structure. They look at questions such as the ways in which an unequal structure constrains or affects women's as well as men's lives, and how this inequality can be addressed. They ask how women's voices can be heard within a political system that is generally patriarchal as well as hierarchical, and how the lack of women's voices affects the decisions that are made. This must move beyond the notion of "peace as a women's issue" to focus instead on how any country can best use and represent *all* its citizens and be aware of the impact of decisions on those citizens as well.

When we discuss feminist IR and seek to understand the role that gender plays in the field, it is also important to note that not all work that deals with women is inherently feminist, nor do we need to assume that all women's political action is feminist. For example, there are groups of women who work for peace at the community level in countries in conflict, such as Northern Ireland or Israel and Palestine. When asked, these women do not think of their work as "feminist" action per se, or even necessarily political. They simply look at it as working to make their community and their country a better place in which to live and to raise their children. However, looking at their activities seriously takes into account the fact that women have an important role to play in issues of peace and conflict without judging their motives.

Like the other theoretical approaches in the field, Tickner notes there are many strains of feminist thought within IR. There is *liberal feminism*, which claims that "discrimination deprives women of equal rights to pursue their self-interest; whereas men have been judged on their merits as individuals, women have tended to be judged as female or as a group."[51] This approach assumes that women have the potential to be participants in the political system but that it would take work and a restructuring of that system. Furthermore, liberal feminists do not necessarily agree that the inclusion of women would change the nature of the political system.

Radical feminists claim that "women were oppressed because of patriarchy or a pervasive system of male dominance, rooted in the biological inequality between the sexes and in women's reproductive roles, that assigns them to the household to take care of men and children."[52] Thus, women are blocked from participating in the public sphere, where policy is made, and are relegated to the realm of the private sphere, which is seen as far less important. Yet women have shown that they can have an impact and make a contribution to important policy discussions, such as about war and peace, by glorifying their roles as wives and mothers. While this runs the risk of "essentializing women" (that is, identifying them based on their traditional roles), it also acknowledges the contributions they can make.

The main point here is the acknowledgment that women's lives, roles, and experiences are different from those of men, who are the primary decision makers, and therefore that they must be considered, if not as central to, certainly as part of our understanding of international relations. Therefore, understanding the structure of the state and the political system, and specifically introducing gender as a concept, should give us another and broader understanding of the state and therefore of the international system.

Limitations and Critique of Feminist Theory

One of the major critiques leveled against the feminist IR theorists is that there really is no single theory, but rather it is more a critique or series of critiques of the primary theories in IR. As noted above, even within the feminist perspective there are significant differences in approaches and understanding regarding the roles of women, specifically the role of feminism as a motivator of women in the political sphere. Does it really matter whether women's political actions are a feminist statement or are the result of a desire to right a wrong? Are all women's political actions feminist by virtue of the fact that they are women? And, more important, how do the answers to these questions help us understand international relations?

Another issue that needs to be considered in injecting the feminist perspective is whether doing so essentializes women. That is, women's actions are defined because they are women, or, put another way, it reduces them to a single common denominator. For example, in understanding issues of war and peace, it is easy to look at peace as a "women's issue" because of the underlying assumptions about women's nature, whereas men are presumed to be warriors and more warlike. This oversimplification minimizes the roles of *both* men and women in international relations.

SUMMARY

This chapter offered an introduction to ways of understanding international relations and some of the theoretical approaches and frameworks that help you understand the international system. As has been stressed throughout this chapter, it is important to remember that no one approach is right or wrong and that no single approach will give you a broad or complete understanding of international relations. Rather, the point that we want to make is that the particular approach you choose should be dependent on the questions you want to ask. The theory, in turn, can then help guide you to an answer to those questions.

Box 2.7 provides a grid that gives some guidance to each of the theoretical approaches and what they can tell you. Remember that the answer to any question you ask is only as good as the material and approach you use to answer it.

BOX 2.7

COMPARISON OF THEORETICAL APPROACHES

Theoretical perspectives	Realist	Liberal	Constructivist	Marxist	Feminist
Assumptions	Human nature; seeks power	Humans are cooperative	Dynamic relationship between the state and the environment	Dialectic and class struggles	Need for "gender-sensitive lenses"
Individual	Decision maker, affected by quest for power	Critical actor; basically moral and good	Range of important players with own identities	—	Impacted by decisions
Culture/ society	—	—	Affect the context within which decisions are made	Class struggle	Who is affected by decisions?
Government	—	Liberal democratic	—	—	Who makes the decision?
Nation-state	Primary actor; monolithic	Cooperative	Relationship with environment	Rich versus poor; dependency	Role that women play
International system	Stability comes from balance of power.	All benefit from cooperation, trade, and interaction.	Dynamic with relationships shifting.	Inevitability of conflict between rich and poor, powerful and powerless.	—

FURTHER READINGS

These additional readings are worth exploring and elaborate on some of the points raised in this chapter. This list is not meant to be exhaustive but only illustrative.

Allison, Graham. *Destined for War: Can America and China Escape Thucydides's Trap?* New York: Houghton Mifflin Harcourt, 2017.

Doyle, Michael. "Liberalism and World Politics." *American Political Science Review* 80, no. 4 (December 1986): 1151–69.

Singer, J. David. "The Level-of-Analysis Problem in International Relations." *World Politics* 14, no. 1 (October 1961): 77–92.

Snyder, Jack. "One World, Rival Theories." *Foreign Policy*, November 1, 2004, 52–62.

Tickner, J. Ann. *Gendering World Politics: Issues and Approaches in the Post–Cold War Era.* New York: Columbia University Press, 2001.

Waltz, Kenneth. *Man, the State, and War: A Theoretical Analysis.* New York: Columbia University Press, 1954.

———. "The Stability of a Bipolar World." *Daedalus* 93, no. 3 (Summer 1964): 881–909.

Wendt, Alexander. "Anarchy Is What States Make of It: The Social Construction of Power Politics." *International Organization* 46, no. 2 (Spring 1992): 391–425.

———. "Collective Identity Formation and the International State." *American Political Science Review* 88, no. 2 (June 1994): 384–96.

Youngs, Gillian. "Feminist International Relations: A Contradiction in Terms? Or: Why Women and Gender Are Essential to Understanding the World 'We' Live In." *International Affairs* 80, no. 1 (2004): 75–87.

NOTES

1. Christine Sylvester, *Feminist International Relations: An Unfinished Journey* (Cambridge: Cambridge University Press, 2002), 161.

2. Charles W. Kegley Jr., *World Politics: Trend and Transformation* (Belmont, CA: Wadsworth Cengage Learning, 2009), 28.

3. Barry Hughes, *Continuity and Change in World Politics: The Clash of Perspectives*, 2nd ed. (Englewood Cliffs, NJ: Prentice Hall, 1994), 79.

4. Richard Haass, *A World in Disarray: American Foreign Policy and the Crisis of the Old Order* (New York: Penguin, 2017), 129.

5. J. Ann Tickner, *Gendering World Politics: Issues and Approaches in the Post–Cold War Era* (New York: Columbia University Press, 2001), 3.

6. Tickner, *Gendering World Politics*, 3.

7. Gillian Youngs, "Feminist International Relations: A Contradiction in Terms? Or: Why Women and Gender Are Essential to Understanding the World 'We' Live In," *International Affairs* 80, no. 1 (2004): 77. In a footnote attached to the title of the article, Youngs also states that "the aim [of the article] is to stimulate productive debate about the nature and contribution of feminist approaches to International Relations." Youngs, "Feminist International Relations," 75.

8. J. David Singer, "The Level-of-Analysis Problem in International Relations," *World Politics* 14, no. 1 (October 1961): 77–92.

9. Kenneth N. Waltz, *Man, the State, and War: A Theoretical Analysis* (New York: Columbia University Press, 1954).

10. Singer, "The Level-of-Analysis Problem," 78.

11. Singer, "The Level-of-Analysis Problem," 90.

12. Singer, "The Level-of-Analysis Problem," 90.

13. See David Easton, *A Systems Analysis of Political Life* (New York: Wiley, 1965).

14. See Joseph S. Nye Jr., *The Paradox of American Power: Why the World's Only Superpower Can't Go It Alone* (New York: Oxford University Press, 2002).

15. Nye, *Paradox*, 8–9.

16. Joseph S. Nye, *The Future of Power* (New York: Public Affairs, 2011), 22–23.

17. See Walter Russell Mead, *Power, Terror, Peace, and War: America's Grand Strategy in a World at Risk* (New York: Knopf, 2004).

18. V. Spike Peterson and Anne Sisson Runyan, *Global Gender Issues in the New Millennium: Dilemmas in World Politics*, 4th ed. (Boulder, CO: Westview Press, 2014), 82.

19. Peterson and Runyan, *Global Gender Issues*, 82.

20. Tickner, *Gendering World Politics*, 47.

21. Brian C. Schmidt, *The Political Discourse of Anarchy: A Disciplinary History of International Relations* (Albany: State University of New York Press, 1998), 27.

22. Hans J. Morgenthau, *Politics Among Nations: The Struggle for Power and Peace*, brief ed. (Boston: McGraw-Hill, 1993), 5.

23. See Graham Allison, *Destined for War: Can America and China Escape Thucydides's Trap?* (New York: Houghton Mifflin Harcourt, 2017).

24. See Thomas Hobbes, *Leviathan*, http://www.oregonstate.edu/instructs/phl302/texts/hobbes/leviathan-a.html.

25. Paul R. Viotti and Mark V. Kauppi, *International Relations and World Politics: Security, Economy, Identity*, 4th ed. (Upper Saddle River, NJ: Pearson Prentice Hall, 2009), 59.

26. It must be remembered here that virtually all references to states*men* are tied to the assumption that diplomats and generally decision makers will be male. In fact,

in Ken Waltz's *Man, the State, and War*, women are only mentioned once and in a rather gendered way: "And J. Cohen, another psychologist, believes that the cause of peace might be promoted if women were substituted for men in the governing of nations." Waltz, *Man, the State, and War*, 46.

27. Morgenthau, *Politics Among Nations*, 5.

28. Morgenthau, "Six Principles of Political Realism," *Politics Among Nations*, 6.

29. John Mearsheimer is a prolific author who remains one of the most prominent realist thinkers in political science today. His published works are too numerous to list here. For more detail, see his website, http://mearsheimer.uchicago.edu.

30. Kenneth N. Waltz, *Realism and International Politics* (New York: Routledge, 2008), 73.

31. Waltz, *Realism and International Politics*, 73–74. It is well worth reading Waltz's entire essay, "Realist Thought and Neorealist Theory," for his critique of realist theory and as a way to better understand the evolution of his thinking regarding neorealism. See "Realist Thought and Neorealist Theory," in *Realism and International Politics*, 67–82.

32. See Kenneth Waltz, "The Stability of a Bipolar World," in *Realism and International Politics*, 99–122.

33. See John Mearsheimer, *The Tragedy of Great Power Politics* (New York: Norton, 2001). Also see Allison, *Destined for War*.

34. *Realpolitik* is a German term that refers to foreign policy tied primarily to power and practical considerations in decision making. When he was secretary of state, Henry Kissinger was known for pursuing U.S. foreign policy based on Realpolitik.

35. J. Ann Tickner, *Gender in International Relations* (New York: Columbia University Press, 1992), 14.

36. Tickner, *Gendering World Politics*, 24.

37. Thucydides, "The Melian Conference," in *History of the Peloponnesian War*, chapter 17, http://www.mtholyoke.edu/acad/intrel/melian.htm.

38. Michael W. Doyle, "Liberalism and World Politics," *American Political Science Review* 80, no. 4 (December 1986): 1152.

39. Viotti and Kauppi, *International Relations and World Politics*, 92.

40. Tyler Marshall, "Bush's Foreign Policy Shifting," *Los Angeles Times*, June 5, 2005, http://articles.latimes.com/2005/jun/05/world/fg-democracy5.

41. Preamble to the North Atlantic Treaty, April 4, 1949, at NATO homepage, http://www.nato.int.

42. Alice B and Matthew J. Hoffman, "Making and Remaking the World for IR 101: A Resource for Teaching Social Constructivism in Introductory Classes," *International Studies Perspectives* (2003), 4, 15.

43. Alexander Wendt, "Anarchy Is What States Make of It: The Social Construction of Power Politics," *International Organization* 46, no. 2 (Spring 1992): 393.

44. Tickner, *Gender in International Relations*, 16–17.

45. V. Spike Peterson and Anne Sisson Runyan, *Global Gender Issues* (Boulder, CO: Westview Press, 1993), 5.

46. Peterson and Runyan, *Global Gender Issues*, 7.

47. Tickner, *Gender in International Relations*, 3.

48. Peterson and Runyan, *Global Gender Issues*, 7.

49. Tickner, *Gender in International Relations*, 18.

50. Tickner, *Gendering World Politics*, 4.

51. Tickner, *Gendering World Politics*, 12.

52. Tickner, *Gendering World Politics*, 13.

3

The Nation-State Level

With the broad theoretical frameworks outlined, we are now going to move through the various levels of analysis in order to focus on the major actors that can help us better understand the international system. We are going to begin by focusing on the nation-state level, which is the primary actor in international relations. After defining the concept and putting it into historical perspective, we will move into an analysis of it, including understanding some of the major questions that have influenced the field of IR and that pertain to the nation-state: issues of peace and war. As we do this, it will be important to bear in mind the different theoretical approaches we raised in the previous chapter (i.e., realism, liberalism, constructivism, Marxism, and feminist perspectives) so that you can better understand how each can help explain aspects of the behavior of the nation-state within international relations. We will conclude the chapter with a discussion of war and peace—understanding what they are, why nations resort to war and how they end, what the concept of "peace" really means, and how difficult it is for a country to transition from a situation of war to one of peace.

DEFINITION OF *NATION-STATE*

Much of contemporary international relations theory is tied to the nation-state, known as a country, as the primary actor. Furthermore, as noted in chapter 2, there are assumptions made about the ways in which this actor behaves and reacts to other nation-states that can help explain major concepts such as why countries go to war or how countries seek to influence the behavior of one another. Realism and structural realism explicitly address the nation-state as the critical actor in international relations. Liberalism similarly focuses on the nation-state as a primary actor, but it looks within the state as well in order to get a more complete picture of the state's behavior. Constructivism focuses on the nation-state, but as an entity affected and constrained by the social and political structures within which it interacts. The critiques of these theories are often tied to flaws that are perceived as coming from the use of the nation-state as the primary unit of analysis.

Given the central role of the concept *nation-state*, it is important to begin this discussion with a definition. When we look at a nation-state, we are looking at two separate yet interrelated concepts, both of which have emerged as especially relevant in the international system today. *Nation* denotes a group of people with a common history, background, and values, all of whom accept the primacy of the state. The *state*, in turn, represents the formal trappings of the political system, such as the government and defined borders, and it in turn accepts certain responsibilities for the people who live within those borders. Hence, a nation-state is an entity that we usually think of as a country, made up of groups of individuals who live within a defined border and under a single government. Even though there might be different groups of people with their own cultures and ideas, they form a single society that has certain values and beliefs in common.

Along with the emergence of the nation-state came another core principle, that of *nationalism*. Nationalism ties the identification of the group with a common past, language, history, customs, practices, and so on. Author Fareed Zakaria sees the concept this way:

> When I write of nationalism, I am describing a broader phenomenon—the assertion of *identity*. The nation-state is a relatively new invention, often no more than a hundred years old. Much older are the religious, ethnic, and linguistic groups that live within the nation-states. And these bonds have stayed strong, in fact grown, as economic interdependence has deepened. (emphasis added)[1]

Hence, Zakaria believes that the globalization of the world today has contributed directly to the growth of nationalism, or to the importance of "core identities" as he calls them, which has replaced loyalty to the nation-state as a whole. This is one of the contributors to conflict, as different nations seek rec-ognition or *self-determination*, the belief that each group of people should be allowed to determine who is responsible for leading or governing them. This in turn can lead to the disintegration of the nation-state into various parts, as noted above—peacefully or, more often, as a result of civil conflict (ethnic, religious, tribal, etc.) as different groups within the country seek to establish their independence and autonomy separate from the larger state structure and establish a state of their own.

Another concept that is important in this discussion is the notion of *legiti-macy*, which grows from the idea articulated in the seventeenth century by philosopher John Locke that political power ultimately rests with the people rather than the leader. According to Locke, the political leader derives his or her power from "the consent of the governed," which became part of the *social contract*. It is this acceptance that grants legitimacy to a government.[2]

In fact, one of the problems with the nation-state as a central concept of in-ternational relations is that there are often many nations or groups of people who live within a state and do not necessarily recognize the legitimacy of that single state. This suggests some of the weaknesses in focusing on the nation-state as the basis for international relations. As we will see in chapter 5, the problem becomes more acute when we look at nonstate actors and stateless peoples. An example of this can be seen with a group such as the Palestinians, who are in effect a "stateless people." That is, they have some of the trappings of statehood, including a governmental structure and a single dominant na-tion, but they do not have a defined state. Therefore, there is no logical place for them to fit within the levels of analysis, yet they cannot be discounted as unimportant players internationally. The Kurds, who straddle a number of different countries (Turkey, Iraq, and Iran, primarily), are another example of a single group that seeks its own state. In fact, in September 2017, Iraqi Kurds held a referendum on independence for that group. Despite overwhelming results in favor of independence, this will not equate to statehood for a host of political reasons. This raises yet another important issue: how to account for such groups, especially as they seek independence and statehood. This is one of the dilemmas facing students of international relations today.

Despite some of these structural issues, understanding the nation-state and the central role it plays in international relations is critical to understanding IR theory.

As we saw in chapter 1 and our overview of globalization, the current international system has evolved over time from one in which empires interacted based on trade and economics to the emergence of the nation-state and the quest for colonies that resulted in another stage of globalization as the world started to get smaller, to the truly globalized and interdependent world that we know today. Included in the changing structure of the current international system are the concepts of integration and disintegration. *Integration* suggests the merging of ideas and policies so that individual sovereign states start to blend into a unified whole. Although each state keeps its individual identity, it is also part of a single larger bloc. An example of this is the European Union (EU), which as of this writing was composed of twenty-eight sovereign states,[3] each with its own government and political system, that agreed to merge into a single entity with a parliament and a president, which arrives at a single set of policies on a number of issues. Although the countries agreed to join and develop policies together, only some (seventeen) have adopted the euro as a common currency, while others (such as the United Kingdom, Denmark, and Sweden) chose not to do so. How can twenty-eight states each remain sovereign and still be part of a larger bloc with a single set of policies? The answer is that they cannot always do so. The "Brexit" vote of June 2016, in which a majority of the people of Great Britain voted to withdraw from the EU, makes this question especially relevant and illustrates what happens when the sovereignty of one member state appears to conflict with the decisions made by the whole. The end of the Cold War has witnessed examples of the *disintegration* of single sovereign states to create any number of others. In this case, the notion of disintegration refers to the breakup of a single nation-state into two or more entities that seek statehood. Some of this has been done peacefully; for example, in 1993, the country of Czechoslovakia split into two countries, the Czech Republic and Slovakia, in what was known as "the Velvet Divorce" because of the relative absence of bloodshed. In 1991, the Soviet Union broke up into fifteen nations, and although the initial disintegration was relatively peaceful, periodic uprisings continue in Chechnya, with ongoing conflict among a number of other republics. At the other extreme, the country of Yugoslavia was racked by civil war and ethnic violence from 1991 until 1996, and violence escalated again in 1999 over the status of the autonomous Serb province of Kosovo which subsequently declared its independence. Initially Kosovo's situation was contentious, with some countries in the international system, including the United States and members of the EU, recognizing it as an independent sovereign nation. However, other countries (Serbia and those allied with it, including Russia) do not. By 2017, 115 states recognized Kosovo's sovereignty, and although Serbia still officially does not, the two have entered into negotiations regarding normalization of relations. This case also stands as an example of the formal processes associated with official international recognition and statehood.

The real underlying question here is, why do some countries choose to integrate with others, thereby forming a larger bloc, while other countries break apart? To answer such questions, we need to have a better understanding of the nation-state as a concept. It is important to note that as we explore some of these questions, our focus is on the nation-state itself, not on the individual leaders or the impact of the policy decisions on the people within the state. That will come later.

HISTORY OF THE NATION-STATE

The approach to understanding the nation-state level and the basic concepts that are inherent in it (such as sovereignty) are derived from the 1648 Treaty (or Peace) of Westphalia. Here the treaty itself serves as an important resource, and it is easily accessible online.[4] What is critical about the document is that it outlines the concept of the *sovereign nation-state* and reminds all states of the importance of recognizing the sanctity of national borders. Since the time of that treaty, we have seen not only the emergence of the modern sovereign nation-state, which is the primary actor in the international system, but also the emergence of nonstate actors, which have also come to play a major role in international relations. Our focus here is on the nation-state; nonstate actors will be discussed in more detail in chapter 5.

As we look back in history prior to 1648, we see a world that was made up not only of city-states but also empires. The Greek city-states that Thucydides wrote about in his *History of the Peloponnesian Wars*, which we talked about in chapter 2, were at the height of their power around 400 BCE. These city-states were characterized by relatively small populations with limited territory, usually found behind city walls. Although they existed in close proximity, each was independent. Inevitably, some became more powerful than others. Over time, Sparta and Athens emerged as the two major city-states, thereby creating a *bipolar system* in which power was roughly balanced between the two. Under the leadership of Athens, many of the Greek city-states united in what became known as the Delian League, an early idea of *collective security* that brought the Greek city-states together so that they could defend themselves from the Persian Empire, which had been trying to expand into Greek territory.

Relations between Athens and Sparta deteriorated, ultimately leading to armed conflict between them. A truce was reached after six years, with each recognizing the power of the other and acknowledging domination over their respective spheres of influence. This truce was short-lived, however, and its failure led to the outbreak of the Second Peloponnesian War, which was documented by Thucydides, as noted in chapter 2.

Why is this ancient history important? The creation of the Delian League, designed to protect against the perceived aggression of Persia, was one of the earliest documented examples of what was later known as collective security. What took place during the Peloponnesian War was also an example of realist politics and the balance of power, both of which we will return to later in this chapter. And since so much of what happened then has been repeated since that time, it is an important lesson about the behavior of states.

Following the period of the domination of the Greek city-states, we really see the emergence of the age of empires. An *empire* (as opposed to a nation-state or a city-state) can be defined as an entity composed of separate units, all of which are under the domination of one single power that asserts political and economic supremacy over the others, which formally or informally accept this relationship. Thus, the separate units or groups have some independence, but they remain under the domination of a supra-entity. One of the major goals of an empire, like any system, was to ensure that it perpetuated itself and continued to expand its domain and therefore its wealth. Because of its size, often the ruler of the empire had to depend upon local officials to carry out his or her bidding.

There were a number of empires throughout history, including those in Europe, such as the Holy Roman Empire and the Austro-Hungarian, and in Eurasia, such as the Persian and later the Ottoman. In Asia, the Chinese empire was in place from 221 BCE to 1911 (with some periods of disruption) and was characterized by centralized rule with allegiance paid to the emperor in Beijing. The Chinese empire was especially enduring.

The end of the Roman Empire in approximately 500 CE led to what became known as the Middle Ages in Europe. During this time, we see the growth of the power of the Christian church, which melded political power and religion to solidify its empire. In Europe in the twelfth and thirteenth centuries, we also start seeing a flourishing of municipalities that functioned like the old Greek city-states. Venice, Florence, Paris, Oxford, and so on each became established centers of law and behavior, focused primarily on universities. Many became the center of important trade patterns and commerce, as well as diplomacy. Eventually this also led to a clash between secular rule and the church, and by the late Middle Ages, we start seeing the rise of what we now refer to as *nationalism*, specifically, commitment to a central identity or consciousness rather than loyalty to the ruler or state. We also see the emergence of strong monarchs who reigned over their domain, sometimes with the support of the church and sometimes in opposition to it, such as Henry VIII in England. This was also the start of the age of exploration and colonization, as states looked for ways to expand their wealth and fortunes by going outside the limited territory of Europe, leading to the early era of globalization. And in a Marxist interpretation of events, this was also the start of the exploitation of colonies by the major powers of the time.

But as we also saw earlier, the growth of the city-states contributed to competition and eventually conflict between and among many of these states, especially regarding the role of religion and political power within the area that was known as the Holy Roman Empire. Eventually this led to the Thirty Years' War, which lasted from 1618 to 1648. The war "devastated Europe; the armies plundered the central European landscapes, fought battles, and survived by ravaging the civilian population. But the treaty that ended the conflict had a profound effect on the practice of international relations."[5]

Treaty of Westphalia

The Thirty Years' War ended with the signing of the Treaty (or Peace) of Westphalia in 1648. This treaty established some of the basic principles that govern international relations today, as well as firmly establishing the nation-state as the primary actor in the international system with certain responsibilities and powers. The treaty established the European political system that we are familiar with and redrew the map of Europe so that a core group of states became dominant, primarily Austria, Russia, Prussia, England, France, and the northern area that would become Belgium and the Netherlands, although the borders of some of the specific countries have since changed and new ones have been created. It ended the Holy Roman Empire and replaced it with a system of sovereign states with the monarch as the primary political leader with authority over his people, supplanting the role of the church. Thus, as a result of this treaty, secular rule superseded the rule of the church. This in turn led to the notion that each national leader has the right to maintain his own military in order to protect himself and his territory. This also contributed to the growth of centralized control of the political system, since each monarch now had an army to support it, not only as protection from external threats but to maintain internal order, collect taxes, and so on. In fact, the monarch had a monopoly on the use of force for both domestic and external purposes.[6] Thus, the individual state and the monarch or leader of the state became more powerful, with that power backed up by the use of force.

Along with the legacy of the modern nation-state, the Treaty of Westphalia also gave us some of the major concepts that govern the relationship between and among nation-states. Paramount among those is the concept of *sovereignty*. K. J. Holsti, in his classic text on international relations, notes that

> the principle [of sovereignty] underlies relations between all states today. . . . The principle of sovereignty is relatively simple: Within a specified territory, no external power . . . has the right to exercise legal jurisdiction or political authority. This establishes the exclusive domestic authority of a government. That authority is based on a monopoly over the *legitimate* use of force. (emphasis added)[7]

Holsti then notes in a corollary to his definition that "no state has the right to interfere in the domestic affairs of another state. This prohibitive injunction has been breached frequently, but it is assumed and observed most of the time by most states."[8]

Although, as Holsti notes, there have been frequent violations of this norm, on the whole it provides the basic framework for relations between and among nation-states (i.e., international relations). Yet it is the breaching of this concept that provides for some interesting questions and discussion. For example, are there times when one country has the right, even the obligation, to intervene in the affairs of another sovereign state—for example, to stop genocide or other human rights abuses? Should countries have intervened to prevent or stop the genocides in Rwanda or Bosnia or Darfur? What about the U.S. invasion of Iraq in March 2003? Was this a justifiable violation of the sovereignty of that country, since evidence showed that Iraq had no responsibility in the 9/11 attacks, which was one of the alleged reasons for the invasion? These types of questions can both help us understand the behavior of a country and provide the grist for important discussions that will contribute to a better understanding of the application of IR theories.

The important point to remember is that the current international system dominated by nation-states grew from events that took place almost four hundred years ago. Although some specifics have changed as new countries were created and as different political systems, such as democracies, evolved to replace the monarchy that was then the norm, the basic structure and concepts governing the nation-state and its actions in the international system remain in place. And questions such as the sanctity of sovereignty and if and/ or when it should be violated remain very much a part of the discourse of international relations today.

BALANCE OF POWER AND ALLIANCES

We have just been looking at the evolution of the nation-state from a historical perspective in order to understand how the current international system and the reliance on the nation-state as the primary actor evolved. Now we are going to move from the historical perspective to the present time and focus on the nation-state system today, specifically looking at concepts such as balance of power and the role of alliances. Both of these concepts have come to play a prominent role in contemporary international relations.

We initially alluded to the concept of balance of power in the discussion above about the Delian League and the ways in which the Greek city-states united as a way of protecting themselves from Persia, which was a larger and more powerful empire. (We also saw this in chapter 2 in the excerpt from the "Melian Dialogue," which explicitly references the idea of enlisting allies.) The idea was that if the Greek city-states worked together, they could counter the power of Persia and deter it from trying to attack. Or, if Persia did decide to attack, they would work together to respond. In effect, what they did was try to balance the power of one of the *hegemons*, or major powers, of the time.

According to realist theory, if unchecked, countries will seek to increase their power. So the dilemma facing countries is how to make sure that the power of the hegemon is balanced.

Interestingly, the concept of balance of power is steeped in realist thought. Yet the concept of alliances, which was applied often in the Cold War period, has a serious liberal and constructivist core. Again we see an apparent contradiction here. On the one hand, realist theory assumes that countries will always seek to maximize their power—"interest defined as power," in Morgenthau's terms. Therefore, countries will do whatever they need to, including making temporary alliances with other countries, if that will help them maximize their own power. To the realists, then, entering into alliances is a pragmatic policy decision that enables nation-states to get something they need (more power) that is greater than what they could achieve on their own. On the other hand, the liberal theorists would say that alliances bring countries with common interests together in order to pursue policies that are in their collective best interest. Thus, they *all* benefit from working together. Similarly, the constructivists would place alliances into a broader structural framework of the international system and would offer the policy decision for countries to join together as a response to structural constraints and realities.

With this quick overview, we will now look at the idea of balance of power and the concept of alliances from a variety of theoretical perspectives in more detail as another way of understanding the behavior of nation-states in the international system.

Balance of Power

The realist perspective portrays world politics as a struggle for power in anarchy by competitive rivals acting for their own self-interests (and *not* for moral principles and global ideals such as improving the security and welfare of *all* throughout the globe). International politics to realism is a war of all against all, to increase national power and national security by preparing for war and seeking advantages over rivals such as by acquiring superior military capabilities. (emphasis in original)[9]

Inherent in this is the idea not only of acquiring power, but of balancing the power of hegemons in order to ensure the country's own security. Or that's the way it's supposed to work, in theory.

The classical balance-of-power system is generally traced back to approximately 1815 and the Congress of Vienna, which contributed to the changing role and power of the major countries in Europe. During that time, there were a number of powerful states that were emerging. The belief was that the only way to balance or constrain their power, and therefore to ensure security, was for a number of countries to join together and align against another country, thereby countering its power. In effect, this was an updated version of what we saw earlier in the case of the Greek city-states. So, for example, Britain and Russia joined together to counter the perceived growing power of France. The idea was that *if countries joined together, their combined power would offset the power of any one dominant nation and thereby hold it in check.* In doing so, the stability of the system would be ensured, as evidenced by an absence of conflict.

Britain was often seen as playing the role of balancer because of its economic and military (naval) strength. That means that it shifted its allegiances to make sure that there was a general perception of balance among the states of Europe. Not only did this allow Britain to maintain an important position internationally, but Britain's military power also ensured that other states did not interfere in European conflicts, at least not in Europe proper. Instead, the European countries in effect divided up the rest of the world, and after the Spanish-American War, the United States became an important player as well.[10] Thus, we see the major countries each with its own sphere of influence.

Most political scientists see the classic balance-of-power system as coming to an end at the start of the twentieth century, when Britain broke from its role as balancer to join Japan in its war against Russia (the Russo-Japanese War of 1904–1905). This was the first time a major European country had aligned with an Asian country against another European ally (in this case, Russia). This is an indicator of how much smaller the world was getting, but also of the difference in the ways in which countries were perceiving their role: internationally and not just regionally.

It was the outbreak of World War I that really ended the balance-of-power system that had dominated European politics for about a hundred years to that point. The war also pointed out the dangers in this system. Some see World War I as the result of a struggle between competitive alliances "made all the more dangerous by the German position. . . . Germany still sought additional territory," even if that meant redrawing the map of Europe.[11] With the assassination of Archduke Ferdinand, the heir to the throne of the Austro-Hungarian Empire, in Sarajevo in 1914, Germany encouraged Austria to fight Serbia. But by that time, since virtually all of Europe was involved with one alliance or another, once one country went to war, the whole continent was in effect brought into the war. And therein lies one of the dangers of alliances.

By the end of World War I, under the leadership of U.S. president Woodrow Wilson, the quintessential liberal thinker who believed that war could best be averted in the future if all countries worked together (collectively), the idea of the League of Nations was born. Even though it proved to be unsuccessful, it served as a model, and the concept of collective security remained an important one.

In effect, the idea of collective security was premised on the notion that "if one country behaved aggressively . . . other states had a legal right to enforce international law against aggression by taking collective action to stop it."[12] Rather than focusing on the realist idea that countries would seek to maximize their own power, this approach was steeped in the liberal notion that cooperation was in all countries' best interest and therefore that countries would work together to pursue their goals. But this only works if countries behave as anticipated. When the United States, which was one of the most powerful countries at that time, did not join the League of Nations, it undermined the entire concept. When Japan went into Manchuria in 1931, the League was powerless to stop it, since any action required unanimous approval, which was virtually impossible to achieve. Similarly, when Italy invaded Ethiopia in 1936, although both countries were members of the League of Nations, that organization proved unable either to control Italy or to protect Ethiopia. Hence, one of the lessons was that collective security would work only if the countries involved all bought in and were willing to take a stand.

Clearly, the notion of *collective defense* did not stop the outbreak of World War II. However, the weaknesses of the collective defense concept that were exposed through the failures of the League and then the outbreak of World War II gave way to a system of *collective security*, which was a modification of the earlier concept. One distinction that can be drawn between the two concepts is that "collective security is based on international law-enforcement obligations whereas collective defense is merely a form of balance-of-power politics."[13] However, often the two concepts are used interchangeably.

Collective Security, Alliances, and the Cold War

This updated notion of balance of power was embodied in Article 51 of the UN Charter and Article 5 of the NATO Treaty and became especially important during the Cold War. Much of the Cold War was premised on the need to maintain a rough balance of power between the United States and its allies, on the one hand, and the Soviet Union and its allies on the other. The perception at the time was that if there were a rough approximation of balance, then neither side would be willing to attack the other, and therefore peace (or a balance of terror, as it was often known) would be maintained. The balance was tied to each country's capabilities, especially its nuclear arsenal, and its ability to inflict grave damage on the other side should an attack occur. The assumption here was that both countries not only had the weapons (*capability*) but also the willingness to use those weapons should it become necessary (*credibility*). It was the combination of these two factors—having the weapons and the perceived willingness to use them—that ensured that balance was maintained and that neither side would attack the other.

It is also important to note that much of this balance was tied to the idea of *perceptions*, specifically the perception that the two sides were roughly balanced in number of weapons as well as willingness to use them. While it was possible to get a rough count of things like number of aircraft or submarines deployed, it was the perception that their weapons arsenals were roughly balanced and that they would be used against the other side that became especially critical. Or, in the world of international relations, perceptions became reality as they were translated into policy decisions.

Throughout the Cold War (from roughly 1945 until the Soviet Union ended in 1991), much of international relations was tied to the need to maintain this perceived balance of power between the two major blocs, each anchored by a single nuclear nation-state (the United States or the USSR). In addition to asserting dominance by building up their respective nuclear arsenals and alliances, both countries also engaged in arms control negotiations, which is a cooperative strategy. In this case, the goal was for the two sides to agree on a level of weapons that would ensure that there would be stability and predictability, rather than relying on relations based on an increasing arms buildup. Such a buildup would only contribute to insecurity (the security dilemma, referred to in chapter 2) rather than making countries feel safer.

BOX 3.1

COLLECTIVE SECURITY

The notion of collective security was embodied in the Charter of the United Nations, where Article 51 explicitly states, "Nothing in the present Charter shall impair the inherent right of individual or collective self-defense if an armed attack occurs against a Member of the United Nations."[1]

It is similarly embedded in Article 5 of the Washington Treaty that created the North Atlantic Treaty Organization (NATO):

The Parties agree that an armed attack against one or more of them in Europe or North America shall be considered an attack against them all and consequently they agree that, if such an armed attack occurs, each of them, in exercise of the right of individual or collective self-defense recognized by Article 51 of the Charter of the United Nations, will assist the Party or Parties so attacked by taking forthwith, individually and in concert with the other Parties, such action as it deems necessary, including the use of armed force, to restore and maintain the security of the North Atlantic area.[2]

NOTES
1. "Charter of the United Nations," Article 51, http://www.un.org/en/charter -united-nations.
2. "The North Atlantic Treaty," Article 5, http://www.nato.int/cps/iw/natohq/ official_texts_17120.htm?selectedLocale=en.

Now that the Cold War is over, one can ask whether alliances remain important. Clearly they do, because countries still enter into alliances, albeit for more than just security or defense reasons, although those continue to remain important. But countries now recognize that aligning or uniting with other countries can bring them more benefits than just security; increased trade and other economic benefits have contributed to various alliance relationships. Thus, nations continue to work together and to enter into formal relationships for any number of reasons.

Why do we need to understand alliances in the context of understanding the nation-state? As noted above, alliances are part of understanding the ways in which nation-states behave. In addition, they straddle a number of important theoretical perspectives, and they have played an important role in the international system in virtually all of modern times.

UNDERSTANDING NATIONAL INTEREST

In theory, all interactions between and among nation-states are designed to further the *national interest*. This means that there needs to be an understanding of what is in the national interest and how to protect and preserve it. In this discussion, it is important to remember that defining national interest is done by an individual leader or members of the government (within the nation-state level). Yet it is the policies of the nation-state as a whole that become the focus for our understanding of national interest and the types of actions states engage in to further that national interest.

Generally, a nation-state begins with a clear statement of its own goals, that is, what is in its perceived "national interest." National interest might be protecting the country from external aggression (security), enhancing trade with other countries (economics), or cleaning up the environment and protecting the population from the spread of disease (human security). From that starting point, there are a range of possible options open to countries as they seek to protect the national interest. Since these all deal with one country's relationship to other countries, these are called *foreign policy orientations*. The particular option chosen should reflect the country's needs at that particular time. What that means in theory is that the national leader(s) understand what the country's priorities are and how those priorities and needs can best be met through its interactions with other countries. The goal, then, would be to formulate policies that help a country move toward achieving its defined national interest through its interactions with other countries and actors in the international system.

Clearly, these needs and priorities can change as both domestic and international circumstances change, which means that countries are constantly evaluating and adapting their policies while always bearing in mind what is in the national interest.

Foreign Policy Orientations

Countries have various foreign policy orientations or options that are available to them. All involve making a decision within the country that requires or affects its interaction with another nation-state or actor beyond its borders.[14] Theoretically, the option chosen should reflect what is in the country's national interest within the context of the time during which the policy is formulated.

One option for a country is to pursue a policy of *isolationism*, the desire to turn inward and to minimize political or military involvement with other countries. Or, put another way, isolationism is a policy decision to be removed from the international system. Often the only exception to this policy is in trading or economic relationships; even the most isolationist country, such as North Korea, recognizes the need to trade and interact economically with a small number of countries beyond its own borders, albeit in a limited way. A complement to this is the policy of *unilateralism*, the policy that the United States engaged in from its founding until the First World War. Similar to isolationism, unilateralism advocates a policy of political and military detachment from other countries, but unilateralism explicitly acknowledges the need to interact with other countries in a range of areas, such as economics and trade. Thus, this policy of unilateralism gave the United States the freedom to engage openly with other countries economically while keeping it out of formal alliances or agreements that could have dragged it into foreign wars.

A country can choose to be *neutral*, which means it does not commit its military forces or engage in a military or security alliance with other countries. This does not mean that a neutral country is removed from the international system; rather, neutral nations are often quite engaged because the status of neutrality gives them certain rights and responsibilities in the eyes of the international system. For example, Switzerland, a neutral nation, has become an international banking center as well as the location for many international negotiations.

Or, depending on its national interest, a country can choose to become *engaged* internationally. This too can take on a number of characteristics, depending on the country and the international circumstances. For example, countries can choose to enter into military alliances or security arrangements of various types. These can be bilateral (between two countries) or multilateral (among three or more). Often the goal underlying the creation of these alliances is the belief that countries acting together can wield more power internationally than any country can if it were acting alone. NATO is one example of a multilateral alliance; it was created in 1949, early in the Cold War period, to unite the countries of Western Europe with the United States as a way to deter Soviet aggression. It remains in place today and has expanded its mandate to include missions outside its formal area, including the war in Afghanistan. Being part of an alliance or multilateral organization requires a constant balancing act as the goals of each individual member state must be weighed against the priorities and policies of the whole group. The Brexit vote is an example of what happens when the policy goals of a country and the larger organization are perceived to be at odds with one another. We will return to this point again in chapter 5.

In general, a country will choose which foreign policy to pursue in order to best assure its own national interest and security. However, countries also have to determine how best to respond to any particular set of actions taken by other countries in the international system. Again, they may choose to act unilaterally, bilaterally, or multilaterally. In most cases, however, the greater the number of countries acting together, the more effective a policy decision will be, although the more difficult it might be to reach agreement.

Here we need to inject our understanding of the theoretical perspectives as they apply to the nation-states and their foreign policy orientations. Realist thinkers will address foreign policy defined in terms of power. President Nixon and Henry Kissinger, who served first as Nixon's national security adviser and then as secretary of state, are both seen as quintessential realist decision makers who used the threat—or application—of military force to achieve U.S. foreign policy goals when they deemed it necessary. But they were also masters at knowing how to play one actor (the Soviet Union) against another (China) to the advantage of the United States. In that case, they used the United States as a balancer nation to exact concessions from both sides.

The foreign policies advocated by Woodrow Wilson are clear examples of the application of liberal thinking to foreign policy decisions. Wilson's advocacy for an organization, the League of Nations, that would thwart expansionist tendencies of other countries was steeped in classic liberal ideals of cooperation. President George W. Bush, with his belief in the importance of spreading the values of freedom and democracy, is another more recent example of this way of thinking. In this case, the emphasis was not as much on cooperation as it was on perpetuating liberal values that, in theory, should result in a more peaceful world.

These cases are illustrations of the ways in which a leader applies a particular theoretical perspective that results in the policies of a particular nation-state regarding other states—that is, international relations.

Negotiation as a Tool of Foreign Policy

When we talk about the nation-state, one of the critical questions is, how do nation-states talk to one another? That is, how do they communicate in order to avoid a conflict or to resolve one that is under way? That is the role of *diplomacy* and *negotiation*, two important tools that are used by nation-states in the international system.

Diplomacy and negotiation represent alternatives to the use of force in the settlement of potential or actual disputes between countries. Negotiation between and among the various parties is often used to help avoid a conflict before it starts or escalates, or to resolve a conflict once it is under way. International negotiation is a phased process predicated on expectations of reciprocity, compromise, and the search for mutually beneficial outcomes. All parties to a negotiation must prepare their positions carefully, looking for a balance between national (domestic) considerations tied to national interest and political realities.

Negotiation is one tool of foreign policy available to countries as a way of addressing their concerns. According to realist international relations theory, countries will behave in a way that maximizes their national interest. But the notion of negotiation, which is premised on the idea that countries can and will cooperate because all will benefit from doing so, is steeped in liberal thinking.

Generally, when entering into any negotiation, a country will begin by ensuring that its core values are maintained. Those values are the ones that guarantee continuity, and a country's security—military and economic—and are often not negotiable. A country's national interest, however, might also include protecting its heritage and its history, its culture and traditions. What we are seeing increasingly in the post–Cold War world, however, is that there are variations within a country as to what these are or how they are interpreted. Hence, ethnic or religious conflict can result when different groups within a country have conflicting interpretations of what its national interest is or how it can be defined and protected.

Negotiations can be among allies or adversaries. Generally, negotiating with allies is easier because the countries start with common values. But this does not necessarily mean they will be easy. For example, the United States alienated some of its NATO allies by its decision to invade Iraq in March 2003, and no amount of negotiations or discussion could get France or Germany to agree with the U.S. position. In that sense, sometimes negotiating with an enemy or adversary might be a more straightforward task. For example, the bilateral arms control negotiations that took place throughout the Cold War between the United States and the Soviet Union—political and military adversaries—were seen as having a positive outcome. Even when the two sides didn't reach an agreement, the very process of negotiating ensured ongoing communication, which meant that they were talking to one another. The belief was that the more they communicated, the less likely the two sides were to go to war. In that case, the *process* of negotiating had a beneficial impact regardless of whether or not an agreement was reached.

Thus, another lesson of negotiation as a tool of communicating between and among nation-states is to understand what the negotiation is really about. Is it about the product, or getting a defined outcome, or the process—specifically, making sure that there is ongoing communication, which is especially important when the negotiation is between or among adversaries?

Negotiations can be used to avoid a conflict by having states discuss areas of disagreement to see if they can arrive at a compromise, or at least a point at which they can agree to disagree. Examples of this might range from trade disputes to trying to keep North Korea or Iran from building a nuclear weapon. Or they can be used to reinforce a positive relationship, such as the 2008 agreement between India and the United States facilitating nuclear cooperation. This agreement went beyond just providing assistance from the United States to India to aid its civilian nuclear energy program. It also strengthened the ties between the two countries, which had often had an uneasy relationship. This was seen as important to both countries politically.

Countries have a range of policy options available to them that can be placed along a continuum from positive (rewards) to negative (punishment) (see figure 2.2). In all cases, the country decides which particular course of action to pursue by weighing the relative costs and benefits. A government, acting rationally, would be most likely to choose the option that promises to give it the desired outcome at the least possible cost.

Thus, *negotiation* is a tool of foreign policy that can be and is used at all points along the continuum. In "normal" (i.e., noncrisis) situations, negotiations can be quite routine and might involve nothing more than determining the ways in which two or more countries can implement an ongoing agreement. However, in times of crisis, negotiations can be used to help manage the situation and avoid armed conflict. Even during times of war, negotiations can be involved as a way to bring the conflict to a halt, to dictate the terms of a cease-fire, and to determine what happens after the conflict ends. The specifics of crisis decision making will be discussed in more detail in chapter 4.

One of the major challenges facing any government involved in a negotiation, however, is separating out the diplomatic from the political. *Diplomacy* is the formal process of interaction between countries and is usually carried out by diplomats who are asked to *implement* a government's policy or policies. This is different from the work of politicians or government bureaucrats, many of whom are also engaged in negotiations of various types but whose main job is to *formulate* policy (rather than carry it out). Both of these play an important role in the world of international negotiations, although the functions are different.

One of the other challenges in any negotiation lies in understanding the culture and perspective of the country or countries with which you are negotiating. Different countries have different negotiating styles, and these must be considered in formulating a position and in determining how to approach another country.[15] In addition, there is a strategy involved with any negotiation: whether to begin the negotiation or wait for another country to initiate it and then to respond; how much to reveal about your own position and at what point; how much you are willing to compromise in order to reach an agreement; and, most important, what your own desired outcome of the negotiation is. These must be determined by each country in advance of the negotiation so that it will know how to begin and/or how to respond to another country's overtures.

That said, ideally all countries approach negotiations by bargaining in good faith. This means that they have a sincere desire to compromise so that an agreement can be reached. But there are cases where that has proven to be impossible. For example, the country of Cyprus has been divided into two parts, Greek (south) and Turkish (north), since 1974, with the United Nations patrolling the border, known as the "Green Zone." Despite many attempts at negotiations to unite the island, they have all failed, in part because neither side would make any concessions. So the island remains divided and in a state of low-level conflict, thereby making it an intractable problem that could not be solved by negotiating. What the negotiations were able to do, however, was to make clear what the issues are and to have in place ongoing procedures that can help ensure that the conflict does not escalate into a case of armed violence.[16]

Thus, negotiations are important ways for countries to communicate either bilaterally or among a group (multilaterally) in order for them to pursue policies that are in their national interest. Before we move beyond this section and our understanding of negotiations, two other points are important to stress. First is that negotiations should always be used to further national interest, which suggests that the nation-state has clearly defined priorities and sees negotiations as an important and cooperative way for it to achieve that end. The second point ties directly to the first, and that is that negotiation is a foreign policy tool. Those who negotiate are often diplomats who do not necessarily make policy but help implement it. This is a fine distinction but an important one.

If negotiation is one foreign policy tool that countries can use to try to avert conflict, then why do so many countries seem to go to war? And what is war, anyway?

WAR AND PEACE

In order to understand international relations and the nation-state level of analysis, it is essential to understand and tackle big questions. Among the biggest questions that we explore in international relations are issues of war and peace. Wars tend to be between states (interstate) or, increasingly, within states (intrastate), such as civil war. We are going to look at the concepts of war and peace, beginning with definitions of each, and then move into the particular cases of intrastate wars, which are often tied to questions of nationalism and self-determination and thereby threaten the traditional concept of the nation-state.

What Is War?

Different theoretical approaches and most political scientists have their own definition of war. One definition of war is "organized armed conflict between or among states (*interstate war*) or within a given state or society (*civil war*)" (italics in original).[17] Another definition of war is "a condition arising within states (civil war) or between states (interstate war) when actors appear to use violent means to destroy their opponents or coerce them into submission."[18] A third defines "general war" (as opposed to more limited types of war) as "armed conflict involving massive loss of life and widespread destruction, usually with many participants, including multiple major powers."[19] Morgenthau, the great realist thinker, makes the point that "both domestic and international politics are a *struggle for power*, modified only by the different conditions under which this struggle takes place in the domestic and international spheres." He also notes that "most societies condemn killing as a means of attaining power within society, but all societies encourage the killing of enemies in the struggle for power which is called *war*" (emphasis added).[20]

In his classic book *Man, the State, and War*, Kenneth Waltz, a neorealist, writes that "the locus of the important causes of war is found in *the nature and behavior of man*. Wars result from selfishness, from misdirected aggressive impulses, from stupidity" (emphasis added).[21] Here Waltz equates state behavior with human behavior: both can sometimes behave badly. But if the natural state of the international system is anarchy, which is what most realists think, then there is nothing that can stop the bad behavior of either states or people from prevailing, resulting in war. In another piece written many years later, Waltz draws on the work of Immanuel Kant when he says, "The natural state is the state of war. Under the conditions of international politics, war recurs; the sure way to abolish war, then, is to abolish international politics."[22] Hence, Waltz notes, "to explain war is easier than to understand the conditions of peace. If one asks what might cause war, the simple answer is 'anything.'"[23]

You can arrive at your own definition that would probably be as descriptive or even explanatory. But generally *war* as a concept involves acts of armed conflict or violence involving two or more parties designed to achieve a specific objective. The objective could be political, economic (over and for resources), competition for the acquisition of territory, or even ascendancy of ideas—all of these or none of these. So, while there are certain traits that are common to the definition or categorization of war, there are countless possible objectives or reasons for it—or, as Waltz notes, the cause can be "anything."

Before we continue this discussion, it is also important to make a distinction among the following concepts: *conflict, armed conflict,* and *war.* The realists would say that *conflict* is an inevitable part of any interaction, which is often a struggle for power. But it is also important to note that not all conflicts lead to armed violence. So too in international relations there is often conflict between and among states, or even among different individuals or groups of people within states. But most are resolved peacefully, without escalating to violence, armed conflict, or, on a larger scale, war.

This leads to a question often asked by political scientists and historians who study war: is (or was) war inevitable? One response to that question is that while it is not inevitable, generally it is also something that does not happen overnight.[24] For example, historian Paul Kennedy notes that the underlying conflict between Britain and Germany that contributed to World War I had been going on for fifteen or twenty years. That point is elaborated on by Graham Allison, who writes about how the underlying conflict between those two countries was really about competition for hegemonic status in Europe, which could not ultimately be resolved without the two going to war.[25] The reality is that generally warning signs pointing to the outbreak of armed conflict exist prior to the time that war actually breaks out. They are just easier to see in retrospect than they were at the time.

Carl von Clausewitz, the Prussian general, military theorist, and author, developed a major theory of war and the use of force. He served in both the Russian and Prussian military fighting against France in the Napoleonic Wars, which ended in the defeat of France in 1815. His most famous piece, *On War,* was published in 1832, one year after his death. He opens the book with his definition of war which grows out of his basic philosophy and understanding of international relations. He is very clear that the conduct of war is a military opinion, but the decision to go to war is a political one. In other words, in his formulation, war is another way nations engage with one another; it is a means to achieve a policy option that has not been accomplished in any other way. It is not an end! Put another way, war should not be a policy goal but an action only of last resort when all else has failed.

As a general, Clausewitz had his own understanding of war and its relationship to policy (the decision to go to war) and strategy (the conduct of war). According to him, a country is justified in going to war when other

BOX 3.2

CLAUSEWITZ *ON WAR*

Carl von Clausewitz's most famous piece, *On War*, was published in 1832, one year after his death. He opens the book with his definition of war, seeking to distill it to its simplest and most basic form: "War is nothing but a duel on an extensive scale . . . [where] each strives by physical force to compel the other to submit to his will: each endeavors to throw his adversary, and thus render him incapable of further resistance. *War therefore is an act of violence intended to compel our opponent to fulfill our will*" (emphasis in original).[1]

Writing as a military officer and theorist, Clausewitz is very clear that *the conduct of war is a military opinion, but the decision to go to war is a political one*: "War is a mere continuation of policy by other means. . . . War is not merely a political act, but also a real political instrument, a continuation of political commerce, a carrying out of the same by other means."[2] In other words, in his formulation, war is another way nations engage with one another; it is a means to achieve a foreign policy option that has not been accomplished in any other way. Put another way, war should not be a policy goal but an action only of last resort when all other policy options have failed.

NOTES

1. Carl von Clausewitz, *On War*, ed. Anatol Rapoport (Middlesex, UK: Penguin, 1968), 101.

2. Clausewitz, *On War*, 119.

policy options fail. But there are other ways to approach the decision to go to war that are tied to moral values. In other words, when is war the *right* thing to do? Is it ever the correct and moral decision? These are important questions that continue to be asked today.

That aspect of war and the decision to go to war is embedded in theology and not necessarily just in politics.

Just War Doctrine

It is virtually impossible to study war, and especially war as an instrument of policy, without talking about *just war doctrine*. Given what we have been talking about regarding war, the question becomes whether going to war is ever a rational decision for a country to make and, if so, under what set of circumstances? At what point *should* a country resort to war (a normative question)? When is it justified? How does a country know that all other policy options, as advocated by Clausewitz, have been exhausted and war remains the only one left? In answering these questions, countries have long been guided (at least in theory) by the concept of *just war*, another idea that must be placed into historical context.

The classical idea of just war is normative in scope and is steeped in Western and Christian doctrine and morality. Just war doctrine, interpreted most broadly, pertains to the moral criteria that states *should* use when justifying armed aggression or war against another state. The precepts of just war doctrine are most often attributed to St. Augustine, who wrote in the fourth century about the apparent contradictions between Christian morality and beliefs ("Thou shall not kill") and the violations of that commandment by the state authorizing killing in its name. In the thirteenth century, St. Thomas Aquinas outlined his concept of what has become known as traditional just war theory in his *Summa Theologica*. In this, he discusses not only the justification for war but also the kinds of activities and behaviors that are permissible in the course of war.

Those ideas in turn led to the work of Hugo Grotius, a Dutch reformer who wrote during the Thirty Years' War. His *Law of War and Peace*, originally published in Latin in 1625, outlined the moral and basic principles that we now think of as the laws of war. These can be further broken down into component parts that distinguish between "the rules that govern the justice of war, that is, when a country can go to war (*jus ad bellum*), from those that govern just and fair conduct in war (*jus in bellum*), and the responsibility and accountability of warring parties after the war (*jus post bellum*)."[26] These precepts have led to a series of accepted principles known collectively as just war.

Many of the ideas of conflict, and especially of combat, that grew from our modern understanding of just war doctrine, such as protecting civilians, were embodied in the Geneva Conventions of 1949 and its various protocols.[27] But it is also clear that many of the distinctions outlined clearly in just war

BOX 3.3

BASIC PRECEPTS OF JUST WAR DOCTRINE

Jus ad bellum (justice of war):

- War can only be waged as a last resort, after all other alternatives have been exhausted.
- War can only be waged by a legitimate government or authority.
- War can only be undertaken to correct a wrong, and never for revenge; or it can be waged to restore justice after an injury has been inflicted.
- War must have a reasonable chance of succeeding.
- War can be used to defend a stable political order or a morally just cause against a real threat.

Jus in bellum (conduct of war):

- Negotiations to end the conflict must be continuous.
- Civilians are never legitimate targets of war. Population, especially noncombatants, should be protected.
- The damage incurred by the war must be in proportion to the injury suffered.

Jus post bellum (after the war):

- The ultimate goal of the war is to reestablish peace. "The peace established after the war must be preferable to the peace that would have prevailed if the war had not been fought."[1]

NOTE

1. "Principles of the Just War," https://www.mtholyoke.edu/acad/intrel/pol116/justwar.htm.

doctrine have broken down with the advent of weapons of mass destruction, as well as the occurrence of civil conflicts of various types. Furthermore, although the United Nations has taken a stand at various times when there have been violations, the international system really has no mechanism to enforce the principles, nor to punish states that violate them. Rather, it is up to the states and the governments to determine when—or whether—a war is just.

This highlights one of the failings of current international law. For example, when U.S. president George H. W. Bush authorized the use of U.S. troops in response to Iraq's invasion of Kuwait, a U.S. ally, in 1991, he made it clear that this was an act of aggression that "would not stand." A range of diplomatic options were tried to resolve the situation through the United Nations, and only after those failed and Iraq still did not withdraw from Kuwait was military action deemed necessary.[28] The U.S. ability to pull together a "coalition of the willing" to help fight the war suggests that other countries agreed with the necessity of the use of military force.

This example stands in contrast to the circumstances surrounding the invasion of Iraq authorized by U.S. president George W. Bush in 2003. In this case, the evidence that Iraq was developing weapons of mass destruction, which justified the invasion, was ambiguous at best. Some of the U.S. NATO allies, most notably France and Germany, opposed the decision, causing a rift in the alliance. And the decision to use military force was made in defiance of the United Nations. Hence, in this case there were none of the moral imperatives that were present in the case of the first Gulf War. Nonetheless, the war went forward, and the international community was virtually powerless to prevent it.

Feminist Theory and War

As you might expect, feminist theorists address issues of war and peace in great detail. Charles Tilly in his book *Coercion, Capital, and European States* reminds us that the modern nation-state was born from war and that the military was integral to the continued success of and even existence of the state.[29] But according to feminist IR scholars, it is the militaristic essence of the state that builds into it a gendered perspective, especially because of the connection between masculinity and war. It is in this discussion that we can really get a clear understanding of the feminist perspective and how it changes the discussion in international relations.

Governments often garner support for war by appealing to masculine characteristics but resorting to symbolism associated with women, such as the need to fight for the "motherland."[30] Women, as members of the society, are directly affected by war but are generally excluded from the decision to go to war. Especially in the civil and ethnic conflicts that have proliferated since the end of the Cold War, not only are women increasingly likely to be killed as more civilians are targeted, but war takes other tolls on them: they are often displaced by war; they are violated physically, psychologically, and emotionally; and the social structure that they inhabit is totally disrupted. There is a high incidence of sexual violence against women, as rape has become one of the weapons of war. Furthermore, even if the women themselves are not literally wounded by the violence, many will have lost family members—husbands, sons, fathers—during the war. Thus, war has a direct effect on women as individuals and as members of the society of a nation at war.

There are other impacts of war on women. Any society in war goes through economic and social disruptions and dislocation. What we often see is women having to take on new roles and responsibilities during war to keep the society going. But they then have to give them up and return to secondary status after the war ends and the men return home. At that point, society returns to the "natural" order, which displaces women once again.

However, the effects of war are often felt by women long after the conflict ends. For example, there is a direct correlation between conflict and domestic violence against women. Incidents of domestic violence increase during but especially after war, which is a consequence of a militarized society. Since that violence takes place at home, which is seen as private space, it is not always perceived as a consequence of conflict or war, but feminist authors have documented the relationship.[31]

War destroys the natural environment, resulting in environmental degradation that has health consequences for women and children long after the conflict ends. And of course, if the government is spending money to fund a war, it is not supporting the social services that many women depend on—that is, "guns versus butter." Thus, while the decision to go to war, the conduct of it, and often the reconstruction of society after the war ends is often left to men as decision makers, the impact of all these decisions is felt by women.

The impact of war or violence is felt especially by women during civil conflict, or war that takes place within the state (intranational conflict), which pits one group against another within a single nation. Thus, the growth of ethnic, religious, tribal, and national conflicts within a single state means that those who had lived together within a culture and society turn on one another; former friends can quickly become enemies, and even family members who are from different ethnic or religious groups can become adversaries.[32] Not only does this put women into positions where they must choose sides, but it can also give them the greatest opportunities to become politically active as they work for conflict resolution and peace, or as combatants supporting one side or the other.

On the other hand, because civil conflicts take place close to home, they give women greater opportunity to make a difference, whether at the national or, more likely, the grassroots or community level. Although the fact that women have been active in working for causes pertaining to peace is not a new phenomenon, civil conflicts can accelerate this process, often drawing on women's traditional roles as wives and mothers as the basis for commonality that allows women to be active participants. And the literature has also documented the fact that women not only work for peace but are also engaged as combatants during civil and ethnic conflict in which, like men, they feel it is their responsibility to fight for a cause they believe in.[33]

Thus, understanding women's roles and their relationship to war and conflict adds another and broader dimension to our understanding of the reasons countries go to war, how it pertains to their national interests, and who is affected by war—all important questions in international relations.

ISSUES OF PEACE AND NATION BUILDING

We have talked a lot about issues of war and conflict, including when and whether countries are justified in going to war. We have also talked about negotiations as an instrument of policy and particularly how difficult it is to end a conflict, especially one that is considered intractable, such as the Israel-Palestine situation that is often in the news or the case of Cyprus, the island nation that has been divided into two parts since 1974.

Yet, if conflict is an inevitable component of international politics, as the realists argue, then one can justifiably ask where the concept of peace fits in the framework. The liberals would argue for the importance of cooperation in pursuit of the greater good, such as peace. Constructivists focus on normative structures and the beliefs of the value system of the elites to lead the nation onto the right path, which is assumed to be peace. But the realists make little accommodation for understanding peace within their theoretical framework.

What we are going to explore here are the large issues of how conflict can be resolved to create conditions of peace, and then what are the various steps related to the reconstruction of society after a conflict ends in order to ensure that the country does move toward "peace."

What Is Peace?

When we talk about war, we also need to talk about peace. It is important to define the various terms as we use them—as we did with the definition of *war*, starting with what we mean by the concept of *peace*. At the most simplistic level, the term *peace* can be defined in the negative—that is, the absence of war. However, in order to get a full understanding of the term, we need to broaden the definition considerably. At a workshop on peace through human rights and international understanding held in Ireland in October 1986, the workshop record summarized the results of a discussion group built around the question of "What is peace?" as follows: "Peace does not mean a lack of conflict—conflict cannot be avoided, but can be resolved. Conflict arises from a fear of losing that in which one has a vested interest. Removal of fear [i.e., creation of trust] brings peace."[34] The UN-sponsored Third World Conference on Women, held in Nairobi in 1985, arrived at a definition of peace that includes "not only the absence of war, violence and hostilities at the national and international levels but also the enjoyment of economic and social justice, equality and the entire range of human rights and fundamental freedoms within society."[35] And a range of feminist authors "define peace as the elimination of insecurity and danger" and as "relations between peoples based on 'trust, cooperation and recognition of the interdependence and importance of the common good and mutual interests of all peoples.'"[36]

What all these definitions have in common is the broad understanding that peace must be seen as more than the absence of violent conflict and that it should also address broad issues such as equality, social justice, and ensuring basic freedoms and fundamental rights for all people in society. Thus, the concept of peace pertains not only to a situation characterized by an absence of hostility, but in a more positive sense, it is a situation of trust, a sense of security, and cooperation among peoples. It is this larger understanding of the concept of peace that has allowed the concept to be seen as a "feminine" or "feminized" notion, which is all too often dismissed as unrealistic and un-attainable in the "real world."

Peace can be achieved through *peacemaking*, which can be defined as "the process of diplomacy, mediation, negotiation or other forms of peaceful settlement that arranges an end to a dispute and resolves the issues that led to conflict."[37] This definition obviously involves two separate but inter-related pieces. First is ending the dispute, and one of the important points, going back to just war doctrine, is that negotiations to end a war should be under way during the war. But the second part, which in many ways is the more critical, pertains to resolving the issues that contributed to the conflict in the first place. It is in the latter case that the role of women becomes most important. While men often look at peacemaking as ending the fighting, including disarming the belligerents, women strive for addressing the issues that contributed to the conflict initially, also known as "structural violence."[38]

As articulated by Johann Galtung, the concept refers to the idea that

> violence is built into the structure and shows up as unequal life choices. . . . *Resources* are unevenly distributed, as when income distributions are heavily skewed, literacy/education unevenly distributed, medical services existent only in some districts and for some groups only, and so on. Above all, *the power to decide over the distribution of resources* is unevenly distributed. (emphasis in original)[39]

The point that Galtung is making is that as long as there is an unequal distribution of resources and unequal access to the power that distributes those resources, then there will always be an element of conflict within the society. So although the society might not exist in a situation of armed violence or conflict, it is really not "at peace." As a result of this structural violence, in general, when working for peace, women see it as an opportunity to address those inequalities that will help remove some of the factors that contributed to the conflict in the first place.

In addition to peacemaking, we can look at a number of other concepts directly related that pertain to finding ways to make sure that peace is maintained and future conflict avoided. Here we have two more concepts. One is *peace building*, which pertains to "postconflict actions, predominantly diplomatic and economic, that strengthen and rebuild governmental infrastructure and institutions in order to avoid renewed recourse to armed conflict."[40]

BOX 3.4

THE NORTHERN IRELAND WOMEN'S COALITION

The Northern Ireland Women's Coalition (NIWC) stands as one example of the ways in which women have worked together not only to help bring about peace (i.e., an end to violence) but also to address the underlying causes of that violence within the society. The NIWC was created in 1996 as "a cross-community party, founded on human rights, inclusion and equality."[1] But what is more important, it was created specifically to help give women a voice in the process of negotiating an end to the violence in Northern Ireland known as "the troubles." One of the things that set the NIWC apart in the negotiations was the belief that "solving the political problems are only one part of addressing the broader issues plaguing Northern Ireland and especially those within the society who have suffered the most, primarily women."[2] Hence, while the other groups involved with the negotiations believed that getting the groups to put down arms (decommissioning) would lead to peace, the members of the NIWC wanted to address the structural issues that led to the divisions within the society and to the violence.

The Belfast (Good Friday) Agreement, which brought an end to the violence, was signed in April 1998. Once the agreement was signed and the troubles that had plagued the country since the early 1960s ended, the NIWC was no longer able to win any local elections. The NIWC held its final meeting on May 11, 2006, and then disbanded.

NOTES

1. http://www.niwc.org (accessed June 13, 2007).

2. Joyce P. Kaufman and Kristen P. Williams, *Women, the State, and War* (Lanham, MD: Lexington Books, 2007), 183.

The third concept that is important to understand is that of *peacekeeping*, which involves active efforts by third parties, such as the United Nations, to keep the warring parties apart so that they do not resort to hostilities. Often peacekeeping forces can be inserted during the process of negotiating an end to a conflict. However, the danger here is that once they are in place, if an agreement cannot be reached, the forces remain. The UN is currently involved with fifteen peacekeeping operations around the world.[41] But, as we can see, having a peacekeeping operation in place is no guarantee that there will continue to be peace.

Ending a War?

Often the future of a country following a conflict depends heavily on how the war ended. This is especially critical in cases of civil/national/ethnic conflict, where groups within a single nation-state are at war with one another. The challenge then becomes how to knit the society back together, if that is at all possible, in order to once again establish a stable nation-state. Part of that will depend on how the war ends.

Political scientist Monica Duffy Toft identified different ways in which wars might end. As we will see below in the examples, the different ways in which wars end have implications for what follows the war. According to Toft, "The most common type of ending is when one side wins so you have a military victory."[42] This is not unlike Japan's surrender after World War II. The United States prepared for the military victory by sending in an occupation force under General MacArthur, who had the troop strength to keep the peace but also helped put in place a political structure for a democratic Japan that would continue after U.S. forces left. Ultimately, the U.S. occupation force was able to leave, and the groundwork for a stable democratic Japan was in place.

Toft continues, "The second most common is negotiated settlements, and that's when the two parties agree to stop hostilities and form a common government."[43] A negotiated settlement is what happened with the Dayton Agreement that ended the war in Bosnia, which was the result of the major leaders coming together and meeting under U.S. leadership. As a result of the agreement, Bosnia-Herzegovina was divided into two parts, the Serb Republic and the Muslim-Croat Federation, two entities that exist together within a single state. So, in that case, the way to end the conflict and deal with the ethnic divisions that led to it was to divide the country into two parts, each of which was made up primarily of one nation or ethnic group.

The third way a conflict or war might end would be a cease-fire or stalemate. In that case, "the violence ends but the war itself, we don't talk about it having ended, because it could re-ignite at any moment."[44] Thus, we are looking at something that might be a temporary cessation of hostilities, although that situation could last for a very long time. This situation of a cease-fire or stalemate can be seen in Korea, where the Korean War ended in 1953 with an armistice that drew a line between North and South. That armistice largely brought a halt to the armed conflict, with the demilitarized zone (DMZ) dividing the two belligerents patrolled by UN forces to this day. In that case, no one won, and no side lost; rather, the status quo was codified. The divided island of Cyprus is another example of this, where the Green Zone that divides the Turkish north from the Greek south remains in place today. Despite the talk in both of these cases of how there will one day be a unified Korea or a unified Cyprus, the real question remains, how might that be possible?

In 2008, the PRI radio show *Marketplace* did a series on "how wars end."[45] What this show concluded was fascinating, and it raised many examples of how *not* preparing for peace contributed to future conflict. For example, it looked at the case of Iraq after the U.S. invasion in March 2003 and the subsequent fall of Saddam Hussein and his regime. Baghdad fell to U.S. troops, and President George W. Bush declared victory. Since "regime change" was one of the reasons given for the U.S. invasion of Iraq, the war should have been over then, with an authoritarian government replaced by a democratically elected one. But, as we can see, many years later, that was not the case. To that we can ask why.

One answer given is that the United States did not plan for the peace, or what would happen after the invasion.[46] The focus was on the conflict, not on what would happen after the United States "won." This means not only preparing for a new government but preparing to win over the population in the country that was at war. Rather than accepting defeat, the Sunni forces initiated an insurgency that has bedeviled the United States for years. The lesson here is in the importance of preparing for the peace during the war.

In another example, while the end of the First Gulf War in 1991 looked like a great success, many would argue that the way that war ended actually contributed to the subsequent problems in Iraq. From the U.S. perspective, that war in 1991 ended quickly with a relatively low loss of life. However, it looked different from the Iraqi perspective. Then-president George H. W. Bush encouraged the Iraqi people to rise up and overthrow President Hussein, which some of the Iraqi Kurds and Shiites tried to do. But even with forces in Iraq, the United States did not come to their aid. Hussein's forces crushed the rebellion, and tens of thousands died. So even though this was a military victory for the United States in that Iraq left Kuwait, which was the justification for the invasion, Hussein was still in power with military forces like the Republican Guard backing him, which allowed him to take retribution against his own people. In many ways, the lack of preparing for that peace set the stage for the war against Iraq that actually took place years later.

There are any number of examples of how ending a war does not guarantee that peace will follow, nor that there will be a real peace. In fact, the way the war ends might actually pave the way for more conflict. The armistice that ended the war in Korea remains in place, but with ongoing tensions between the North and the South remaining. And the various agreements that have been negotiated to end the conflicts between Israel and its neighbors have not assured peace in the Middle East or security for Israel.

There are important lessons to be learned here, not least of which is that if there is to be a real peace, the groundwork needs to be started during the period of war. And for a nation-state in civil conflict, the reconstruction and rebuilding process will determine whether the state will be able to endure as a stable entity.

The Disarmament, Demobilization, and Reintegration (DDR) Process

The end of formal hostilities is one step in transforming a society from a situation of armed conflict to one of peace. "Such post-conflict transformation processes include negotiating the formal peace agreement as well as instituting legal and political reforms; security sector reforms; transitional justice mechanisms; reconciliation measures; and disarmament, demobilization, and reintegration, (DDR) programs."[47] These interrelated processes are critically important in ensuring the success of a country as it seeks to move from a situation of war or conflict to one of peace. According to the UN, "DDR activities are crucial components of both the initial stabilization of war-torn societies as well as their long-term development. DDR must be integrated into the entire peace process from the peace negotiations through peacekeeping and follow-on peacebuilding activities."[48]

Just as war affects men and women differently, so do these postconflict transformation processes. Because wars are typically fought by men, most of the DDR programs are geared toward men, including things like how to reintegrate (male) combatants back into society after a war ends. However, it is also clear that unless women are a part of the rebuilding process that follows the end of war, it is unlikely that the peace that follows will be successful.

In order to ensure that women have a formal role in the DDR process, on October 31, 2000, Resolution 1325 on Women, Peace and Security was adopted by the UN Security Council. This resolution was the international community's recognition of the impact of war on women as well as recognizing the contributions that women can make in the processes of conflict resolution, peace negotiations, and peace building. In addition to explicitly recognizing the importance of women's contributions to the peace process, it also acknowledges the importance of including women and girls in DDR programs. While 1325 and subsequent resolutions also designed to shore up women's roles in postconflict transformation are seen as important steps for women, the reality is that their implementation has been problematic, meaning that women too often continue to remain outside the processes that are necessary for a society to move from war to a situation of peace.

SUMMARY

This chapter focused on the nation-state level of analysis, beginning with a definition of *nation-state*. It is important to understand the nation-state and the concepts that govern state behavior, such as sovereignty, by putting them into historical context and understanding the evolution of the state. That was the starting point for our discussion of this level of analysis.

Also looking from a historical perspective, we talked about issues of *balance of power*, what that means, and how that concept has been realized using the different theoretical perspectives. Thus, we see the realists who look at all relations in terms of power and, therefore, to the inevitability of conflict, and the liberal thinkers who look at cooperation as the most effective foreign policy tool. Constructivists look at the ways in which the existing social and political structures affect the relationships among nation-states and ways to alter those structures for more positive ends. And the feminists would admonish us to look not only at the states but also at the impact of the actions of those nation-states.

We also talked about some of the "big questions" pertaining to the nation-state level: What is war and why do countries go to war? What is peace and how can peace be realized? How do countries communicate, and what options are available to countries as they are determining their foreign policy or their relations with other nations? These are all big and important questions to think about, and they make up an important element of international relations.

However, understanding international relations means understanding *all* of the critical levels of analysis. In the next chapter, we will start looking within the nation-state at the component parts: the *nation*, and what that means, and the *state*, or the trappings of the government. When we look at the nation, we also have to look at the people, the society, the culture, and ultimately the individuals. By understanding these, we can better understand how and why nations behave as they do, but also why so many nation-states break up or end up in civil, ethnic, or religious conflict. These are all critical pieces of understanding international relations.

FURTHER READINGS

These additional readings are worth exploring and elaborate on some of the points raised in this chapter. This list is not meant to be exhaustive but only illustrative.

Galtung, Johann. "Violence, Peace, and Peace Research." *Journal of Peace Research* 6, no. 3 (1969): 167–91.

Jones, Anne. "Wars Abroad Continue at Home." http://www.tomdispatch.com/blog/175053/tomgram:__ann_jones,_wars_abroad_continue_at_home.

Snow, Donald. Chapter 2, "National Interests and Conflict: Russian Oil and U.S.-Russian Relations." In *Cases in International Relations: Principles and Applications*, 7th ed. Lanham, MD: Rowman & Littlefield, 2018.

"Treaty of Westphalia." http://avalon.law.yale.edu/17th_century/westphal.asp.

NOTES

1. Fareed Zakaria, *The Post-American World* (New York: Norton, 2009), 38.

2. Locke's belief in the inherent goodness of man stands in marked contrast to the ideas of Thomas Hobbes, outlined in chapter 2, and makes Locke one of the founders of modern liberalism. See John Locke, especially his *Two Treatises of Government* and his *Essay Concerning Human Understanding*, in which he outlines his understanding of human nature and the role of government. Both are widely available.

3. As a result of the Brexit vote, Britain invoked Article 50 of the Treaty of Lisbon, which binds all EU states to certain rules, including a process for any country that decides to leave the EU. Under the terms of Article 50, the British government had to notify the EU of its intent to leave and then agree to enter into negotiations with

the EU regarding the British exit (Brexit). Britain notified the EU of its intention to leave in March 2017, and the talks started in June 2017. Under the terms of Article 50, the EU and Britain have two years to reach an exit agreement unless all EU countries agree to an extension. For a quick overview of Brexit and the process, see Alex Hunt and Brian Wheeler, "Brexit: All You Need to Know about the UK Leaving the EU," BBC News, July 13, 2017, http://www.bbc.com/news/uk-politics-32810887.

4. Although the treaty is difficult to wade through, it is interesting to see how the modern nation-state and concepts such as sovereignty have their origins here and how its impact is felt to this day. See "Treaty of Westphalia," http://avalon.law.yale.edu/17th_century/westphal.asp.

5. Karen A. Mingst, *Essentials of International Relations*, 4th ed. (New York: Norton, 2008), 24.

6. In describing the origins of the modern state, Charles Tilly asserts that it was born from war and that the military was integral to the continued success, or even existence, of the state. Specifically, Tilly places "the organization of coercion and preparation for war squarely in the middle of the analysis, arguing . . . that state structure appeared chiefly as a by-product of rulers' efforts to acquire the means of war," and tied to that, "relations among states, especially through war and preparation for war, strongly affected the entire process of state formation." Charles Tilly, *Coercion, Capital, and European States, AD 990–1992* (Cambridge, MA: Blackwell, 1992), 14.

7. K. J. Holsti, *International Politics: A Framework for Analysis*, 7th ed. (Upper Saddle River, NJ: Prentice Hall, 1995), 46.

8. Holsti, *International Politics*, 47.

9. Charles W. Kegley Jr., *World Politics: Trend and Transformation* (Belmont, CA: Wadsworth Cengage Learning, 2009), 458–59.

10. As I note in *A Concise History of U.S. Foreign Policy*, "The Spanish-American War unambiguously made the United States an imperial power, rivaling the major powers of Europe." Joyce P. Kaufman, *A Concise History of U.S. Foreign Policy*, 4th ed. (Lanham, MD: Rowman & Littlefield, 2017), 43.

11. Mingst, *Essentials of International Relations*, 32–33.

12. Paul R. Viotti and Mark V. Kauppi, *International Relations and World Politics: Security, Economy, Identity*, 4th ed. (Upper Saddle River, NJ: Pearson Education, 2009), 70–71.

13. Viotti and Kauppi, *International Relations and World Politics*, 537.

14. For a more detailed discussion of foreign policy orientations, see Joyce P. Kaufman, *A Concise History of U.S. Foreign Policy*, 15–18.

15. For more examples of the ways in which culture affects negotiations, see Raymond Cohen, *Negotiating Across Cultures: International Negotiation in an Interdependent World* (Washington, DC: United States Institute of Peace Press, 1997).

16. The most recent talks took place between January and early July 2017 but ended without a resolution. For a quick overview of the talks and the situation in Cyprus, see BBC News, "Cyprus Talks End without a Peace and Reunification Deal," July 7, 2017, http://www.bbc.com/news/world-europe-40530370.

17. Viotti and Kauppi, *International Relations and World Politics*, 555.

18. Kegley, *World Politics*, 382.

19. Mingst, *Essentials of International Relations*, 218.

20. Hans J. Morgenthau, *Politics Among Nations: The Struggle for Power and Peace*, brief ed. (Boston: McGraw-Hill, 1993), 37.

21. Kenneth N. Waltz, *Man, the State, and War: A Theoretical Analysis* (New York: Columbia University Press, 2001), 16.

22. Kenneth N. Waltz, *Realism and International Politics* (New York: Routledge, 2008), 199.

23. Waltz, *Realism and International Politics*, 199.

24. There are exceptions to that statement, of course. Although there are allegations that Franklin Roosevelt and others in his administration were aware of the possibility of the Japanese attack on Pearl Harbor, that theory has been refuted as discussed in a story on NPR's *Morning Edition*, "No, FDR Did Not Know the Japanese Were Going to Bomb Pearl Harbor," December 6, 2016, http://www .npr.org/2016/12/06/504449867/no-fdr-did-not-know-the-japanese-were-going-to -bomb-pearl-harbor. Of course terrorist attacks, such as 9/11, rely on surprise to have the maximum impact, but that is a different case. That said, most interstate conflicts are preceded by periods of tension and even low levels of armed violence prior to the outbreak of major war.

25. Graham Allison, *Destined for War: Can America and China Escape Thucydides's Trap?* (Boston: Houghton Mifflin Harcourt, 2017), 83.

26. "Just War Theory," *Internet Encyclopedia of Philosophy*, http://www.iep/utm/ edu/justwar/print.

27. Although the first Geneva Convention was adopted in 1864, the one that is generally referred to regarding protecting civilians is the fourth Geneva Convention, adopted in 1949. The principles embodied in this grew from the experiences of World War II; it was the first to deal explicitly with civilians. For a discussion of this and the other Geneva conventions, see "The Geneva Conventions of 1949," https://www.icrc .org/eng/war-and-law/treaties-customary-law/geneva-conventions/overview-geneva -conventions.htm.

28. For President Bush's own account of the events, see George Bush and Brent Scowcroft, *A World Transformed* (New York: Knopf, 1998).

29. See Charles Tilly, *Coercion, Capital, and European States* (Cambridge, MA: Blackwell, 1992).

30. It should be noted that one of the few exceptions to this moniker was Hitler's Germany during World War II, where the fight was for the "fatherland."

31. See, for example, Ann Jones, "Wars abroad Continue at Home," http://www.tomdispatch.com/blog/175053/tomgram:__ann_jones,_wars_abroad_continue_at_home; Cynthia Cockburn, *The Space Between Us: Negotiating Gender and National Identities in Conflict* (London: Zed Books, 1998); and Joyce P. Kaufman and Kristen P. Williams, *Women, the State, and War* (Lanham, MD: Lexington Books, 2007), 173–74.

32. Women in ethnically or religiously mixed marriages was one of the variables that we examined in *Women, the State, and War*. Marriage is one way that states gender citizenship, and as we saw in the cases we examined, generally it is the woman who suffers when she marries outside her group. She is often ostracized by her own family for marrying outside the group and is never really accepted by her husband's family because she is one of "the other." In some cases, as we saw in the case of the former Yugoslavia, this led directly to violence against women. See Kaufman and Williams, *Women, the State, and War*, 96–103.

33. There are a number of authors who have studied women as combatants. For example, see Laura Sjoberg and Caron E. Gentry, *Mothers, Monsters, Whores: Women's Violence in Global Politics* (London: Zed Books, 2007); Miranda H. Alison, *Women and Political Violence* (New York: Routledge, 2009); Mia Bloom, *Dying to Kill: The Allure of Suicide Terror* (New York: Columbia University Press, 2005); and Joyce P. Kaufman and Kristen P. Williams, *Challenging Gender Norms: Women and Political Activism in Times of Conflict* (Sterling, VA: Kumarian Press, 2013).

34. Workshop summary, "Workshop on Peace through Human Rights and Understanding," Navan, Ireland, October 12–17, 1986, 13. Accessed at the Women's Library, London, June 2008.

35. Inger Skjelsbaek, "Gendered Battlefields: A Gender Analysis of Peace and Conflict," PRIO Report (Oslo: International Peace Research Institute, 1997), 7.

36. Tami Amanda Jacoby, *Women in Zones of Conflict: Power and Resistance in Israel* (Montreal: McGill-Queen's University Press, 2005), 13.

37. Kegley, *World Politics*, 578.

38. Johann Galtung, "Violence, Peace, and Peace Research," *Journal of Peace Research* 6, no. 3 (1969): 167–91. Also see Galtung, *Peace by Peaceful Means: Peace and Conflict, Development and Civilization* (London: Sage, 1996).

39. Galtung, "Violence, Peace, and Peace Research," 171.

40. Kegley, *World Politics*, 578.

41. United Nations Peacekeeping Operations, http://www.un.org/en/peacekeeping/operations/current.shtml.

42. Quoted in Public Radio International, "How Wars End," part 1, introduction, October 6, 2008, https://www.pri.org/series/how-wars-end.

43. Quoted in "How Wars End."

44. Quoted in "How Wars End."

45. This was a five-part series, broadcast October 6–10, 2008. The entire series can be found at https://www.pri.org/series/how-wars-end.

46. For more detail on this point, see George Packer, *The Assassins' Gate: America in Iraq* (New York: Farrar, Straus & Giroux, 2005). See also Thomas E. Ricks, *Fiasco: The American Military Adventure in Iraq* (New York: Penguin, 2006).

47. Joyce P. Kaufman and Kristen P. Williams, introduction to *Women, Gender Equity, and Post-Conflict Transformation*, ed. Joyce P. Kaufman and Kristen P. Williams (New York: Routledge, 2017), 1.

48. "United Nations Peacekeeping: Disarmament, Demobilization and Reintegration," http://www.un.org/en/peacekeeping/issues/ddr.shtml.

4

Within the Nation-State

In the last chapter we looked at the nation-state—specifically, what it is, how it evolved, and the critical role that nation-states play in the international system. What we are going to do now is look *within* the nation-state, as we continue to move from the macro to the more micro levels of analysis. (As a reminder, you might want to look back at figure 2.1 on the levels of analysis.) If the international system is the most macro level—it encompasses the entire system at its broadest—then we are moving toward the most micro level, the individual. Why is this important? Nation-states are the products of their component parts: the government and political system that run it; the cultures and societies of the people within it; and the individuals who make up the government, cultures, and societies. In fact, only by understanding all these interrelated parts is it really possible to understand why some nations (such as the United States) hold together despite the disparate groups of peoples it comprises, and why others (such as the former Yugoslavia) fall apart, often leading to bloody conflict. Understanding these pieces is critical to understanding international relations.

We will proceed in this chapter by going through the levels of analysis that are found within the nation-state, ultimately ending at the individual level. It is important to remember that even though we address these as if they were individual pieces, the reality is that they are parts of an integrated whole. For example, the nation-state is composed of the government, the culture, and society, all of which are made up of individuals. But this does not mean we need to know how every individual thinks. Rather, as we will see later in this chapter, what is most important is how the individual leaders think, as they are the ones who steer the course for the nation-state. That said, at a time of political transition in parts of the world, it is important to think about how individuals, acting together, can change the course of political action in any one country, as they did in Tunisia, Libya, and Egypt during the Arab Spring, for example, and the impact of such actions on the government.

We will begin with an overview of government in general and of the role that government plays in international relations. From there, we will look at the "nation" part of the nation-state, with an eye toward understanding the culture and societies. Just as we examined large questions of peace and war when we talked about the nation-state level, there are important questions to be asked about conflict when we look within the nation-state. Rather than looking specifically at wars between or among nation-states, here we will try to understand and get a better grasp of what causes civil or intrastate conflicts or wars. We need to look within the nation-state at the nations, culture, and societies in order to understand a little bit more about why one group within a country turns on another, and also why these types of conflicts are often so difficult to resolve.

We will conclude the chapter with a discussion of the individual level and what role the individual plays in international relations under different sets of circumstances.

THE GOVERNMENT

In chapter 3, we gave the definition of the nation-state as comprising two separate but interrelated concepts. As noted in our definition of *nation-state*, it has two component parts, the nation, or the people, and the state, which includes the boundaries or borders that define the territory but also the government. Every nation-state has a government that is responsible for ensuring the collective well-being and security of the state and the people within it. Looking at it another way, for a government or the political system of the country to be considered *legitimate*, the people within the borders of the state (i.e., the nation) must feel an allegiance to the state. There are any number of different types of political systems or governments, some of which are considered more legitimate than others both by the people within their borders and by those outside them. The latter is an especially important point; if a government is not considered to be legitimate, then other countries and governments will not want to interact with it for fear of the appearance that doing so will be granting it legitimacy.

This might seem confusing, so let's put it a different way. If a dictator takes power through illegitimate means such as overthrowing an established government, other countries will not want to deal with that leader as a sign that they cannot support the methods used to take control. Hence, another country might not want to grant the country diplomatic recognition or will try to isolate it from interacting with other countries in the international system through measures such as imposing a trade embargo or economic sanctions. We have seen this with the imposition of sanctions against North Korea as "punishment" for moving forward with its nuclear weapons testing. Does that mean the leader does not exist or will go away, or that the country will change its policies? Not really. But it does send a signal regarding that country's place within the international system.

It has also been shown that even if a country opposes the policies of another or the means by which a leader took power, they might continue to work with the leader if they feel it's in the national interest. Here again, some examples might prove helpful. Although the United States did not support many of the repressive policies of Joseph Stalin, during World War II the United States and Stalin were allies against Hitler, who was seen as a greater threat. It was after the war ended and Hitler was defeated that there was a huge ideological and military divide between the United States and the then USSR that grew into the Cold War. More recently, we can look at the case of North Korea, which is a closed, isolationist regime—yet the UN Conference on Trade and Development estimates that "foreign direct investment in 2010 was $38m (£24m; 29m euros) and that the total amount invested in North Korea over the past few decades comes to $1.475bn (£940m; 1.13bn euros)."[1] Most of that investment was from China, due in part to the fact that North Korea has resources that China wants and needs for its own development. Neighboring South Korea has been investing in the North, and other countries, including Russia, India, and Germany, also see North Korea as holding potential for investment.

Countries will also isolate another country when a leader with whom they have problems ideologically takes power. For example, after then–Chinese leader Mao Tse-tung officially declared the creation of the People's Republic of China as a communist country on October 1, 1949, the United States would not recognize that country as "China," preferring instead to recognize the nationalist government on Formosa (Taiwan) as China. The United States had backed the nationalist leader Chiang Kai-shek against Mao during the civil war and preferred to make a statement about their allegiance to that leader, as well as against communism. It was not until many years later, in 1979, that the United States officially recognized what we now know as "China." U.S. nonrecognition of China did not mean that the country did not exist; clearly it did. But the policy sent a signal that the United States was continuing to support its ally, Taiwan, which in turn alerted China that should it decide to attack Taiwan and try to annex it, it would have to deal with the United States.

Now let's look at another, more recent example here in the United States. The presidential election of 2016 brought Donald Trump into office. Although he fell far short of Democratic candidate Hillary Clinton in the popular vote, he won the Electoral College, thereby giving him the presidency. From the time he came into office, despite the fact that the election was consistent with the U.S. electoral process, there were cries of "not my president," thereby questioning his legitimacy. When information started to become public that Russia had meddled with the election through hacking and other electronic means, it raised further questions about his legitimacy. Objectively, whether one liked the outcome of the race or not, the U.S. electoral process was followed, and therefore Trump became the legitimate president. Should information subsequently be revealed that the process was tampered with in any way, then the legitimacy can be questioned. But that would be a case to be made by the special prosecutor (Robert Mueller) and/or the Congress in their investigations. Hence, in this case, the process grants legitimacy unless or until that process has been proven to be flawed. And the questions that emerged are not about the legitimacy of the government but the individual (i.e., Donald Trump), which in this case is conflated with the government.

Clearly, there are many different types of governments and political systems. Some impose their will (and the hope of legitimacy) from the top down. These tend to be autocratic or authoritarian governments whose continuity within the country is often assured through means of coercion, such as the use of the military. Another type of government is a democracy, which is generally a participatory system in which the citizens have some say in choosing their leaders

BOX 4.1

RUSSIA AND "DEMOCRATIC ELECTIONS"

It is important to remember that holding an election does not equate to democracy. For example, in Russia, former president Putin's role was formalized when he was again elected president in March 2012, succeeding Dmitry Medvedev, his handpicked successor. But Putin's election in 2012 was not without controversy, leading to street protests that started even prior to the elections and grew violent at times. In many ways, the protests underscored how much Russia had changed in the period since Putin was last elected president in 2000 and again in 2004. Although Putin "won" 64 percent of the vote in 2012, he was not recognized as the legitimate president by many in Russia. According to one report, "The election was neither open nor honest. . . . [And] by some estimates vote-rigging added at least ten percentage points to Mr. Putin's tally."[1] As also reported, the election results of more than 50 percent ensured that Putin did not have to face a runoff election and was a demonstration to the bureaucracy and security services that he remains in charge and can mobilize whatever resources he needs to stay in power. "Yet the fact that the Kremlin was forced to use more elaborate means to rig the election was also testimony to the growing pressure from civil society."[2] Nonetheless, as the "elected" leader, he represents his country at most international meetings, which is one way of granting him legitimacy.

The election of Putin in 2012 serves as an example of a case where an election does not equate to democracy and the will of the people. Yet Putin continues to serve as the recognized president of Russia.

NOTES

1. "Russia's Presidential Election: Moscow Doesn't Believe in Tears," *The Economist*, March 10, 2012, 62.
2. "Russia's Presidential Election," 62.

and, therefore, in the decisions that are made. Democracies are supposed to reflect the will of the masses (that is, the non–decision makers), since one of the characteristics of this form of government is that if the people are dissatisfied, they can throw out the decision makers in the next election. Democracies can be parliamentary systems, such as the United Kingdom, or presidential, such as the United States. Both of these variations *empower* their people.

We are not going to go into these different types of governments in depth here—that is really the purview of comparative politics—beyond noting that different types of governments have implications for international relations. Each political system has a different process for making decisions, including decisions on foreign policy. Since foreign policy is the process through which one nation-state interacts with another, foreign policy decisions and the ways that these are made have important implications for understanding international relations. It is this set of points that we will be exploring in more detail here.

What does all this tell us about the level of the government? It means that even though a government is something that exists within the nation-state specifically to govern the people, there are implications for the ways in which other states see the government of that country and interact with it. In other words, what happens within the country has implications for foreign policy, which is also international relations.

Democratizing the State

One statistic suggests that "approximately thirty countries shifted from authoritarian to democratic systems during the 1970s and 1980s; this so called 'third wave' of democratization, defined as a move toward competitive electoral politics, was most successful in countries where Western influences were strongest."[2] For example, this can be seen in the transition that took place in the countries of Eastern Europe, as they moved beyond Soviet-era communist systems to embrace both democratic political systems and capitalist economies. Ultimately, this was also manifested in their individual desire to join both NATO and the EU, as proof that they were indeed part of the family of "Western" countries.

This transformation to democracy spurred a greater interest in understanding democratization, especially as it was also connected to the growth of free-market capitalist economies and an emphasis on improved human rights, both of which are tied to liberal values. Going back to our earlier discussions of theory, realists assume a unitary actor, which in turn makes assumptions about the behavior of states—specifically that they will always act in their own best interest to maximize power. On the other hand, liberal theorists are more interested in looking at the ways in which the transition to democratic systems has played out, not only economically but also as it affects a country's foreign policy. This is especially important, as the liberal theorists see a direct connection between economics and politics. The constructivists would want us to understand the relationship between the various social and political structures and the country's policy decisions, and of course the Marxists see a direct link between economics and politics.

The feminists would alert us to think about the concept of democracy through gender-sensitive lenses. Doing so alters the perspective still further. The feminist literature reminds us that even in democratic systems, generally women do not have the same access to power that men do, and that political agendas that benefit women are not always put forward. Even liberal definitions of citizenship are grounded in the social contract of seventeenth- and eighteenth-century Europe, which were based on "male, property-owning heads-of-households . . . [and] thus, democratic theory and practice have been built on the male-as-norm engaged in narrowly defined political activities."[3] We will return to the ways in which the state genders citizenship later. But the point to remember is that while we often think of democracy as a political form that the people can contribute to and benefit from, we still need to ask who participates and who benefits. Thus, each of the theoretical approaches would have something to contribute to this part of the discussion.

Accompanying the apparent move toward increased democratization has also been the assumption that democracy is a "better" form of government because of the apparent benefits derived: people have a vested interest; government will protect the "national interest"; human rights will be protected; theoretically, decisions will benefit the greater good or the collective; and so on. There is also the emergence of theories such as the "democratic peace," which makes assumptions about the supposedly peaceful nature of democracies, explored in more detail below. This too has reinforced the idea of democracy as the "best" form of political system.

However, it is also important to remember that democracy brings with it certain responsibilities and requirements. Democracy assumes an educated

BOX 4.2

CAN DEMOCRACY BE IMPOSED? PRESIDENT GEORGE W. BUSH AND DEMOCRACY IN IRAQ

By looking a series of speeches made by the Bush administration, it is possible to track the rhetoric leading to the war against Iraq, justified initially by the alleged presence of weapons of mass destruction, to the need for regime change, and ultimately the hope of creating a democratic form of government in Iraq.

In his State of the Union speech in January 2002, Bush identified Iraq, Iran, and North Korea as an "axis of evil," and he stated that "some governments will be timid in the face of terror. . . . If they don't act, America will."[1] While this foreshadowed the eventual attack on Iraq, the rationale for doing so continued to change. In August 2002, Vice President Dick Cheney, in a speech to the Veterans of Foreign Wars, set the stage by stating that "there is no doubt that Saddam Hussein now has weapons of mass destruction."[2]

By October 2002, President Bush addressed the country to prepare it for an attack against Iraq, now justified not only by the presence of weapons of mass destruction but by painting Saddam Hussein as "a ruthless and aggressive dictator," "a threat to peace," and "a student of Stalin," who has "links to international terrorist groups." According to Bush, "*regime change* in Iraq is the only certain means of removing a great danger to our nation" (emphasis added).[3] The attacks began in March 2003.

In December 2005, when the war against Iraq had been under way for almost three years, President Bush was speaking explicitly of the imposition of democracy in Iraq: "Today I am going to speak in depth about another vital element of our strategy: our efforts to help the Iraqi people build a lasting democracy in the heart of the Middle East."[4]

A paramount goal for both the United States and Iraq was to stress the importance of Iraq as a sovereign nation headed by a *democratically elected government* once U.S. troops had withdrawn and a sense of "normalcy" had returned to the country. The fighting continues as of this writing, and when—or whether—that will happen remains uncertain. This raises the question of whether democracy can be imposed by an outside nation.

NOTES

1. Joyce P. Kaufman, *A Concise History of U.S. Foreign Policy*, 2nd ed. (Lanham, MD: Rowman & Littlefield, 2010), 146.

2. "Full Text of Dick Cheney's Speech," August 27, 2002, http://www.guardian.co.uk/world/2002/aug/27/usa.iraq.

3. "President George W. Bush's Address Regarding Iraq, Cincinnati Museum Center," October 7, 2002, http://www.johnstonsarchive.net/terrorism .bushiraq. html.

4. President George W. Bush, "The Struggle for Democracy in Iraq: Speech to the World Affairs Council of Philadelphia," December 12, 2005, http://www. presidentialrhetoric.com/speeches/12.12.05.html.

citizenry, who are aware of the issues and are willing participants in the process. In addition to voting, among a citizen's responsibilities are paying taxes; making their voices heard through the political process; serving in the military if required; obeying laws; and, of course, owing allegiance to the government, among other things. The government, in turn, has its responsibilities, which include providing for the common defense; engaging with other countries (foreign policy); providing for "human security," such as clean air, food, and water; ensuring that the budget is apportioned wisely; and so on. Because of the range of responsibilities associated with democracy, it can be argued that it cannot be *imposed* on any state but must grow organically from within the state. Thus, the countries of Eastern Europe, which had been under Soviet domination, *chose* democracy as their preferred political system and pursued a capitalist market economy when they had the opportunity. This stands in contrast, for example, to cases like Iraq, where one of the stated reasons for the U.S. invasion in 2003 was to rid the country of a dictator and to encourage (impose) democracy in its place. This assumption that because it was the preferred form of political system and would contribute to a more peaceful world led to the liberal notion that democracy could be imposed on another country as a foreign policy goal.

The liberal belief in the primacy of democracy goes back to Immanuel Kant, who in 1795 argued that "the spread of democracy would change international politics by eliminating war."[4] In his view, the best way to ensure peace was to encourage the growth of republics, or representative democracies, which he felt would take international law more seriously than any other

BOX 4.3

EXCERPTS FROM "PERPETUAL PEACE:
A PHILOSOPHICAL SKETCH," BY
IMMANUEL KANT

SECTION I. CONTAINING THE PRELIMINARY ARTICLES FOR PERPETUAL PEACE AMONG STATES

3. *"Standing Armies (miles perpetuus) Shall in Time Be Totally Abolished"*
"For they incessantly menace other states by their readiness to appear at all times prepared for war; they incite them to compete with each other in the number of armed men, and there is no limit to this. For this reason, the cost of peace finally becomes more oppressive than that of a short war, and consequently a standing army is itself a cause of offensive war waged in order to relieve the state of this burden."

SECTION II. CONTAINING THE DEFINITIVE ARTICLES FOR PERPETUAL PEACE AMONG STATES

"The state of peace among men living side by side is not the natural state (*status naturalis*); the natural state is one of war. This does not always mean open hostilities, but at least an unceasing threat of war. A state of peace, therefore, must be *established*, for in order to be secured against hostility it is not sufficient that hostilities simply be not committed; and, unless this security is pledged to each by his neighbor (a thing that can only occur in a civil state), each may treat his neighbor, from whom he demands this security, as an enemy."

FIRST DEFINITIVE ARTICLE FOR PERPETUAL PEACE

"The Civil Constitution of Every State Should Be Republican"
"The only constitution which derives from the idea of the original compact, and on which all juridical legislation of a people must be based, is the republican. This constitution is established, firstly, by principles of the freedom of the members of a society (as men); secondly, by principles of dependence of all upon a single common legislation (as

subjects); and thirdly, by the law of their equality (as citizens). . . . Is it also the one which can lead to perpetual peace?"

SECOND DEFINITIVE ARTICLE FOR PERPETUAL PEACE

"The Law of Nations Shall Be Founded on a Federation of Free States"
"Peoples, as states, like individuals, may be judged to injure one another merely by their coexistence in the state of nature (i.e., while independent of external laws). Each of them, may and should for the sake of its own security demand that the others enter into a constitution similar to the civil constitution. . . . This would be a *league of nations*." (emphasis added).

Source: Immanuel Kant, "Perpetual Peace: A Philosophical Sketch," https://www.mtholyoke.edu/acad/intrel/kant/kant1.htm.

forms of government, which at that time were monarchies and empires. "The republican constitution, besides the purity of its origin (having sprung from the pure source of the concept of law), also gives a favorable prospect for the desired consequence, i.e., *perpetual peace*" (emphasis added).[5]

Democratic Peace

From this eighteenth-century notion about the peaceful nature of democracies grew one of the basic principles of international relations: *democratic peace*. This idea was introduced into IR thinking in the 1980s, put forward by Michael Doyle, among others. Doyle, an important liberal thinker in international relations, wrote in 1986 that "the predictions of liberal pacifists . . . are borne out: liberal states do exercise peaceful restraint, and a separate peace exists among them."[6] He drew on the work of Kant and also Joseph Schumpeter to conclude that although liberal states will fight when they must—when they are attacked and/or threatened in some way—they have established a "separate peace—but only among themselves."[7] This has contributed to the incorrect notion that democracies are more peaceful than other types of governments, although the more accurate representation is that democracies do not fight one another. The reality is that democracies fight as many wars as authoritarian states do, *but not against other democratic states.*

"No major historical cases contradict this generalization, which is known as the *democratic peace*" (emphasis in original).[8]

Political scientists continue to ponder why this is the case. Is it a coincidence, or is there something inherent in the democratic system of government that is more peaceful, or at the least, less likely to engage in war as a means of settling disputes? Since democracies depend on "the consent of the governed," are they more hesitant to engage in war, which will not be popular at home, will require public support, and will result in loss of lives and great monetary expense? Or as democratic peace proponents argue, is it because the spread of democracy helps negate the inherent anarchy of the international system as understood by realists? Perhaps the existence of more democracies would help alleviate if not eliminate the "security dilemma," or the insecurity that comes with a buildup of weapons, thereby making war less likely.

New York Times columnist Thomas Friedman put forward a slightly different understanding in his thesis that "no two countries that both have a McDonald's have ever fought a war against each other." His "Golden Arches Theory of Conflict Prevention" suggests that "when a country reaches a certain level of development, when it has a middle class big enough to support a McDonald's, it becomes a McDonald's country, and people in McDonald's countries don't like to fight wars."[9] In other words, a country that can support a McDonald's, or any other major multinational corporation that requires a strong economic/middle-class base, has achieved a certain level of development economically and is probably integrated with the larger global community. Those characteristics alone mean that it is a country that is less likely to engage in war than a country that has not yet achieved those qualities. This also introduces an economic component to the understanding of democratic peace, which in many ways makes it a more complete package.

Militarizing the State

Political scientist John Mueller argues that it is not democracy that "causes" peace, but there are other conditions internal to a nation as well as external circumstances that contribute to both democracy *and* peace. For example, attitudes toward war have changed, such that "the appeal of war, both as a desirable exercise in itself and as a sensible method for resolving conflicts, has diminished markedly."[10] But in some countries, including the United States, there has also been significant militarization, which started during the Cold

War and has continued. The growth of the defense sector and its impact on the U.S. economy was something that President Eisenhower warned about in his farewell address to the nation:

> This conjunction of an immense military establishment and a large arms industry is new in the American experience. The total influence—economic, political, even spiritual—is felt in every city, every State house, every office of the Federal government. We recognize the imperative need for this development. Yet we must not fail to comprehend its grave implications. Our toil, resources and livelihood are all involved; so is the very structure of our society.
>
> *In the councils of government, we must guard against the acquisition of unwarranted influence, whether sought or unsought, by the military-industrial complex.* The potential for the disastrous rise of misplaced power exists and will persist.
>
> We must never let the weight of this combination endanger our liberties or democratic processes. We should take nothing for granted. Only an alert and knowledgeable citizenry can compel the proper meshing of the huge industrial and military machinery of defense with our peaceful methods and goals, so that security and liberty may prosper together. (emphasis added)[11]

The changes that Eisenhower identified, which can be thought of as the *militarization of the state*, have continued, and as the technology has improved, the costs of war, especially the human costs, have changed. So while technology has allowed technologically developed countries like the United States to wage war using technology like drones to replace soldiers, the collateral damage to civilians has increased.[12] Another aspect to this, as Eisenhower warned about almost sixty years ago, is that the defense industry is now an important part of the U.S. economy; according to a 2016 study, the aerospace and defense industries generated "$300 billion in economic value, representing 1.8 percent of total nominal Gross Domestic Product in the U.S., and 10 percent of manufacturing output."[13] Thus, the military-industrial complex is a real phenomenon in the United States that has an impact on policy decisions.

Moving beyond the United States in particular to the international system in general, Mueller also argues that although there has been a proliferation of what he calls "local wars," there is also a marked diminishing of countries resorting to war as a means to settle disputes and differences. And he also makes the distinction between war and conflict, noting that although war

BOX 4.4

"DEMOCRATIC PEACE"

Liberalism has gained momentum with the emergence of the "democratic peace," the idea that countries that are democracies do not fight one another. Note, this does not suggest that democracies do not go to war, but rather that *they do not go to war against one another!* So the question here is why that is the case. Some argue that shared democratic norms and values mean that democratic countries are not only less likely to have conflict, but they are also more likely to use peaceful means (negotiation) to resolve any differences.

Another possible reason can be drawn from Thomas Friedman's "Golden Arches Theory of Conflict Prevention," which suggests that countries that have McDonald's have never fought a war against one another.[1] This is not as silly as it sounds, for it reminds us that countries that have a McDonald's also have a certain level of economic development and that they are an integrated part of the international economic system. It would then be irrational for a country that is tied to other countries economically to go to war against them.

NOTE

1. See Thomas L. Friedman, "Foreign Affairs Big Mac I," *New York Times,* December 8, 1996, http://www.nytimes.com/1996/12/08/opinion/foreign-affairs-big-mac-i.html. Friedman developed this idea further in his book *The Lexus and the Olive Tree: Understanding Globalization* (New York: Farrar, Straus & Giroux, 1999).

has declined, "it certainly does not mean that conflict has been eliminated."[14] However, this also does not necessarily mean that war is the only means by which these conflicts can be resolved. In fact, looking at some of the NATO nations, for example, there can be very extreme disagreements about policy, such as the U.S. decision to go to war in Iraq, but they can be addressed without resorting to armed violence.

In examining the materials about democracy and the democratic peace, it does appear that from the perspective of international relations, this form of government has emerged as the most cooperative and beneficial, not only to the individual nation but to the direction of the international system as a whole. That said, the transition from another type of political system to democracy can be difficult and even violent. We know that it cannot be imposed from outside but that the desire for this form of political system must originate from within and that the country must have the infrastructure (e.g., an educated citizenry, open access to media, a fair election process) to support it.

Democracy and Feminist Perspectives

In order to truly understand democracy, though, we also need to put on our gender-sensitive lenses and ask who makes the decisions and who is affected by the decisions even in a democratic system. As suggested above, feminist theorists, such as Ann Tickner, warn us that the movement toward democracy can actually have a detrimental effect both within and across states. Across states, decisions made by some of the more powerful democracies of the northern developed tier of states can limit the options available to the developing countries of the South. Often, the decisions of the major developed or industrialized states are made with consideration as to what is in their best interest, even if that means that the decisions will have a detrimental effect on developing countries. For example, an environmental policy that was designed to improve the air or water quality of developed countries can be more costly for a developing country to implement or might even be irrelevant to a country struggling to feed its own people. The imposition of values by one country or group of countries onto another (something the countries of the developed West have increasingly been accused of doing) is often called *cultural imperialism.*

Within a country, while democracy promotes equality among all citizens in theory, the reality is that often these are patriarchal governmental structures, where power is concentrated in the hands of wealthy men who have the wherewithal to gain access to high office. Further, these same leaders often promote and mentor younger people who look and think just as they do. Thus, it can be argued, this is a system that can limit progress for women, rather than allowing them to advance.[15] So, in order to really understand democracy in practice as well as in theory, we need to ask who has access to the system of governance and who participates in it.

Another point that Tickner and other feminists make—and it is one that keeps women out of decision making—has to do with the differentiation between the public and the private spheres, where politics is associated with the public, and the private sphere of running the household and the family is the domain of women. In fact, Tickner notes that "historically . . . terms such as *citizen* and *head of household* were not neutral but were associated with men."[16]

What this suggests is that no matter how democratic a political system might appear to be, it can exclude women from decision making and positions of power. This too has implications for the foreign policy decisions that a country makes, including issues of war and peace.

CULTURE AND SOCIETY

In the section above on the government, we talked about the "state" part of the concept of the nation-state. The *state* represents the formal trappings such as the government and defined borders, and it in turn accepts certain responsibilities for the people who live within those borders. We will now move into a discussion of the "nation" part, which is the people. It is the people as a whole who not only represent the nation but also define the culture and the society. Therefore, the *nation* denotes a group of people with a common history, background, and values, all of whom accept the sanctity of the state. While this level might seem to exist outside the purview of international relations per se, it is important for a number of reasons, not least of which is that it can determine whether a nation-state will endure peacefully or dissolve into civil, ethnic, or religious violence.

Ideally, any nation-state has one culture and one societal set of norms, or if there is more than one, they are compatible. These might be characterized by a common language, set of values, and traditions. Or in some countries, there might be more than one group within a larger set of cultural and societal norms. For example, within the United States, the majority of people speak English (although a lot speak Spanish), but within the country there are ethnic enclaves, such as the Cajun areas of Louisiana, where the dominant language is a patois based on French. There are groups that hold on to their original ethnic heritage; they may speak Russian and worship in a Russian Orthodox Church or live in Chinese enclaves and worship in Buddhist temples. The point is that although there are these subgroupings, they are found within a dominant cultural tradition that understands and expects certain behaviors that transcend any one cultural tradition and are "American." Thus, members of these various subgroups will all celebrate the Fourth of July or Thanksgiving as a common tradition, while they may also celebrate the Orthodox Easter or the Chinese New Year. Thus, various nations can live in harmony within one state.

These various "nations" need not be tied to ethnic background or traditions, religion, or culture but may be considered an artifact of "identity"—that is, issues of belonging. Sociologists, anthropologists, and other social scientists as well as political scientists have explored various aspects of this concept to try to get a broader understanding of what it is, what it means, and where it comes from. It might be tied to religion, ethnicity, culture, or even region. But in many ways it is the broader understanding of a common identity that holds groups of people within the state together.

For our purposes, though, the question remains, how does this affect international relations? The fact of the matter is that it does affect it. For example, look at the strong pro-Israeli group within the United States, which has a powerful lobby that has had a direct influence on U.S. policy toward Israel. This group of people advocates support for Israel as an important component of U.S. foreign policy. Although they are Americans, they also have a strong sense of identity with the Jewish religion and feelings of loyalty to the state of Israel, and therefore they want the United States to support that country. This does not mean they want to leave the United States for Israel, but simply that they also feel strongly about the need to support Israel as a plank of U.S. foreign policy and are willing to lobby for that policy. Or, taking another example, we can look at the impact of the large number of Cuban émigrés who have settled in Florida. They might see themselves as Americans—one first-generation American whose parents left Cuba, Marco Rubio, was elected to the U.S. Senate from Florida—but they also feel strongly about their Cuban identity and follow events on the island, which translates into their interpretation of U.S. foreign policy. Not only has this group of émigrés had a marked impact on the domestic politics of the United States because of the strength of their votes, but they have also influenced U.S. foreign policy toward Cuba.

And the United States is not unique in this regard. Many of the former colonial powers in Europe, such as the United Kingdom, France, Belgium, the Netherlands, and Spain, not only have trade and political ties with their former colonies, but they also have relatively large immigrant populations who, if they don't directly affect the country's foreign policy, certainly affect its culture. Anyone who has traveled there has seen the large number of Indian restaurants in London or the North African restaurants found throughout Paris. Clearly, those immigrants bring with them their own cultural traditions that spill into and affect their adopted homeland in general, making it a culturally richer and more diverse place. But this also affects their sense of identity and belonging, not only to their new or adopted country, but also to what had been their home country. And, as we have seen, it can also contribute to feelings of nationalism and anti-immigrant sentiment that also affects the politics of the home country as well as toward other countries. One of the benefits of a democratic form of government is the belief that these various identities should not be contradictory, although in reality they sometimes are.

Clearly this is not to suggest that assimilation of these immigrant groups into the dominant culture and society is always peaceful and/or easy. As noted above, they are often accompanied by a growth in nationalist feelings that can be fueled by political leaders and contribute to a sense of division and exclusion within a country. Donald Trump's "America First" campaign and anti-Muslim rhetoric contributed to the growth of nationalism among some in the United States during and following the 2016 presidential election. Marine Le Pen, leader of the National Front party in France, similarly based her presidential campaign on nationalism and anti-immigrant sentiments. The main point is that these various groups exist *within* a larger cultural and social setting, and they are expected to conform to the norms of that larger culture even though they may still hold on to their own traditions. When they do not, or when even a small and fringe group is perceived as not conforming, it can be threatening to the majority, and conflict can result.

One of the challenges facing all nation-states now is how to handle issues of the integration of different groups of people. Perhaps the old "melting pot" model is no longer appropriate in a globalized world, where no matter where people move internationally, they can easily retain ties to their home country, friends, family, culture, and traditions. The real issue then becomes, what happens when a group's loyalty is to or their identity is with the *nation* as opposed to the state? That can lead to the growth of nationalism, which ultimately can lead to conflict. That has important implications for international relations.

Nationalism and Conflict

Nationalism can be defined as the promotion of national identity to the exclusion of other identities. It promotes the common characteristics of the group and allegiance to that group. In short, nationalism moves beyond patriotism (loyalty to the nation-state) to promote commitment to one's own group over others, including the broader interests of the state. This also alerts us to the fact that as students of international relations, it is important to look *within* the state if we are really going to understand the origins or root causes of intrastate civil conflict.

Nationalism is often tied to the principle of *self-determination*, which suggests that the peoples of a nation have the right to form a state and therefore to have control over their own affairs. But in this idea is an inherent theoretical conflict. If states are sovereign entities (a notion that goes back to the Treaty of Westphalia), then how can a group of people *within* the state declare themselves to be independent and able to make rules that govern only themselves?

Tied directly to this conundrum and to the idea of self-determination is the concept of *territory*. When the claim of nationhood is contested within a state, then who has primacy over the territory within which the "nation" resides? To address this, we can bring together different theoretical models or approaches, although none can really explain or address all sets of circumstances.

For example, the realists look at the international system as inherently anarchic, and as such, there are few rules as to how to deal with competing claims over territory. Therefore, in realist thinking, war will inevitably break out as a way to settle the dispute, and the group that is more powerful will win. By that logic, the conflicting claims that both Israel (a formal nation-state) and Palestine (a nation or stateless people) have to the land known as "Palestine" will inevitably lead to war, as there is no other way to settle the claim to the contested territory except by military might. The realist approach would argue that there is no single system-level arbiter that these groups can turn to in order to resolve this conflict, nor can they really negotiate directly—especially since the role of the Palestinians, who do not have a state, does not fit neatly into the model of international relations, which presumes that contact will always be state to state.

The liberal theorists would approach the issue differently. Initially, liberals would say that there are viable alternatives to settling disputes beyond war. The liberals especially would argue that the two sets of actors (Palestinians and Israel) *can* negotiate to see whether it might be possible to settle their dispute peacefully by beginning with what they might have in common rather than their differences. Here the role of individuals can be important. For example, there are grassroots groups such as Women in Black, which started in 1988 when ten Israeli women held a vigil in Jerusalem to protest Israel's occupation of the West Bank and Gaza and to show their solidarity with the Palestinian people. As the movement spread, it started to incorporate Palestinian as well as Israeli women, who were united by a common cause.[17] In this case, then, what started as a small group of women grew to encompass individuals around the world who have joined together to work for peace and justice and against violence. While this might not carry much weight officially or influence government policy, it can draw public attention to the issue, thereby building pressure on the government to settle the conflict.

At a more macro and official government level, working to settle the conflict can be done by direct negotiations, or there can be a mediator or neutral third party involved, as we have seen so often in the Arab/Palestinian–Israeli case. In that case, the role of the mediator would be to hear each side's position and see if there is any common ground upon which they can build.

It was this type of mediation process that was used to arrive at the agreement that became known as the Camp David Accords, signed in September 1978 between enemies Egypt and Israel. Mediated by the United States under the direction of then-president Jimmy Carter, the result was the first major peace agreement between Israel and an Arab state (Egypt), which resulted in the resolution of the disputed territory of the Sinai, which Israel had taken in 1967 following the Six-Day War. In that case, consistent with liberal ideas, resolution was possible because of cooperation between the two countries, albeit with U.S. mediation, and because both countries saw peace as in their national interest. This confluence of views allowed both countries to arrive at an agreement that was consistent with the priorities of the members of the groups within the country, thereby ensuring support for the agreement both within and outside the country. However, not all within Egypt were pleased with the outcome. The then president of Egypt, Anwar Sadat, was assassinated in October 1981 by a group of fundamentalist officers who were opposed to his policies. Although the long-term international impact of the agreement was peace between Israel and Egypt, it cost the president his life and created rifts between the more fundamentalist members of the population and those who wanted peace. And there were groups within Egypt who similarly felt that it had given up too much in order to achieve an agreement. In the long term, however, the relationship between the two countries has been peaceful.

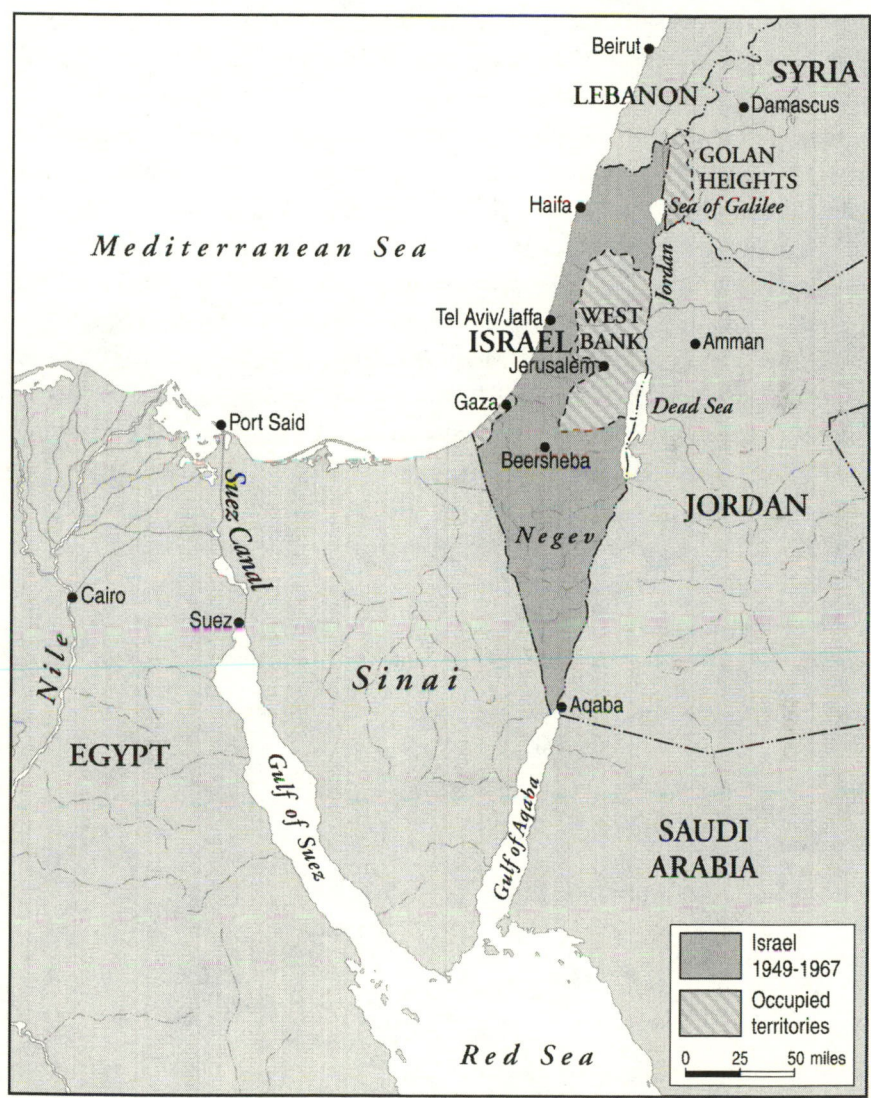

MAP 4.1
Israel's Borders, 2010

Intractable Conflicts

In some cases, a conflict is so intractable and deep seated that the issue of the disputed territory cannot be resolved by mediation or negotiation. The example of Jerusalem, a city claimed as sacred by all three monotheistic religions, is a case in point. Since both Israel and the Palestinians lay claim to the city as part of their dispute over land, and since each feels that it has a legitimate right to Jerusalem, peaceful resolution seems impossible in this case. Further complicating the possibility of resolution is the fact that the Palestinians see Jerusalem as the capital of a future Palestinian state. Hence, here we have issues of self-determination and territory coming together, exacerbated when placed within the context of the larger issues that the two groups have.

There are a number of other apparently intractable conflicts that can be seen today in addition to the case of Israel and the Palestinians. The divided island of Cyprus is another example of two groups of people who share the island of Cyprus, but with each group aligned with a different country, Greece in the south and Turkey in the north, which is the result of a conflict and division of the island that took place in 1974. Since that time, there have been any number of negotiations, both formal (Track I) and informal (Track II) to address the status of the country and to see if there is a way to unite the island. It is important to remember that the division of the island is not only political but also economic. Although the island as a whole was admitted to the EU in 2004, its status is as a "de facto divided island," which means that the northern part of the island administered by

MAP 4.2

Cyprus. *Source:* iStock/Peter Hermes Furian

Turkish Cypriots and known as the "Turkish Republic of Northern Cyprus" (TRNC) is exempt from full implementation of all EU treaties, obligations, and regulations. It is the southern part of the island, which has the majority of the population and territory, that is seen as "Cyprus" and is represented in the EU. The market-based economy of the north is roughly 20 percent of that of the southern part of the island. Ironically, because the southern part of the island is tied heavily to Greece, it suffered economically as a result of Greece's financial crisis, while the north, which is tied to Turkey, weathered the economic crisis relatively well. This disparity makes issues of reunification even more difficult as the issues are not only those of identity (Greece versus Turkey) but economics as well.

We can look at other cases of these deep-seated intractable conflicts that are the result of nations seeking self-determination or statehood. This issue will come up again when we talk about stateless peoples in chapter 5.

The main point about these deep-seated conflicts is that in all cases they pit one group against another, and they either threaten to destroy an existing state or they push for the creation of a new one by carving out territory of existing nation-states, which directly threatens sovereignty.

The Kurds

The case of the Kurds stands as another example of this type of conflict between a nation (the Kurds) and, in this case, a number of states. The Kurdish people share a common language, culture, and so on and increasingly support the creation of an independent state of Kurdistan. But as a people, they can be found in parts of Turkey and Iraq primarily, but also in Iran and Syria. Each of the states in which there is a significant Kurdish population refuses to give up any part of its territory in order to create such a state, which they see as a violation of their own sovereignty. This resistance became even more apparent with the uprising that became the civil war in Syria, where Syrian Kurds have been fighting with the rebels against President Bashar al-Assad's government. Part of the rationale for their fighting is the hope of creating an autonomous Kurdish region in Syria as a step toward the creation of an independent state of Kurdistan. But, as noted in one newspaper account, that hope "threatens to draw a violent reaction from those other nations [Iraq, Turkey, and Iran]. They have signaled a willingness to take *extreme actions* to prevent the loss of territory to a greater Kurdistan" (emphasis added).[18]

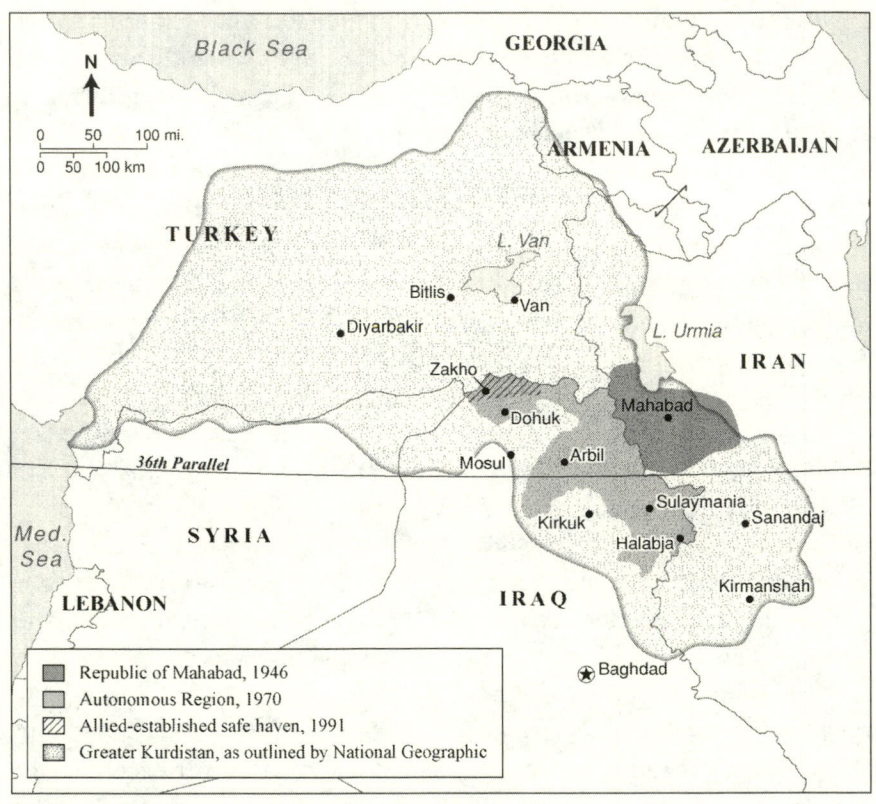

MAP 4.3
Kurdish Regions, 1946–Present

Within Iraq, the Kurds, who were brutally massacred under Saddam Hussein in an act of genocide, have been able or been allowed to maintain a degree of autonomy since the fall of Hussein in 2003. The Iraqi constitution of 2005 recognizes Iraqi Kurdistan as a federal region within Iraq, and it recognizes Kurdish as an official language of Iraq. Despite what appears to be a resolution of the issue, tensions remain over issues of borders and governance outside the formal boundaries of Iraqi Kurdistan, especially in Turkey. Turkey does not want to cede any of its territory to create a country of Kurdistan, and any movement in that direction is perceived by Turkey as a threat to its sovereignty and territory. Thus, while the situation appears to have been stabilized in Iraq, it remains far from resolved in Turkey. The Kurds' quest for self-determination at best and recognition of its identity within Turkey at a minimum has manifested as a low-level conflict with Kurdish guerilla forces, known as the PKK (Kurdistan Workers' Party), which was founded in 1974, fighting against the government of Turkey.

The issue of the Kurds and how they should be treated and recognized is not a new one, as the Kurdish people as a nation pre-dated the drawing of the current national boundaries that divided up the group. That situation becomes even more complicated when a semiautonomous group declares itself independent of its host state and seeks to create a new state. We have used the Kurds as just one example of a nation that straddles multiple states and the issues this creates for the international system.

The real question is one of self-determination and belonging, and it is complicated when states are in conflict, a situation we can see today with the conflict between Russia and Ukraine.

Russia and Ukraine/Crimea

A return to the ideological battles of East versus West that characterized the Cold War was played out in Ukraine beginning in mid-December 2013 when Ukraine's then-president Viktor Yanukovych signed a series of deals with Russia instead of working with the EU as promised. This decision to turn toward Russia coalesced opposition to Yanukovych, and literally thousands of Ukrainians turned out to protest in Kiev's Maidan Square. Their opposition was to Yanukovych's decision to support Russia and to turn away from the EU, but more specifically, it was to call for the president's resignation. By the end of January 2014, the protests went from peaceful opposition to violent uprisings, which were met by violent police crackdowns. Western leaders condemned both the passage of the repressive laws and also the increase in violence. Russia, in turn, accused the West of meddling in an internal issue in Ukraine.

One of the things that made the Ukraine situation especially difficult is the fact that the country itself is split linguistically, culturally, and politically between the Russian-speaking east and the pro-European west, or a conflict between national groups and allegiances. It was the western part of the country that was bolstered initially by what appeared to be the decision to move closer to the EU and then was deflated by Yanukovych's decision to side with Russia instead. That, in turn, bolstered the pro-Russian faction while simultaneously undermining the group tied to the West.

Yanukovych fled the country on February 22, 2014, and he asked Russia for asylum. An interim government was put in place until elections could be held at the end of May. Yanukovych's escape did not do anything to address Ukraine's dire economic situation, nor did it stabilize the country politically. The situation in fact grew worse when Russia annexed the Ukrainian region of Crimea in March 2014. Part of Russia until 1954, Crimea's largest city, Sebastopol, is populated largely by Russians and is the home to Russia's Black Sea fleet. Russia claimed that it was simply reclaiming a land that should have been Russia's. But this, too, posed a dilemma for the Western countries as to how to respond. Russia's involvement first in Crimea and then into the eastern parts of Ukraine was justified by Putin by the need to ensure the safety and protection of all Russian-speaking peoples. But in doing so, he abrogated a treaty between Russia and Ukraine, signed in 1994, to respect Ukraine's border.

What these two examples illustrate clearly is how difficult issues of self-determination are for the international system because they deal directly with

MAP 4.4
Ukraine and Crimea. *Source:* iStock/Peter Hermes Furian

sovereignty and the supremacy of the nation-state, two inviolate principles of international relations. How can the international system recognize "Kurdistan" when it would mean authorizing the annexation of parts of existing sovereign states? In this case, the country maps that were drawn by the then colonial powers had little regard for the Kurdish people, and the impact of those decisions are being felt decades later. In the case of Russia, Ukraine, and Crimea, once again, we see peoples with different loyalties all within a single state. The conflict that took place within Ukraine only exacerbated those loyalties, leading eventually to conflict and Russia's decision (rationale) to annex Crimea. Furthermore, as you can now see, such conflicts are extremely difficult to resolve, with tensions often festering for years. They also show how nationhood can conflict with the concept of the nation-state. The end result can be armed conflict that could involve the international community.

Ethnic Conflict

Nationalism can contribute to conflict in other ways. The concept of ethnic conflict is tied directly to the issue of nationalism. In countries in which there are a number of ethnic groups—nations—a leader often emerges who encourages the supremacy of one group at the expense of another. This can be carried to an extreme and has led to what we now call *ethnic cleansing*, or the systematic extermination of one ethnic group by another (i.e., genocide), often with the approval and support of the state. This is extremely difficult for the countries in the international system, since the issue pits the sovereignty of one state against the need to protect a group against human rights violations and, at its most extreme, genocide.

It was ethnic conflict that ripped the former Yugoslavia apart, with Serbs, Croats, and Bosnian Muslims engaged in war over the area of Bosnia-Herzegovina. In this case, the ethnic cleansing was encouraged by nationalist leaders (Slobodan Milošević in Serbia, proclaiming the need for a "Greater Serbia," and Franjo Tudjman in Croatia), and it was directed primarily against the Bosnian Muslims.[19]

This can also be seen in Rwanda, where approximately eight hundred thousand people were massacred in about a hundred days between April and June 1994. In Rwanda, the hatred against Tutsis had been building for decades and finally exploded in April 1994 following the death of Rwandan president Juvenal Habyarimana, a Hutu, when his plane was shot down above Kigali airport. The blame for the rocket attack was placed on a Tutsi rebel leader, and within hours, the genocide by Hutus against Tutsis started and quickly spread.[20]

There are other examples of such ethnic conflict and genocide, which seems to have become more commonplace. One of the ironies of ethnic conflict, though, is that often there is no ethnic difference between the groups. For example, in the case of Rwanda, "the two ethnic groups are actually very similar—they speak the same language, inhabit the same areas and follow the same traditions."[21]

In the former Yugoslavia, Serbs, Croats, and Bosnian Muslims are ethnically the same, although their religions vary. Serbs tend to be Eastern Orthodox, Croats Catholic, and Bosnian Muslims obviously are Muslim. Yet the war in Yugoslavia was not about religion but about nationality commingled with "ethnicity." What that tells us is that often a conflict is attributed to one thing, such as religion or ethnicity, but there are other factors that actually are equally if not more important. So we must really look within the country in order to understand the full set of circumstances related to a civil conflict.

The lesson here is that when we try to understand the roots of violent civil conflict, we often have to look deep within the state to the government, culture, and society and even individuals if we are to really identify all the factors involved.

The Importance of Looking at Culture and Society

These cases all serve to remind us why it is important to look within the nation-state and to focus on the "nation" (culture and society) if we are really going to get a complete picture of why a nation-state behaves the way it does. Especially since the end of the Cold War, we have seen a decline in the number of major wars but an increase in violent national, ethnic, and civil conflicts. If we are to understand the origins of these conflicts, we need to look at the cultural and social issues that exist within the nation-state as a whole.

The realists would claim that the decline in major wars within the international system is the result of the security commitment of the United States and its emergence as a global hegemon that has kept other countries in check. They would also argue that although we are seeing the emergence of other major powers, such as China, there is no conflict between the hegemons.

BOX 4.5

NORTHERN IRELAND: RELIGIOUS CONFLICT?

Northern Ireland is an example of a country that had to face violent civil conflict that seems to have its root in religious differences. But in many ways, calling it a conflict between Catholics and Protestants becomes a shorthand that summarizes a host of other issues that really are at the heart of the divide between the two groups. Limiting it to a religious conflict also obscures some of the issues that would help us explain civil conflict in general: economic and political inequalities, issues of power, and what Johann Galtung would call "structural violence."[1] For example, the Protestants generally are tied to Great Britain and want to remain part of the UK. Historically, the Protestants, with their ties to England, were also the privileged group, and they were the land and business owners as well as the members of the government. As the land and property owners, they could discriminate against the Catholics. In contrast to the Protestants, the Catholics, who were tied politically to the independent Republic of Ireland, suffered economically. They were often discriminated against in housing and education, and they were not able to gain power politically. The root of "the troubles" that divided Northern Ireland from the 1960s until the signing of the Belfast (Good Friday) Agreement in April 1998 was economic and political as well as religious. The reality is that all three factors intertwined to work against the Catholics, who sought power through violence.

NOTE

1. Johann Galtung, "Violence, Peace, and Peace Research," *Journal of Peace Research* 6, no. 3 (1969): 167–91.

Rather, each is asserting its presence in different places and parts of the world, so there is no conflict.[22]

The liberals argue that the decline in major interstate war is the result, at least in part, of the growth of democracies that are unlikely to go to war against one another (the democratic peace). Not only are democracies less likely to go to war against one another, but the fact that they generally have capitalist economic systems and that they trade with one another means that they are also more economically interdependent. This, too, suggests that they are less likely to engage in war with one another.

The constructivists would claim that the relative decline in major war is due to a change in the predominant values of decision makers and the people within the nation from those that support war as a means of settling disputes to those that promote ideals of peace, as well as understanding that countries do not need to compete for material advantage. But this certainly does not explain the increase in intrastate war.

While the major theoretical approaches could all provide some explanation for the decrease in major wars, how well can they also explain the increase in civil wars? As noted above, the realists would simply argue that this is just another manifestation of the conflict for power. Different groups within the state all seek to maximize their power and position, even if that comes at the expense of another group. Marxists would attribute the growth of civil wars to economic inequities and to the desire of one group (the oppressed or less fortunate) to overturn the existing power balances. Liberals and neoliberals would probably argue that the growth of these wars is the result of failures of institutions and cooperative approaches, and constructivists would similarly look at the failures of the structures that would otherwise have held these aggressive tendencies in check.

So, in understanding the increase in the incidence of civil wars, one can look at the reasons as being the inherent competitive nature of the leaders or as the failures of the state and national structures that would emphasize cooperation among groups rather than conflict. But the important lesson is that in trying to get an answer to questions like why there is ethnic violence, or why there is conflict between groups within a country, it is important to look within the country at the various actors involved, their priorities and expectations, what the distribution of power actually is, and who is making the decisions.

It is also possible to examine this question from a broader levels-of-analysis perspective. For example, in focusing within the state on the emergence of national groups and the concomitant rise in nationalism, are we overlooking the possibility that we are witnessing the diminishment of the state as a major actor in international relations? As Charles Tilly notes, the state was born from war, and the growth of civil conflicts might mean that the militarized state carries within it the seeds of its own destruction.[23]

Regardless of which theoretical perspective seems most appealing or how one would interpret the rise in conflicts as a lesson about the role of the nation-state, all would suggest at least some need to look within the country and understand the predominant cultures as well as the role and perspectives of the individual decision makers. It is to this last and most micro level of analysis that we now turn.

THE ROLE OF THE INDIVIDUAL

We have been talking a lot about what goes on within the state and the role of government, culture, and society in order to understand some big questions in international relations pertaining to conflict. But one of the other critical variables tied to understanding international relations, particularly the behavior of any nation-state, is the individual or individuals who actually make the decisions that affect foreign policy decision making. To do this, we need to ask ourselves how much influence any individual has. What gives these individuals power? Does a single individual really make a difference?

Here we need to distinguish between the individual decision maker, the "average" person, and truly outstanding individuals, such as Nelson Mandela in South Africa or Mahatma Gandhi in India. What about someone like now deceased Mu'ammar Gadhafi in Libya or Bashar al-Assad in Syria? Each of them was a strong leader who directly influenced the policies of his country. But Gadhafi was overthrown by his own people in 2011, and since 2011 the country of Syria has been engaged in the deadliest conflict of the twenty-first century; as of July 2017, that civil war has resulted in the deaths of more than 465,000 Syrians, more than one million injured, and over twelve million Syrians, half the country's prewar population, displaced from their homes.[24] How does an individual get—and keep—that kind of power? And what changes could threaten that power?

Let's look at this question another way: How much was Mikhail Gorbachev responsible for the end of the Cold War or the fall of the Soviet Union? Or what role did Solidarity leader Lech Wałęsa play in leading to a change in the government of Poland, which in turn became a model for other Eastern European countries' rebellions against Soviet domination? In all these cases, what we are really asking is, what role did the individual play? Or how did the political and/or structural factors within the country and the changing international environment *coupled with* the role of a particular individual at that particular time result in major change? Is it the individual alone who makes the difference, or a strong and powerful leader who emerges when the environment is receptive, thereby providing a context for him or her to facilitate change? These are difficult and important questions that ask us to think about the role of an individual, but also to place that individual into a larger context if we are truly to understand the changes that have taken place within a culture/society/government/nation-state.

The example of Gorbachev is especially interesting. The end of the Cold War has been attributed to President Ronald Reagan's hard-line rhetoric, which pushed an already significantly diminished Soviet Union to the brink. Yet, when he was questioned about the role that he played in facilitating the end of the Cold War, Reagan referred to himself as "a supporting actor." According to one account, when Reagan was asked at a press conference who deserved the credit for the changes in the Soviet Union that ultimately led to the end of the Cold War, he replied, "Mr. Gorbachev deserves most of the credit, as the leader of this country."[25] The reality is that a number of factors came together at the right time to bring about an end to the Cold War, but both Reagan and Gorbachev were receptive to the ideological as well as political changes that affected both their countries.

For his part, Gorbachev had a broader understanding of the West than had previous leaders of the Soviet Union, and he saw Europe and Russia as sharing a common home. He articulated his ideas about *glasnost* (openness) and *perestroika* (economic restructuring away from a command economy) in his book *Perestroika*, which was readily available in the West.[26] And these ideas affected the direction in which he took the Soviet Union.

Reagan, in turn, was receptive to Gorbachev's ideas and was willing to work with him on implementing new policies.

> Reagan believed that a change in the direction of the Soviet Union would be in the best interests of the United States and therefore modified his own approach over time, becoming less "cold warrior" and more the diplomat whose primary goal was to encourage Gorbachev to continue down the road he had chosen. Doing this required *personal contact*, and *the two leaders met periodically to outline areas*

of common interest. Reagan was so successful that by the time his administration ended, the Cold War was on a course to its inevitable end. (emphasis added)[27]

Thus, not only did the individual matter, but it was because of meetings between these two individual leaders that trust was established, leading to political change.

And if one is looking at this major change in policy through "gender-sensitive lenses," some insight can be gained by looking at the impact of both Raisa Gorbachev and Nancy Reagan, who both played important behind-the-scenes roles in influencing their husbands. Although each was, on the surface, a traditional wife, they played a part in the historical events unfolding.[28]

The important point here is that an individual can play an important role in influencing the direction of a country's policy and, in this case, of the international system. However, that individual can be helped considerably by other factors, especially the structures within which the leader acts. Within any given country, these might include the role of the military, an organized opposition (or lack thereof), the economy, and so on—all of which can either contribute to continued stability and legitimacy of an existing government or work in opposition to defy or even overthrow the individual leader.

In addition, as seen with the above example of Raisa Gorbachev and Nancy Reagan, an individual does not have to be the critical decision maker in order to have an impact on a country or even international politics. For example, feminist author Cynthia Enloe in her book *Bananas, Beaches, and Bases* notes,

> In the 1930s Hollywood moguls turned Brazilian singer Carmen Miranda into an American movie star. They were trying to aid President Franklin Roosevelt's efforts to promote friendlier relations between the US and Latin America. When United Fruit executives then drew on Carmen Miranda's popular Latinized female image to create a logo for their imported bananas, they were trying to construct a new, intimate relationship between American housewives and a multinational plantation company. With her famous fruited hats and vivacious screen presence, Carmen Miranda was used by American men to reshape international relations.[29]

Hence, in this case, Enloe would argue that an individual (Carmen Miranda) had a direct impact on international relations through symbolism, even if she

FIGURE 4.1
Carmen Miranda as a symbol. © 2011 United States Postal Service. All Rights Reserved. Used with Permission.

was not a decision maker. But that symbolism played an important role in furthering U.S. policy interests.

But how representative is this case? How much does an individual influence the course of international politics? The individual level of analysis reflects the perceptions of individuals and the choices that they then make. Generally, this refers to leaders, who are in the best position to make decisions that influence international events. But as can be seen with the uprisings of the Arab Spring, individual citizens can have an impact, as can military leaders, people who can influence decision makers (such as lobbyists and members of various interest groups), and even the "ordinary" voter. But in thinking about the individual level, it is also important to remember that it is often difficult to pinpoint the exact impact that any one person has had. According to political scientists Paul Viotti and Mark Kauppi, "While individuals can have a tremendous impact on the short-term course of world events . . . it is extremely difficult to identify such individuals after their impact has been felt." In fact, they argue, "most people who want to influence world politics do so in an indirect manner through collective actors such as states."[30]

The fact is that although we speak of "nation-states" and "governments" and "societies" and "cultures," all of these are collectives of individuals. States do not make the decision to go to war; the individuals within the government do. It is for this reason that political scientists argue that every international event ultimately is the result of decisions made by individuals. And most individuals, regardless of how powerful they are, still operate within and are subject to the constraints of the organization or government or structures of which they are a part.

Decision Maker as Rational Actor

When we do focus on the individual as decision maker, or on any individual who makes a decision that has some effect on a government, it is important to ask to what extent these decisions are *rational*. That means asking whether the decision was based on a logical process that includes an assessment and ranking of choices, an understanding of the costs and benefits of the options, and a review of alternatives before arriving at a final conclusion. In international relations, we make the assumption that decision makers will act rationally and that rationality will be reflected in their choices. This may—or may not—be a correct assumption, and it draws heavily on realist thinking. But simplifying the otherwise complex decision-making process in this way allows us to explain in general terms why a particular action was taken or a decision made.

In chapter 2 we talked about the importance of theory because it helps us describe, explain, and predict. The only way in which we can describe what happened and explain why it happened so that we can anticipate future events is to simplify reality. Similarly, when we talk about decision making, it is a complex undertaking that has many component parts. Hence, if we really are ever going to understand that complexity, we need to simplify it. Starting with the assumption of the rational actor is one way in which we can do so.

What is important to note is that decision makers are distinct individuals who have differing beliefs, values, and unique personalities. Therefore, the decisions that they make are the result of their own experiences, belief systems, intellectual capabilities, personal styles, and so on. And here both liberal and constructivist theoretical approaches play a role. While national decisions are constrained by the political system and by precedent, there is also room for any individual to make his or her own mark. For example, you can ask yourself whether the outcome regarding the response to 9/11 would have been the same if Al Gore had been president in 2001 instead of George W. Bush. We know what the outcomes of President Bush's decisions were. But Gore probably would have approached the attacks differently, since he had different experiences, both as vice president and as a long-serving member of Congress, than Bush did, who, before become president, had been governor of Texas and a businessman. We can also see that today with some of the decisions made by President Trump, who had no experience with government or the political decision-making processes prior to taking office. Hence, his approach to the decisions that he has made in office thus far is very different from previous presidents, thereby confounding other policy makers both in the United States and abroad. In other words, we can ask, how did the experience of the individual leader affect the way in which he would have responded or did respond to an event or to the decisions that he or she made?

But looking at decision makers as unique individuals also raises questions about the assumption of the rational decision maker, as every decision will be affected by the decision maker's own perceptions or (perhaps more important) misperceptions. Every person is selective in his or her perceptions, screening experiences and information and often drawing on those that are most consistent with his or her own existing beliefs. But the role of the decision maker is to filter the information received in order to arrive at a decision that also builds in bias. "*Information screens* are subconscious filters through which people put the information coming in from the world around them. Often they simply ignore any information that does not fit their expectations."[31] Thus, most decision makers will look for information or even "evidence" that supports what they already believe. Clearly, this will also change the outcome of any decision. Nor would all decision makers in the same set of circumstances do the same thing, because they would filter everything through their own information screen.

In terms of foreign policy decision making, what this means is that information can and will be screened as it passes from person to person. In the old children's game of "Telephone," one person whispers a secret to the next person, who passes it on to the next person, and so on. By the time it gets to the end of the chain, it is a totally different statement than the one that started. Similarly, when dealing with the interpretation of events regarding other countries and cultures, not only do we have to deal with information screens and perceptions, but also with translation and cultural issues that can further skew or bias the information that is needed in order to make the decision. And of course they will also affect the interpretation of any decision that is made.

But these are not the only biases or issues that can affect a decision maker and therefore a decision. There are also *affective biases*—that is, the impact of emotions. Regardless of how dispassionate or rational decision makers try to be, they will be affected by strong feelings that they have about the circumstances under which the decision has to be made and/or the person or state the decision will affect. This stands in contrast to *cognitive biases*, or "systematic distortions of rational calculations based not on emotional feelings but simply on the limitations of the human brain in making choices."[32] For example, individual decision makers will want to construct models that are consistent with their beliefs so that they can reduce cognitive dissonance. This can lead a decision maker to make a decision on a goal or outcome that he or she has a greater chance of achieving rather than a more grandiose or larger goal that, realistically, is unattainable. No decision maker wants to engage in an action that is likely to fail, nor to admit failure about any policy decision that he or she has made.

Here the work of political scientist Robert Jervis is important, because he not only warns us about the dangers or misperceptions that a decision maker will have, but he also recommends "safeguards" that can be followed by any decision maker who is aware of the possible dangers in decision making that come from biases and expectations.[33] Specifically, Jervis asks,

> Can anything then be said to scholars and decision-makers other than "Avoid being either too open or too closed, but be especially aware of the latter danger"? Although decision-makers will always be faced with ambiguous and confusing evidence and will be forced to make inferences about others which will often be inaccurate, a number of safeguards may be suggested which could enable them to minimize their errors.[34]

That is where the safeguards come in. To a student of international relations, this makes a great deal of sense. For example, in his first safeguard, Jervis notes that "decision-makers should be aware that they do not make 'unbiased' interpretations of each new bit of information, but rather are inevitably heavily influenced by the theories they expect to be verified." Jervis ultimately concludes that knowing their biases and how information is interpreted through these biases "should lead decision-makers to examine more closely evidence that others believe contradicts their views."[35] Or, to put it another way, it is incumbent upon decision makers to look at all points of view. Another safeguard would be to ask whether decision makers' attitudes are consistent and logical and whether they are based on evidence versus belief. All told, Jervis identifies five areas of possible danger and the safeguards that can be used to guard against falling into those traps.[36]

But what a student of international relations also knows and understands about foreign policy decision making is that analyzing the decisions after the fact is very different from the process that a decision maker actually goes through in order to make a decision while she or he is in office. We cannot always know what went on in the mind of any decision maker, nor whether she or he fell into any of the possible traps. This is especially true when decisions are made in times of crisis, when they have to be made quickly and a host of other variables come into play.

What all this tells us is that despite our attempts to arrive at the most rational models of decision making, there are a host of irrational and intangible factors that go into the making of a foreign policy decision *whether the decision maker is aware of them or not.* As students of international relations, if we really are to understand the decisions that are made, at the individual level we need to know who made the decision, something about his or background that might have influenced the decision, the circumstances surrounding the decision (e.g., crisis decision making or not), who else was involved with the decision-making process, and any other information that will provide insight into the variables and factors surrounding the decision. And we do this while holding the other levels constant—that is, we focus on one level at a time.

Crisis Decision Making: The Cuban Missile Crisis

The Cuban missile crisis stands as one of the best examples of foreign policy decision making under crisis circumstances. It is also a case where the situation can best be explained by looking at multiple levels of analysis from the individual through the government. Taking place in October 1962 in the midst of the Cold War, it was one of the most dangerous confrontations, when the two superpowers were said to be "eyeball to eyeball."[37]

Graham Allison, who studied and wrote about the Cuban missile crisis, also reminds us that there are a range of approaches that can be used to explain the events that transpired and why, and that these can be found across a number of levels of analysis. His models, initially articulated in an article in the *American Political Science Review* and then developed further in his classic book *The Essence of Decision*, illustrate what he calls "alternative explanations of the same happening,"[38] which reminds us of the importance of looking at a range of explanations and how various models may be interrelated, all of which can contribute to our understanding of an event.

As we talk about the role of individuals in foreign policy decision making, we have to ask about the Cuban missile crisis how the decisions were made and what happened now that we know how close the world really was to nuclear catastrophe. Clearly we have to begin with the role of President Kennedy, the individual decision maker who was a relatively new president and had already experienced a number of foreign policy failures, both in Cuba with the Bay of Pigs and also in Europe. The result of the confrontation between Kennedy and Soviet leader Nikita Khrushchev was the building of the Berlin Wall. Kennedy was also dealing with an insurrection in Southeast Asia (Vietnam) that was escalating. So the missile crisis emerged amid a climate of confrontation between the United States and communist countries, most notably the Soviet Union, and the president had to make decisions relatively quickly.

In assessing the situation, Kennedy made sure that he had carefully chosen close advisers he could depend on. But this too carried certain dangers. First, we have to understand the psychology of *groupthink*, which clearly came into play. As articulated by Irving Janus, who studied the impact of this phenomenon on foreign policy decisions, the concept refers to "a psychological drive for consensus at any cost that suppresses dissent and appraisal of alternatives in cohesive decision making groups."[39] In this case, all were trusted advisers of President Kennedy who were pulled together as the crisis unfolded to try to arrive at a solution. They met intensively for days to arrive at a decision. Kennedy, aware of the potential problems associated with groupthink, periodically left the room to allow his advisers to have more open discussion. They finally arrived at a range of possible options, from doing nothing to invading Cuba, and settled on a naval blockade as the preferred option. In retrospect, this led to a desirable outcome from the perspective of the United States. But the episode stands as an excellent example of the issues associated with crisis decision making.

In addition to the dangers of groupthink, another point about crisis decision making is that the crisis situation itself alters the process by which decisions are made. The fact that the situation is perceived as critical, with the need for decisions to be made quickly, means that decisions will be made based on the information available at the time, even if it later proves to be incorrect, which was the case here. The time constraints also weigh in, for it means that decision makers will not screen information as carefully as they might otherwise, or they will discard information that is not consistent with their beliefs. Unlike the assumptions we mentioned above for rational actors, in times of crisis, choices might be limited, rather than all options being explored.

Further, the decision makers are affected by the stress of the situation, which can further cloud their rational judgment. In a classic *conflict spiral*, the decision makers often overestimate the hostile intentions of the adversary while underestimating their own hostility toward the adversary. Since so much of decision making depends on the perceptions of the individuals making the decisions, this too tends to alter the options that appear to be available.

As the situation unfolded over those few weeks in October, President Kennedy and his advisers arrived at a plan to place a naval blockade around the island of Cuba. Through back-channel negotiations, the situation was finally resolved peacefully, but not without an escalation of tension and the perception that the world was poised on the brink of nuclear catastrophe.

BOX 4.6

THE CUBAN MISSILE CRISIS AND INDIVIDUAL DECISION MAKING

In October 1962, over a brief period of time, the world was poised on the brink of nuclear catastrophe over a situation that became known as the "Cuban missile crisis." As the situation started to unfold, it evolved relatively quickly, and President John F. Kennedy, who was still recovering from an embarrassing foreign policy defeat in 1961 at the Bay of Pigs in Cuba, assembled a group of advisers around him to discuss what should be done about the missiles that the Soviet Union was deploying to Cuba, ninety miles off the Florida coast. The group of about twenty advisers, who became known as EXCOMM (for "executive committee"), were members of the National Security Council and close advisers to the president, including the secretaries of state and defense, Attorney General Robert Kennedy, the director of the CIA, the chairman of the Joint Chiefs of Staff, and others Kennedy trusted. Meeting regularly, the group charted the course that ultimately led to a peaceful resolution of the crisis and withdrawal of the Soviet missiles from Cuba. But what was most important was that the event was a turning point in the Cold War. No longer was Kennedy perceived as a young and inexperienced president, but as one who was able to face down the Soviet Union and win.

It was thirty years later, in 1992, when there was a conference in Havana that brought together former U.S., Soviet, and Cuban officials to explore the circumstances of the event in retrospect, that former secretary of defense Robert McNamara revealed that "the two nations [the United States and the Soviet Union] were much closer to nuclear conflict than previously realized."[1] McNamara also disclosed that he had learned at that conference that Soviet officials "had sent Havana short-range nuclear weapons and that Soviet commanders there were authorized to use them in the event of American invasion. . . . The short-range nuclear weapons were in addition to medium-range nuclear weapons that would have required authorization from Moscow to use." Given the new information, McNamara concluded that "the actions of all three parties were shaped by *misjudgments*, *miscalculations* and *misinformation*," and that, "in a nuclear age, such mistakes could be disastrous" (emphasis added).[2]

NOTES

1. Don Oberdorfer, "Cuban Missile Crisis More Volatile than Thought," *Washington Post*, January 14, 1992.

2. Quoted in Martin Tolchin, "U.S. Underestimated Soviet Forces in Cuba during '62 Missile Crisis," *New York Times*, January 15, 1992.

From a levels-of-analysis perspective, the three nation-state actors were the United States, the Soviet Union, and Cuba. But in this case, it is what happened *within* the nation-state level that is most critical. It was Kennedy (the individual) and his close advisers who made the decisions, with communication between the United States and the Soviet Union limited to discussions among a few trusted advisers on both sides. Government involvement was limited to the members of EXCOMM (executive committee), most of whom represented the major executive agencies. There was little congressional involvement.

The public (culture/society) was kept informed through the media, but also through speeches made by Kennedy specifically to ensure the ongoing support and cooperation of the public, as well as to reassure them that he was in command of the situation. As noted in a press release from the Kennedy Library, the "public phase covered barely a week (October 22–28, 1962) . . . [and] is one of the key defining events of the Cold War in general and of John F. Kennedy's presidency in particular."[40] In assessing public opinion during and reactions to the missile crisis, the study commissioned by the Kennedy Library found that "similar to responses to other foreign crises both before and since, the Cuban missile crisis drew the country together as people rallied around the president. Presidential approval rose 13 to 15 percentage points, and the public backed the blockade and President Kennedy's resolve to have the offensive missiles removed." The study also found that following the peaceful resolution of the crisis, the public indicated lower fear of nuclear war than it had prior to the event. Thus, although the public was anxious and paid close attention to what was going on, "the public was neither traumatized nor paralyzed by events." And the public saw foreign policy as the most important area for evaluating Kennedy's presidency.[41]

The pattern seen in terms of public support for the president in times of crisis is a pattern that has been replicated in other crisis situations and is often referred to as the "rally-round-the-flag syndrome."[42] Similarly, the fact that the crisis itself galvanized the public has become an established pattern. The author of the Kennedy Library report in fact draws parallels between the missile crisis and the September 11 attacks, noting that

> they were both events of enormous importance that involved a clear and present danger to the country, galvanized the populace, and propelled the political leadership into decided and forceful action. . . . The American people . . .

absorbed the shock, backed their leaders, and carried on with their lives. This may be the hallmark of the American people in times of greatest challenge.[43]

And, one can argue, the individual decision maker and those with whom he or she consults during a time of crisis could not do the job without the support of the public, at least not in a democracy.

In the case of the missile crisis, despite all the things that could possibly go wrong when we look at decision making in general and crisis decision making in particular, the situation was resolved peacefully. But it has become an excellent example of decision making and why foreign policy decision making can be so difficult.[44]

SUMMARY

In this chapter we looked within the nation-state in order to understand how the range of internal factors—the government or political system, society and culture, and the individual—affect international relations and the decisions that are made by one country that affect another. What we learned is that one or all of these factors can have an impact on a nation-state's decisions about any number of factors that are relevant in international relations: going to war; how to avoid or, if it becomes necessary, respond to internal conflict; how to deal with divergent groups within the country; and how individual decision makers approach important decisions.

In the next chapter we are going to return to the macro level of the international system with a special focus on understanding nonstate actors. Although they are not explicitly included as part of the classic levels of analysis, they play an important role in affecting the international system and the nations that make up that system. And, as we will see, it is their very omission from this framework that points out one of the major weaknesses in the approach.

FURTHER READINGS

These additional readings are worth exploring and elaborate on some of the points raised in this chapter. This list is not meant to be exhaustive but only illustrative.

Allison, Graham T. "Conceptual Models and the Cuban Missile Crisis." *American Political Science Review* 63, no. 3 (September 1969).

Doyle, Michael. "Kant's Perpetual Peace." *American Political Science Review* 80, no. 4 (December 1986).

Friedman, Thomas L. "Foreign Affairs Big Mac I." *New York Times*, December 8, 1996. http://www.nytimes.com/1996/12/08/opinion/foreign-affairs-big-mac-i.html.

Jervis, Robert. "Hypotheses on Misperception." *World Politics* 20, no. 3 (April 1968).

"Kennedy Library Releases New Report on Cuban Missile Crisis—Study Documents Impact of Crisis on American Public Opinion." October 16, 2002. http://www .jfklibrary.org/About-Us/News-and-Press/Press-Releases/Kennedy-Library-Re leases-New-Report-on-Cuban-Missile-Crisis-Study-Documents-Impact-of-Crisis -on-Amer.aspx.

Snow, Donald. Chapter 3, "Territorial Disputes: This Land (Palestine and Kurdistan) is *Whose* Land?" In *Cases in International Relations: Principles and Applications*, 7th ed. Lanham, MD: Rowman & Littlefield, 2018.

NOTES

1. Lucy Williamson, "Made in North Korea: Business in a 'Communist Monarchy,'" *BBC News Magazine*, February 12, 2012, http://www.bbc.co.uk/news/maga zine-17046941.

2. J. Ann Tickner, *Gendering World Politics: Issues and Approaches in the Post–Cold War Era* (New York: Columbia University Press, 2001), 96.

3. Tickner, *Gendering World Politics*, 105.

4. Karen A. Mingst, *Essentials of International Relations*, 4th ed. (New York: Norton, 2008), 121.

5. Immanuel Kant, "Perpetual Peace: A Philosophical Sketch," https://www .mtholyoke.edu/acad/intrel/kant/kant1.htm.

6. Michael Doyle, "Kant's Perpetual Peace," *American Political Science Review* 80, no. 4 (1986), 1156.

7. Doyle, "Kant's Perpetual Peace," 1156.

8. Joshua S. Goldstein and Jon C. Pevehouse, *Principles of International Relations* (New York: Pearson Longman, 2009), 72.

9. Thomas L. Friedman, "Foreign Affairs Big Mac I," *New York Times*, December 8, 1996, http://www.nytimes.com/1996/12/08/opinion/foreign-affairs-big-maci.html. This idea was developed still further as part of Friedman's book, *The Lexus and the Olive Tree: Understanding Globalization* (New York: Farrar, Straus & Giroux, 1999).

10. John Mueller, "Is War Still Becoming Obsolete?," paper presented at the Annual Meeting of the American Political Science Association, 1991, 2.

11. President Dwight D. Eisenhower's farewell address to the nation, January 17, 1961, http://avalon.law.yale.edu/20th_century/eisenhower001.asp.

12. For a more complete description of the militarization of the United States, see Andrew J. Bacevich, *Washington Rules: America's Path to Permanent War* (New York: Henry Holt, 2010).

13. Aerospace Industries Association, "2015 Economic Impact Study of the U.S. Aerospace & Defense Industry," http://www.aia-aerospace.org/report/aerospace -and-defense-an-economic-impact-analysis.

14. Mueller, "Is War Still Becoming Obsolete?," 19.

15. Tickner, *Gendering World Politics*, 104–6. It is important to note that the election of Donald Trump and the defeat of Hillary Clinton, the first woman to run for president from a major political party, mobilized a lot of women to political action. For example, the so-called Women's March that took place on January 21, 2017, brought more than two million people, a majority of whom were women, to Washington to protest. An article in the *Los Angeles Times* on May 21, 2017, focused on how Democratic women in Orange County, long a Republican stronghold, have been energized to run for local office. (Sarah D. Wire, "Democrats See New Hope on GOP Turf," *Los Angeles Times*, May 21, 2017, B1.) And similar stories have been reported across the United States in response to the election of Donald Trump.

16. Tickner, *Gendering World Politics*, 106.

17. See Women in Black, official website, http://womeninblack.org.

18. Tim Arango, "Kurds to Pursue More Autonomy in a Fallen Syria," *New York Times*, September 29, 2012.

19. There are a number of sources documenting the genocide and other atrocities committed during the war in Bosnia-Herzegovina. Some that deal specifically with the acts of ethnic cleansing and the nationalist/ethnic struggle include Tom Gallagher, *The Balkans after the Cold War: From Tyranny to Tragedy* (London: Routledge, 2003); Davorak Ljubisic, *A Politics of Sorrow: The Disintegration of Yugoslavia* (Montreal: Black Rose Books, 2004); and Vjeksolav Perica, *Balkan Idols: Religion and Nationalism in Yugoslav States* (New York: Oxford University Press, 2002).

20. For a quick background, see BBC News, "Rwanda: How the Genocide Happened," December 18, 2008, http://www.bbc.com/news/world-africa-13431486. For more detailed background of the conflict, see, for example, Romeo Dallaire and Samantha Power, *Shake Hands with the Devil: The Failure of Humanity in Rwanda* (New York: Carroll & Graf, 2004); and Scott Straus, *The Order of Genocide: Race, Power, and War in Rwanda* (Ithaca, NY: Cornell University Press, 2006).

21. BBC News, "Rwanda: How the Genocide Happened."

22. See, for example, John Mearsheimer, *The Tragedy of Great Power Politics* (New York: Norton, 2001). In this volume, Mearsheimer, who is a quintessential realist thinker, puts U.S. foreign policy and the emergence of the United States as a great

power in a broad historical context that takes into account the emergence of other major powers such as China. Also see Graham Allison, *Destined for War: Can America and China Escape Thucydides's Trap?* (Boston: Houghton Mifflin Harcourt, 2017).

23. Charles Tilly, *Coercion, Capital, and European States* (Cambridge, MA: Blackwell, 1992).

24. The statistics are taken from Al Jazeera, "Syria's Civil War Explained from the Beginning," July 18, 2017, http://www.aljazeera.com/news/2016/05/syria-civil-war-explained-160505084119966.html.

25. The quote is taken from Jack F. Matlock, *Reagan and Gorbachev: How the Cold War Ended* (New York: Random House, 2004), 302. This is an example of how an individual actor in a position of power can play an important role in affecting the direction of a particular nation-state.

26. Mikhail Gorbachev, *Perestroika: New Thinking for Our Country and the World* (New York: Random House, 2004).

27. Joyce P. Kaufman, *A Concise History of U.S. Foreign Policy*, 4th ed. (Lanham, MD: Rowman & Littlefield, 2017), 120.

28. See Matlock, *Reagan and Gorbachev*, for a description of the role played by both women.

29. Cynthia Enloe, *Bananas, Beaches, and Bases: Making Feminist Sense of International Politics* (Berkeley: University of California Press, 2000), 1–2.

30. Paul R. Viotti and Mark V. Kauppi, *International Relations and World Politics: Security, Economy, Identity*, 4th ed. (Upper Saddle River, NJ: Pearson Prentice Hall, 2009), 13–14.

31. Goldstein and Pevehouse, *Principles of International Relations*, 47.

32. Goldstein and Pevehouse, *Principles of International Relations*, 48.

33. See Robert Jervis, "Hypotheses on Misperception," *World Politics* 20, no. 3 (April 1968): 455–79.

34. Jervis, "Hypotheses on Misperception," 462.

35. Jervis, "Hypotheses on Misperception," 462.

36. The potential traps and possible safeguards are outlined by Jervis in "Hypotheses on Misperceptions," section 3, "Safeguards," 462–65.

37. Upon hearing that Soviet ships bearing missiles heading to Cuba had turned around at sea, then–secretary of state Dean Rusk was quoted as saying, "We're eyeball to eyeball and I think the other fellow just blinked." This statement is quoted in any number of sources. The one used for this volume is from Michael Dobbs, "The Price of a 50-Year Myth," *New York Times*, October 15, 2012, http://www.nytimes.com/2012/10/16/opinion/the-eyeball-to-eyeball-myth-and-the-cuban-missile-crisiss-legacy.html. In this op-ed piece, Dobbs uses his analysis of the Cuban missile crisis to draw lessons for more recent foreign policy decisions.

38. Graham T. Allison, "Conceptual Models and the Cuban Missile Crisis," *American Political Science Review* 63, no. 3 (September 1969): 691. See also Graham T. Allison and Philip Zelikow, *The Essence of Decision: Explaining the Cuban Missile Crisis*, 2nd ed. (New York: Pearson, 1999).

39. Irving L. Janis, "Victims of Groupthink: A Psychological Study of Foreign-Policy Decisions and Fiascoes," *Abstracts of the American Psychological Association*, http://psycnet.apa.org/record/1975-29417-000#.

40. "Kennedy Library Releases New Report on Cuban Missile Crisis—Study Documents Impact of Crisis on American Public Opinion," October 16, 2002, http://www.jfklibrary.org/About-Us/News-and-Press/Press-Releases/Kennedy-Library-Releases-New-Report-on-Cuban-Missile-Crisis-Study-Documents-Impact-of-Crisis-on-Amer.aspx.

41. "Kennedy Library Releases New Report on Cuban Missile Crisis."

42. One of the more interesting cases where this can be seen is regarding the taking of American hostages in Iran in 1979 during the Carter administration. In one poll taken in June 1979, before the event, Carter had a 20 percent approval rating. Immediately following that event, public opinion shifted dramatically to become strongly supportive of Carter and also hostile to Iran. For more details, see Rose McDermott, *Risk-Taking in International Politics: Prospect Theory in American Foreign Policy* (Ann Arbor: University of Michigan Press, 1998), especially chapter 3, "The Iranian Hostage Rescue Mission," 45–74.

43. "Kennedy Library Releases New Report on Cuban Missile Crisis."

44. See, for example, Graham T. Allison, *Essence of Decision: Explaining the Cuban Missile Crisis* (Boston: Little, Brown, 1971). This is perhaps the classic book on the missile crisis. Also see Raymond L. Garthoff, *Reflections on the Cuban Missile Crisis* (Washington, DC: Brookings Institution, 1989), and Robert F. Kennedy, *Thirteen Days: A Memoir of the Cuban Missile Crisis* (New York: Norton, 1969), for a fascinating first-person account of the event by someone intimately involved. For a work that draws on previously secret documents from Russian and U.S. archives to offer further insights into the crisis, see Aleksandr Fursenko and Timothy Naftali, *"One Hell of a Gamble": Khrushchev, Castro, and Kennedy, 1958–1964* (New York: Norton, 1997). Also see Michael Dobbs, *One Minute to Midnight: Kennedy, Khrushchev, and Castro on the Brink of Nuclear War* (New York: Knopf, 2008) for a detailed account of the crisis that draws on exhaustive and relatively new research.

5

Nonstate Actors and the International System

Thus far, we have moved through the basics of international relations and the primary actors who are involved with and are part of the international system. We started by looking at the international system as a whole; at the nation-state, which is traditionally the primary actor in the international system; and within the nation-state at the component parts that make up the nation-state. In this chapter, we are going to look at the range of nonstate actors that exist outside the traditional levels-of-analysis framework but which have a marked impact on the international system and the actors within it. These nonstate actors range from international organizations, such as the United Nations and the European Union, which are made up of nation-states, to terrorist organizations, such as ISIS and Al-Qaeda, that are capable of mounting attacks against nation-states, as we saw on September 11, 2001. But we will look at other nonstate actors such as multinational corporations, nongovernmental organizations, and even the media, all of which also play an important role in international political and economic systems today.

By the end of this chapter, you should have a more complete picture of the international system and the range of actors that make up that system and also a better understanding of the strengths and weaknesses of the traditional approaches to international relations.

THE CHANGING NATURE OF THE INTERNATIONAL SYSTEM

What are nonstate actors and why are these actors important? As we noted in chapter 2, the traditional levels-of-analysis approach to understanding international relations *assumes* the nation-state as the primary actor. It *assumes* that the international system is made up of nation-states that interact with one another and conform to certain norms and expectations that can be defined as international law. It also *assumes* that all nation-states have certain characteristics that determine and affect the ways in which they act. And the fact of the matter is, for much of the modern history of international relations, that was the case.

Furthermore, most of the traditional theories that were formulated to describe and explain international relations also assume that the nation-state is the primary actor, even though they vary widely in their understanding of the nation-state and its role. Although more recent theoretical approaches, such as the constructivists, look at the structures that influence nation-states and therefore international relations, they also assume that states have certain characteristics or patterns of behavior that are influenced by factors that were socially constructed. Thus, even though this is a different theoretical approach to and understanding of the nation-state, that actor is still prominently featured.

In thinking about international relations today, it is also true that the norms or patterns of interaction among the nation-states as the major actors has changed, especially since the end of World War II, and exponentially since the end of the Cold War. At the end of World War II, national priorities changed. The world settled into the Cold War, a period also known as "the Long Peace" for the relative stability that came with a bipolar world, but also was kept in check with the knowledge of the devastation that might result if the balance of power were disturbed.[1] Countries that had been colonies sought their independence, resulting in a proliferation of new nations, especially in Africa and Asia. The countries of Latin and South America started to become more assertive at charting their own course of political and economic action, which often did not align with the direction desired by the developed countries of the North, their former colonial powers. Countries also tried to understand why cataclysmic events such as World War II happened, in the hope of preventing them from occurring again in the future.

We see even greater and more rapid changes since the end of the Cold War. The countries of the developing world have moved far beyond their secondary postcolonial status and are now emerging as international powerhouses that even the most developed countries, such as the United States, have to deal with. For example, China is no longer a third world country built on a peasant workforce tied to the land; rather, it is a military and economic force to be reckoned with. The economy of India, the world's largest democracy and one of the BRIC (Brazil, Russia, India, and China, and sometimes including South Africa) countries, is growing at a rate of over 7 percent annually and could soon reach, if not overtake, China. Although many educated Indians are part of the global technology framework, more than half of the population depends on agriculture for its livelihood; agriculture accounts for 16 percent of the country's GDP,[2] which continues to hold India back at this time. Nonetheless, it is quickly emerging as a major player economically as well as politically. The pattern of rapid economic growth and social development that we see in India is not unique but has been repeated in countless other formerly developing countries, such as South Africa and Brazil. Although both of these are facing political issues at the present time, that does not in any way diminish the rapid progress that they have made economically in a relatively short period.

This change in the international order among nation-states has important implications for other aspects of international relations, such as international organizations. With the world no longer divided into developed and developing nations, power blocs have been realigned, and more countries are asserting themselves in discussions on important global issues such as the environment. Within the established international organizations, such as the United Nations, these same countries are demanding more of a say, claiming that the Cold War order that provided the framework for the creation of these organizations and was tied to "major powers" is no longer appropriate. And of course globalization has made it not only possible but easier for more countries to play a role in and have an impact on the international economic system.

We see the changing nature of the international system in other ways as well. For example, in an age in which countries are interdependent, the earthquake and tsunami that hit Japan in March 2011 disrupted life in that country as well as in the countries that trade with it. Help came quickly not only from other countries, but from international organizations whose mission is humanitarian aid and assistance. It is easy to look at that case and to think that help from other countries was forthcoming because they needed Japan; a disruption in trade could easily have had global consequences. But that would hide a more important message. We can also look at the earthquake that struck Haiti in January 2010, resulting in the deaths of more than three hundred thousand people, injury to at least that number, and more than one million people left homeless.[3] Haiti is not a major player in the international system, and yet supplies and aid were coming as quickly as twenty-four hours after the initial event. And the help came from other countries but also from nongovernmental organizations such as the Red Cross and Doctors Without Borders.

It becomes clear, then, that in addition to the realignment in the relative power of nation-states, one of the other major changes that we see in the operation of the international system as a whole is the emergence of nonstate actors who have come to play a role that is in some cases as large as or even larger than that of nation-states. These nonstate actors are also known as transnational actors because they operate across national borders. Some, like nongovernmental organizations (NGOs), provide aid and help in the event of major catastrophes, both natural (such as earthquakes and tsunamis) and man-made (including the devastation caused by wars). They also help influence policy by raising issues to the front of the international agenda, as organizations such as Greenpeace and the Sierra Club do for the environment or Amnesty International has done for issues of human rights. And they advocate for specific positions within countries and across countries on behalf of children, women, animals, the environment, and so on. Others, like multinational corporations (MNCs) and terrorist groups, influence the policies of nation-states for other sets of reasons. Clearly, these nonstate actors influence important aspects of international relations and play a role that nation-states can't or won't play.

What Are Nonstate Actors?

Nonstate actors can fall into a broad range of categories, but on the whole, they exist outside the traditional category of nation-states. Some have nation-states as their members, and others are organizations or groups of individuals whose membership and goals cross the borders of nation-states. Some are organized to advocate for the common good, such as the environment, the rights of children, or health care, while others have expressly political motives, such as terrorist groups. What makes them so perplexing to deal with in IR terms, though, is that the major theories and levels-of-analysis framework have few ways to account for them or their behavior. These organizations don't fall within any of the major theoretical perspectives, yet they have a marked impact on the traditional actors in IR.

International organizations (IOs) are also known as intergovernmental organizations (IGOs), because their members are nation-states, and generally their main role is to help bring order to the international system. This category encompasses a range of organizations, for example, the United Nations (UN) or the European Union (EU), which bring sovereign nation-states together in pursuit of common goals. What becomes most interesting in these cases, however, is how states can join together to pursue common policies *without* infringing on their sovereignty as individual nations. This is a point we will come back to a little bit later in this chapter.

Another group that has become more familiar to many are nongovernmental organizations (NGOs), whose members are individuals or groups rather than nation-states and who generally have a specialized function. Often they try to influence national or international policies and are created specifically to advocate for a specific policy that transcends national borders. Examples of these are Amnesty International, which fights for basic human rights worldwide; Doctors Without Borders (Médecins Sans Frontières), an international medical humanitarian group that provides medical assistance after a natural disaster, political violence, or in cases of extreme poverty; and Greenpeace International, which campaigns to protect the global environment, to name but a few of the better-known organizations. Such NGOs are another form of international organization that exists outside the formal levels of analysis but tries to bring pressure upon the actors in the international system, nation-states, and international organizations in order to effect policy change.

Other entities, such as terrorist groups or even multinational corporations, can also influence actors in the international system and can pose a threat of some kind to the international system and/or the actors within it, especially the nation-state. In the case of terrorist groups, the threat is pretty self-explanatory. However, MNCs are much more insidious in the role they play. While they exist outside the levels of analysis, they can exert a strong influence on the policies of nation-states and the international system as a whole. And for that reason, it is important to explore them.

We also include in this chapter a section on the media. During a period when cable news proliferates, when the Internet is ubiquitous and social media transmits ideas quickly, and when "fake facts" and "alt news" seem to raise questions about what is "real" news and what isn't, we need to think about the role that the media plays as it, too, influences what people think and believe and therefore the policies that can result. In that sense, the media also functions as a nonstate actor.

In this chapter, we will consider each of these types of nonstate actors. Beginning with a general definition or description of each, we will explore their goals, their members, and the role they play in international relations. Since these groups of actors exist outside the bounds of the formal levels of analysis, we need to look at the impact that they do have and on what levels. Thus, one of the major points to think about as we continue through this discussion is what level or levels of analysis they draw from or affect as actors in the international system.

In keeping with the themes of this brief overview of international relations, what we are going to turn our attention to first is at the more macro level, focusing on international organizations as a group of actors that have come to play a role in international relations. They are generally made up of nation-states as well as some NGOs, and they seek ways to bring nation-states together to discuss issues of common concern and to make policy that will affect all of them. In so doing, they help bring about a more stable and regulated order in the international system.

In chapter 3 we talked about the concept of collective security and how it was embodied in the charter of the United Nations. Our approach here will be to identify the purposes or functions that international organizations serve, the role(s) they can—or cannot—play in the international system today, and the type of influence they have. We will also try to see the ways in which different theoretical approaches view international organizations. We will then look quickly at examples of specific organizations in order to apply our understanding of them.

INTERNATIONAL ORGANIZATIONS

Within the subfield of international relations, there is a further subdivision that includes the study of international organizations (IOs). Generally, when we think of international organizations we think of those organizations whose members are national governments; therefore, these organizations are also known as intergovernmental organizations (IGOs). Within this broad category, organizations can be further subdivided; some have virtually universal membership, such as the UN, while others are regional organizations, such as the European Union.

Another way to look at these IGOs is by function. For example, there are organizations that were created to ensure the collective security of their members. NATO is an example of that type and, although on a larger scale, so is the UN. There are other organizations that were created to help stabilize the international economic system, such as the International Monetary Fund (IMF), "an organization of 189 countries, working to foster global monetary cooperation, secure financial stability, facilitate international trade, promote high employment and sustainable economic growth, and reduce poverty around the world."[4] Then there are a plethora of regional organizations designed to facilitate free trade and openness among member nations such as the North American Free Trade Agreement (NAFTA), which unites the United States, Canada, and Mexico into a big trading block. Asia-Pacific Economic Cooperation (APEC) is committed to increasing trade and opening markets in the Asia-Pacific region. APEC is an organization of twenty-one nation-states that border both sides of the Pacific Ocean. Hence, its membership includes the three NAFTA countries, but also Chile and Peru in South America and a range of other countries including China, Japan, Russia, and Vietnam. This illustrates the ways in which membership in organizations can often be overlapping rather than exclusive. And there is no limit to the number or types of organizations that a country can be part of.

These are but a few examples of the types of international organizations that exist and the varied roles that they play internationally. What all of these have in common is that *their members are nation-states* that have joined the organization in the belief that doing so will further their national interest. Nation-states may be, and often are, members of more than one organization that reflect the different interests and priorities that nations have, for example, security, economics, trade, regional, international, and so on.

We will now turn to a more detailed discussion of some of the different types of international organizations that, ultimately, will allow us to draw some important conclusions about the roles they play in the international system.

Intergovernmental Organizations (IGOs)

As noted above, IGOs are multilateral organizations whose members are nation-states. As we have suggested, this raises some interesting questions about the balance between the state's commitments to the organization while also ensuring its own sovereignty. In order to be able to answer that question of balance, we need to begin by determining why states join such organizations in the first place. Here the theoretical approaches can give us some insight, even if they appear to be conflicting.

There are certain general principles that are common to all IGOs and help describe the role(s) that they play in international relations. The assumption underlying the creation of IGOs is that each organization brings together independent states that adhere to the basic principles and goals of the organization and are willing to support its norms. Each organization also has its own set of rules of operation, ways to finance itself, a bureaucratic structure of some type, a voting or decision-making approach among its members, ways to punish member states that don't conform, and membership criteria. Since there is no single means of enforcing international law, IGOs often play an important role in ensuring that such laws, international agreements, and policies are enforced and violators punished. Beyond this set of generalities, however, international organizations vary widely.

The United Nations

The UN is a multilateral organization whose membership includes most nation-states. It is also a major and complex bureaucracy composed of many parts and agencies, with voting of the whole on broad policy issues coming through the General Assembly based on majority vote. So, in that forum, all states have an equal voice. In contrast, the Security Council of the UN has the primary responsibility for issues pertaining to international peace and security and can meet at any time. There are fifteen members, including five permanent members (China, France, Russia, the UK, and the United States), each of which has veto power, and ten additional members that are elected by the General Assembly to serve two-year terms. One of the major items of discussion lately has been whether the makeup of the Security Council is an artifact of the Cold War and needs to be broadened. That argument suggests that the number of permanent members should be expanded to more accurately represent the power distribution beyond the "major powers" of the Cold War period—for example, to include at least one of the BRIC states and/or a representative from different regions, including Latin/South America and Africa. Despite this apparent flaw in membership and the difficulty that the UN in general has had in adapting to changing international realities, it continues to play an important role in the international system as a forum for discussion and also because of the specialized work it does through its various agencies.

One of the unique roles that the UN plays internationally has to do with peacekeeping. An extension of the collective security role that the UN was created for, the peacekeeping mission extends into regions in which there is violent political conflict. Because of its virtually universal membership and the fact that the deployment of UN peacekeeping forces is discussed, debated, and voted on in the Security Council, it is generally seen as playing an apolitical role, responding instead to the particular circumstances and working for the greater good.

UN peacekeeping forces, also known as "blue helmets" because of their headgear, play an important and unique role in supporting missions designated by UN Security Council resolutions or other relevant organizations, such as NATO. In that regard they play a role that no single country can, injecting themselves into conflict situations not as combatants but as representatives of an international organization deployed for a specific purpose and usually of limited duration. For example, UN peacekeeping forces patrol the Green Zone between the north and south in Cyprus and the DMZ separating North and South Korea; supported the implementation of a peace agreement between the government and rebel factions in Sudan; helped maintain civil order in the Democratic Republic of Congo; were based in Kosovo to help administer that area and to support the reconstruction of a political process following the conflict in 1999; and have performed and still perform countless other missions in virtually every part of the world—all authorized by the international system through the United Nations. The forces are drawn from member countries, and their purpose is

to capitalize on the moral authority drawn from their position as peacekeep-
ers accepted in principle by all contending parties. As such, they were not to
intervene in these conflicts, much less take sides. They were only to monitor the
peace and to provide a necessary presence to dissuade the parties from resorting to force against each other.[5]

Ideally, of course, one of the goals of the UN's collective security function
is to provide a forum for discussion and debate that allows for the peaceful
resolution of conflicts before they escalate into armed violence. However,
should the conflict escalate into armed violence, the United Nations can help
play the role of peacemaker and/or peacekeeper as needed.

But the United Nations plays a broader role than just dealing with conflict
and peace. Through its various agencies, the UN performs other important
tasks pertaining to human rights, children, women, social and economic programs, adjudicating international disputes, and other broad international issues as they arise. Each of these has its own structure and specialized mission,
although there can be overlap. For example, if you ever trick-or-treated for
UNICEF, you were raising money on behalf of the UN organization specifically dedicated to helping children worldwide.

In brief, the UN has other agencies within it that address specific issues.
One of the most critical recently has been dealing with the international
refugee crisis that has emerged as people are fleeing conflicts such as the
ones in Syria, Yemen, and other parts of the Middle East and Africa, as well
as economic dislocations due to environmental catastrophes. These have
put more pressure on some of the UN agencies that were created to deal
specifically with these types of issues. An estimated sixty million people were
displaced by World War II, yet the Office of the United Nations High Commissioner for Refugees, created in 1950 following World War II, reports that
"the number of displaced people is [currently] at its highest ever—surpassing
even post–World War II numbers, when the world was struggling to come to
terms with the most devastating event in history. The total at the end of 2015
reached 65.3 million—or one out of every 113 people on Earth, according to
the United Nations High Commissioner for Refugees (UNHCR). The number represents a 5.8 million increase on the year before."[6] And that number
has only increased since 2015. According to a UNHCR report released in June
2016, at that time, about 1 percent of the world's population was either "an

asylum-seeker, internally displaced or a refugee."[7] In short, as a major international organization, the UN is designed to address and to find solutions to major global issues by bringing countries but also NGOs together.

The UN has been subject to the accusation that it is tied too closely to Cold War values and political structures, and it has also been criticized for its inability to confront some of the most difficult international issues. Because of the structure of the Security Council, a veto, or even the threat of a veto, from one of the "big five" countries can limit the types of actions that the organization can take, often while conflict continues to rage. For example, in October 2011 as the civil war in Syria was escalating, China and Russia vetoed a measure proposed by Britain to impose "targeted measures" against the government of Bashar al-Assad. While this response provoked cries of outrage from other countries, the structure of the Security Council means that little could be done to move forward. Subsequently, there have been ongoing negotiations to try to find a way to end this conflict. In December 2016 the members of the Security Council endorsed a resolution proposed by Russia and Turkey to bring about a cease-fire and to jump-start peace negotiations. As of this writing, however, negotiations continue, but so does the conflict.

Criticisms aside, the UN has been able to endure and remain an important symbol of international cooperation and unity, as well as being an established forum for discussion of important issues. For example, through the Millennium Development Goals (MDGs) and its successor, the Sustainable Development Goals (SDGs), the UN has been able to use its influence to raise a number of important human security issues to the top of the international agenda. Many of the conventions and resolutions pertaining directly to women, for example, grew out of major UN-sponsored conferences that brought together political leaders and NGOs. Passage of conventions such as the Declaration on the Elimination of Violence against Women, passed in 1993, and the 1979 Convention on the Elimination of All Forms of Discrimination against Women (CEDAW), described as the international bill of rights for women, brings the weight of the international system to bear on important issues, in this case pertaining specifically to women.

What this illustrates is the way in which the UN can be used to coalesce international opinion behind an issue and can contribute to international agreement.

SUSTAINABLE DEVELOPMENT GOALS

On January 1, 2016, the seventeen Sustainable Development Goals (SDGs) adopted at a summit of world leaders in September 2015 officially came into force. "Over the next fifteen years, with these new Goals that universally apply to all, countries will mobilize efforts to end all forms of poverty, fight inequalities and tackle climate change, while ensuring that no one is left behind. . . . The new Goals are unique in that they call for action by all countries, poor, rich and middle-income to promote prosperity while protecting the planet. They recognize that ending poverty must go hand-in-hand with strategies that build economic growth and addresses a range of social needs including education, health, social protection, and job opportunities, while tackling climate change and environmental protection."[1] Although these are not legally binding, governments are expected to establish national frameworks to achieve these goals. Taken together, these goals will improve the lives of everyone as well as the state of the planet.

Goal 1: End poverty for all.

Goal 2: End hunger, achieve food security and improved nutrition, and promote sustainable agriculture.

Goal 3: Ensure healthy lives and promote well-being for all at all ages.

Goal 4: Ensure inclusive and quality education for all and promote lifelong learning.

Goal 5: Achieve gender equality and empower all women and girls.

Goal 6: Ensure access to water and sanitation for all.

Goal 7: Ensure access to affordable, reliable, sustainable, and modern energy for all.

Goal 8: Promote inclusive and sustainable economic growth, employment, and decent work for all.

Goal 9: Build resilient infrastructure, promote sustainable industrialization, and foster innovation.

Goal 10: Reduce inequality within and among countries.

Goal 11: Make cities inclusive, safe, resilient, and sustainable.

Goal 12: Ensure sustainable consumption and production patterns.

Goal 13: Take urgent action to combat climate change and its impacts.

Goal 14: Conserve and sustainably use the oceans, seas, and marine resources.

Goal 15: Sustainably manage forests, combat desertification, halt and reverse land degradation, and halt biodiversity loss.

Goal 16: Promote just, peaceful, and inclusive societies.

Goal 17: Revitalize the global partnership for sustainable development.[2]

NOTES

1. UN, "The Sustainable Development Agenda," http://www.un.org/sustainabledevelopment/development-agenda.

2. "Sustainable Development Goals: 17 Goals to Transform Our World," http://www.un.org/sustainabledevelopment/globalpartnerships.

North Atlantic Treaty Organization (NATO)

As noted above, there are any number of other IGOs that are either more limited in membership or that take on specific functions. Many of these were created after World War II by the then "great powers" as a way to stabilize and formalize some aspect of international relations. For example, the North Atlantic Treaty Organization was created in 1949 by the then democratic countries of Western Europe, specifically to link them with the United States to serve as a deterrent to Soviet expansion. The assumption was that this alliance would explicitly tie the U.S. nuclear deterrent to the European allies, and it would thereby balance the power of the Soviet Union. The enlargement of NATO in 1993 to include the countries of the former Eastern bloc, beginning with Poland, Hungary, and the Czech Republic, was tangible proof that the Cold War had ended and that these formerly communist countries were now recognized democracies. But perhaps even more important, NATO enlargement has served as an indicator that the old international order was changing, and along with it, so were assumptions about the need for a collective security agreement directed against a single threat.

Especially since the end of the Cold War, the utility of NATO has been questioned. For example, as a candidate for president, Donald Trump referred to the alliance as being "obsolete," although he later retreated from this position.[8] The decision to enlarge NATO in 1993 at the same time that the war in Bosnia was escalating raised serious issues about the role of the alliance after the Cold War. When NATO agreed to go into the Balkans initially in 1992, it was the first "out of area" mission, and it set a precedent for the expanded global role for the alliance that we see today. In December 2001, two months after the decision to attack Afghanistan, NATO created the International Security Assistance Force (ISAF), and in August 2003, NATO assumed leadership of the ISAF operation. At that time, the alliance "became responsible for the command, coordination and planning of the force, including the provision of a force commander and headquarters on the ground in Afghanistan."[9] Hence, NATO has evolved from an organization designed specifically to protect the European allies by tying them to the U.S. nuclear deterrent, as envisioned when NATO was created in 1949, to one that is bringing together many countries to address major security issues in other parts of the world.

Clearly NATO has expanded its role greatly and, as of this writing, is playing a support role in Afghanistan, maintains a presence in Kosovo, patrols the Mediterranean to counter the threat of terrorism, and supports the African Union (AU) in its peacekeeping missions. In other words, as threats and conflict areas have changed, NATO has tried to adapt to meet these new military and security needs.

The International Monetary Fund (IMF) and the World Bank

There are many other examples of the creation of specialized IGOs created after World War II to serve specific purposes as envisioned by the major powers, given the political and economic realities of that time. The International Monetary Fund grew out of the Bretton Woods Conference in 1944, driven largely by the United States to promote international monetary cooperation and stability. The World Bank, which was also created at Bretton Woods, was originally designed to help facilitate the postwar reconstruction efforts in Europe, but it was subsequently expanded to provide loans to assist countries' development efforts. These organizations were designed to help foster financial stability, promote international trade and cooperation, and promote employment and economic growth worldwide through their policies. And many of the ideas underlying these organizations made sense at that time. But the situation has changed since then, leading to questions about their effectiveness today.

One of the major policies that both organizations advocate are structural adjustment programs (SAPs) that "impose specific spending restrictions on governments, especially when it comes to social welfare, health and education programs, while encouraging expenditures on items such as infrastructure, more efficient revenue collection programs, tourist facilities, and tax rebates for foreign investors."[10] While these should lead to economic growth, they often ignore the costs to the people of the country.

The approach taken by these organizations to provide loans to the leaders or governments of countries has raised questions about who really benefits from those loans. In some cases, the loans funded corrupt governments rather than the projects that were designed to reach the people. The structural adjustment programs that were supposed to help a country develop by offering lower interest rates on loans under certain conditions can actually have the opposite effect by putting the country into debt, which can undermine its economic development.[11] And feminist theorists as well as some of the Marxist/radical theorists question "the harsh effects of structural adjustment policies imposed by the International Monetary Fund on Third World debtor nations [which] fall disproportionately on women as providers of basic needs, as social welfare programs in areas of health, nutrition, and housing are cut."[12]

The IMF and the World Bank have also been subjected to international criticism and questions about their role in a globalized world. At the most basic level, both of these organizations were created at a period in time that was quite different from the present, politically and economically. This can be seen in the leadership structure of each; traditionally, the World Bank has been headed by an American and the IMF by a European, representing the "old" order. When IMF managing director Dominique Strauss-Kahn stepped down because of a sex scandal in May 2011, there were questions about whether his replacement had to be a European. In fact, some countries argued that it was time to move beyond that assumption and to have a managing director from one of the emerging countries who could better understand those countries' needs. Although Christine Lagarde, then serving as France's finance minister, was ultimately elected to the post, the head of the Mexican Central Bank was also a contender for the position.

The five countries with the largest number of shares in World Bank capital (the United States, Germany, France, Japan, and the UK) have the greatest say. Again, this reinforces the charges that these institutions are artifacts of the Cold War and do not reflect current international reality. Furthermore, since their members are states, they cannot help but be subject to political rivalries that can call into question their decisions.

Regional Organizations: The European Union (EU) as a Case Study

In addition to international organizations that bring together all or most of the nation-states, such as the UN or the IMF and World Bank, a host of regional organizations have emerged that complement—or challenge—the place of global IGOs. Many of these reflect changing power relationships both internationally and regionally, and they can play an important role for the member countries. Often they are both economic and political in scope, and they exist to foster greater collaboration and cooperation among the member nations.

The oldest among these regional organizations is the Organization of American States (OAS), which entered into force in 1951. Now composed of thirty-five states in the Americas, the United States is represented as simply one of the members, albeit with more resources than most of the other member countries. The OAS was based on four pillars: promoting democracy, defending human rights, ensuring a multidimensional approach to security in the region, and fostering development and prosperity throughout the region.[13]

Another example of an ongoing regional organization is the Organization of African Unity, now called the African Union (AU), which was created in 1963 to promote cooperation and solidarity among the states of Africa and to ensure a better life for the peoples of the continent. One of the underlying goals of the AU is to minimize dependence on the developed countries of the North and West and to further the roles in which African countries can help one another. Both the OAS and the AU serve as examples of regional organizations created to foster cooperation and collaboration among the states of a particular region that would be independent of the major international powers.

Perhaps the most well known and even enduring of the regional organizations is the European Union. Currently, the EU is made up of twenty-eight countries that have pledged to move toward a common economic, foreign, and defense policy, including the seventeen countries that make up the euro zone—those countries that have come to adopt the euro as their common currency, although adopting the euro is not a requirement for being in the EU. By remaining outside the euro zone, which has given it a degree of independence, the UK has been able to emerge as a leader in establishing policy for the EU, and by virtue of its "special relationship" with the United States, it plays an important balancing role. On the other hand, because of its economic power, Germany has emerged as an important player in both the EU and the euro zone and has, in fact, dictated many of the economic policies that the countries in that group have followed. What cannot be overlooked is the fact that in a globalized world, the economic policies and issues surrounding the euro zone have a direct impact on the global economic system. The EU also stands as an example of the growing trend toward regional integration.

The EU has an interesting structure; each of the member nations has its own leader, typically a president, a prime minister, or both. But as an entity, the EU also has a president—actually two: a president of the European Council and a president of the European Commission. The European Council is composed of the heads of state or government of each of the EU member nations, and it meets regularly to review common policies and initiatives. It is headed by a president who is appointed for a two-and-a-half-year term, replacing the previous structure of a presidency that rotated among member nations. This body has been the driving force behind EU integration efforts. The European Commission is the executive body of the EU, and it is responsible for the implementation of policy and the day-to-day running of the EU. There are twenty-eight commissioners, one per member state, with the president proposed by the European Council and then elected by the European Parliament.

Are you confused yet? How can an organization of twenty-eight sovereign states also be a member of another organization that also has its own parliament and president(s) and makes policy that each state is expected to support? The realists would say that states will remain in this organization as long as it is in their national interest to do so. The liberals would say that all countries benefit from this union of democratic countries because of increased trade and the advantages that come from a common security and foreign policy. The constructivists would note the ways in which these states and the people within them have been transformed because of the structural framework within which they are now interacting (the EU) and, in turn, that the structure itself has been transformed because of the member states.

BOX 5.2

THE EU AND "BREXIT"

The EU has its origin in the post–World War II period and the desire to bring some of the recovering European states closer together. The Treaty of Rome was signed in 1957 and officially went into effect on January 1, 1958, creating the European Economic Community. The 1992 Maastricht Treaty officially established the European Union, with the then European Community as one of its foundational pillars. The Lisbon Treaty that followed in 2007, entering into force on December 1, 2009, further amends and updates the previous treaties. In addition to creating the euro zone, which not all EU members need to be part of— the UK retained its own currency, for example—the EU created a European government with the goal of moving all member states toward a common foreign and security as well as economic policy. There has often been tension between the sovereignty of the individual member states, currently at twenty-eight counting the UK, and the goals of the EU as a whole, but those tensions were subsumed by the importance of the larger goals and the many advantages accrued to the individual states by being part of this organization.

In a referendum called by Prime Minister David Cameron, on June 23, 2016, the UK voted by 52 percent to 48 percent to leave the EU in what has become known as "Brexit." What was perhaps most interesting about the result were the differences they revealed within the UK, not only across regions but also generationally. Regionally, Scotland, Northern Ireland, London, and a few other primarily urban areas were strongly for "remain," while much of rural England and Wales as well as some of the aging industrial cities went heavily to "leave." Younger and more educated people (especially under age forty) voted to remain by a significantly larger margin than did older people. In many cases, this pitted members of households against one another. All of this suggests very big differences in the ways in which different groups and regions perceive their own country as well as its relationship to Europe.

In addition to its impact on the UK, especially Scotland and Northern Ireland, the other major question surrounding Brexit is what the withdrawal of the UK will mean for the EU. There was already discontent among some of the member states about the ways in which the various financial crises in Greece and Spain were handled as well as how various EU countries have chosen to deal with the refugee issue. This has led to concern that the UK referendum would set a precedent that other countries might follow, thereby leading to the end of the EU.

The Lisbon Treaty has within it Article 50, which outlines how a country could leave the EU. It states, "Any Member State may decide to withdraw from the Union in accordance with its own constitutional requirements."[1] It then puts the burden on the state that seeks to withdraw to notify the European Council of its intention, and then the EU and the state enter into negotiations regarding the arrangement for the formal withdrawal. Part of those negotiations should include the terms for the future relationship between the individual state and the EU. For the UK, the clock is set at two years to conclude the negotiations unless both the members of the European Council and the state decide to extend the period. Those negotiations started in June 2017.

NOTE

1. Lisbon Treaty, http://www.lisbon-treaty.org/wcm/the-lisbon-treaty/treaty-on-European-union-and-comments/title-6-final-provisions/137-article-50.html.

That is one of the challenges of integration, and it serves as the primary reason that the people of the United Kingdom rebelled and voted to leave in what has become known as "Brexit." The Brexit vote raises important questions about the future of the EU and whether other countries, which are or could become similarly discontent with EU policies that run counter to what is believed to be in their national interest, would also choose to leave the EU.

As it has existed to this time, EU nations have a common foreign and economic policy when they agree, but they generally resort to national policies when they disagree. However, when the member nations disagree, it means that the EU working as a whole can do little or nothing at all. The primary example of this is the U.S. decision to go to war with Iraq in 2003, where some of the member nations, such as the UK, Poland, and initially Spain, were strong supporters of the U.S. decision, as opposed to France, Germany, and Belgium, which were united in opposition. And the EU countries remain deeply divided over the issue of enlargement in general and which countries to admit in particular. This is especially acute over the issue of membership for Turkey, a country that applied for full membership as far back as 1987 but has yet to meet the criteria for membership. The reality, though, is that issues of enlargement take a backseat to the crises that the EU is experiencing as it has to deal with Brexit, an influx of refugees, and economic uncertainty.

What does this brief review of IGOs tell us about the state of international relations today? First, the emergence of regional organizations that parallel the broader global ones suggests that states still believe in the importance of organizations that bring them together to pursue common goals. Yet, as the Brexit example illustrates, when a state sees a conflict between what is in its national interest and the goals of an organization, it has the option to leave, which then threatens the cohesion of the entire organization.

Second, the emergence of regional organizations serves to reinforce the changing power structure within the international system. Countries no longer have to rely on the major powers for security or to ensure their economic well-being. While many organizations include some of the major powers— the United States is a member of many IGOs, including regional ones such as APEC, NAFTA, and the OAS—the organization does not depend on, or even want, a major power like the United States to steer its course. Rather, the United States serves as another member of the group, albeit one with more resources than other members.

Third, many of the IGOs that exist today stress economic cooperation, rather than security, as a core value. Admittedly, this is also an indicator of the changing and broadening understanding of security, which is also a function of the post–Cold War world. It is also a vindication of one of the basic principles put forward by feminist authors that the concept of security needs to be redefined so that it moves "beyond its association with military issues" to include economic and environmental threats, as well as ensuring basic values such as freedom.[14] It is instructive that the websites of so many regional organizations stress these values as fundamental to the organization.

Fourth, despite the criticisms of the global IGOs with their emphasis on the power of the developed countries and their outdated goals, these organizations remain important; they have not been supplanted by other organizations, either regional or functional, but rather they continue to exist and to play a prominent role internationally. One basic assumption of political life is that if an entity, such as an organization, stops being able to meet a need or perform a function, it will cease to exist or it will be supplanted by another entity/actor/organization that can better fill the gap. But that has not happened. Whereas the League of Nations disappeared when it became clear that it could not serve the function it was designed for, the UN continues to exist and to play an important role internationally. While that might not have been the role it was originally designed for, the organization has been able to adapt and evolve and, in doing so, has met other needs that were not necessarily envisioned when the UN was created.

These are important lessons if we really are to understand the role of IGOs today. Where you stand on this issue is, in part, a function of which of the philosophical traditions you support, which in turn will color your interpretation of the issues.

IGOs and IR Theory

If IGOs are an established part of the international system, how do they fit within the theoretical framework that we outlined earlier? As organizations whose members are nation-states, they clearly exist at a unique place in the levels-of-analysis framework and within the international system. They play a role as actors whose decisions and actions affect other actors, including nation-states, in the international system at various levels. And while they represent the interests of the states that make up their membership, they also enact policies that are separate from and influence the behaviors of other nation-states, both those that are their members and also nonmembers.

Realists start with the presumption that all states seek to maximize their own power and that they are rational actors. They would also be skeptical of the utility of IGOs and the role that they play in the international system, since such organizations seem to go against the primacy of the nation-state. Logically, then, the next step would be to conclude that if states enter into such agreements or join IGOs, they do so in the belief that membership will increase their power or leverage or that it would not undermine their power or leverage in any way. That would certainly be the case with some of the examples above.

But there is also a healthy dose of liberal thought inherent in the creation of any IGO. Here the assumption is that countries choose to enter into them because they facilitate cooperation and collective action that all benefit from. All participating countries share basic values and work together to ensure that their values and norms are sustained. These IGOs reinforce the belief in the importance of interdependence and regional integration, which they see as mutually beneficial. Furthermore, also underlying the liberal commitment to such organizations is the belief that the resulting cooperation and interdependence will make war and conflict less likely to occur, which is clearly another benefit.

Constructivists emphasize the structures that influence states, as well as the ways in which states and the individuals within them are altered by the structures with which they interact. So, as we saw above with the case of the EU, the various states in the organization are affected directly by its policies, and the organization (in this case, the EU), in turn, is influenced and affected by the decisions of the states that are its members. In other words, the structure of the organization transforms and is in turn transformed by the actors within it—not only the states, but the individual leaders. Witness the critical role played by Angela Merkel in determining the fiscal policies of the euro zone. Thus, IGOs serve as a way in which the international system can be altered and the actions of that system changed—hopefully in a positive way.

The more radical theorists, such as Marxists, would probably discount the value of such organizations in the belief that even if they were not explicitly created by the more powerful countries, ultimately an unequal power balance will result, creating an outcome that will pit more powerful against less powerful states. In many ways, this is the charge often leveled against the UN, which is seen as perpetuating a structure based on pitting the developed versus the developing nations, even though that now appears to be an outdated political order.

It is also in understanding the role of IGOs that the feminist perspective again offers some important insights. On the one hand, the UN and some of the other IGOs have played an important role in identifying the inequities that exist among members of a population and in drawing attention to ways to address these inequities. The various world conferences on women hosted by the UN have drawn attention to the status of women worldwide and have led to the passage of resolutions specifically to ensure women's representation and that women's views are noted. However, feminists also note that since IGOs represent the views of the governments of the member states rather than the populations, women's views are underrepresented—as are women— in the discussions.

Regardless of which theoretical perspective you accept about the role or utility of IGOs, there can be little discussion or debate about the fact that they do exist as organizations with nation-states as their members, which play an important role in contemporary international relations.

IGOs and Sovereignty

One question we must come back to is, how do states reconcile the apparent contradiction between ensuring their own sovereignty and participating in such an organization? To respond to that, it is important to remember that any state can withdraw from the organization (or, for that matter, from any international agreement) at any time if it feels that participating will not be in its national interest or would undermine its sovereignty. An example of this can be seen with France and NATO and, more recently, with the UK and the EU, explored in more detail in box 5.2.

In the case of France and NATO, France withdrew from the NATO unified military command structure in 1966 in the belief that remaining within the organization undermined its sovereignty and was not in its best interest. France did remain part of the political structure, however, which ensured that it had ongoing ties to the organization. In 2009, French president Nicolas Sarkozy announced that France would be returning to the military structure, claiming that "there was no sense in France—a founder member of NATO—having no say in the organization's decisions on military strategy." Sarkozy also said that "this rapprochement with NATO ensures our national independence. . . . To distance ourselves would limit our independence and our room for maneuver."[15] Thus, Sarkozy was making the case that inclusion, rather than exclusion, offered more options for France and benefited its ability to make policy decisions internationally, rather than constraining it as previously believed.

But Sarkozy also noted, "A solitary nation is a nation that has no influence whatsoever. We need strong diplomacy, a strong defense and a strong Europe."[16] This, in turn, suggests that the country's strength and power would be maximized by being part of NATO. Obviously, then–French president Sarkozy saw that the advantages that accrued from being in the alliance outweighed the possible costs. This is an example of rational decision making. But it also stands as an example of how a country can choose when or whether to join or remain part of an IGO.

This particular case is especially illustrative for a number of reasons regarding the role that IGOs play internationally, but also applying the levels of analysis. From the perspective of an individual nation-state, it shows the ways in which a country's interpretation of sovereignty varied according to the individual leader of the country and also the changing political context. In this case, we can look at the decisions made by then-president Charles de Gaulle in 1966 versus President Sarkozy in 2009. At the nation-state level, it illustrates how the interpretation of the national interest changed, and with those changes came a different relationship to NATO. From the perspective of the IGO, in this case NATO, it also shows that a unified organization is far greater than its individual parts.

In looking at the case of the UN, we can also see some of the apparent contradictions between sovereignty and the IGO. When it was envisioned in 1941, the United Nations was to be an organization that would unite sovereign states, all of which would be equal in terms of voting within the General Assembly. However, as sovereign states, none is bound by any determination made by the UN. Therefore, what binds them to the organization is commitment to international law and the obligations that come with that. However, because of the sanctity of state sovereignty and other central principles of international thinking, it has also proven to be powerless at times to address international crises, such as the genocide that has taken place in a number of countries and the proliferation of nuclear weapons. While it has been successful at bringing countries together to take a stand against such global issues—the imposition of sanctions against North Korea as a way to check its development of nuclear weapons is an example—it has not been able to put a stop to the actions of individual nations in all cases.

Nonetheless, it is also important to remember that the UN does hold moral suasion in that countries want UN approval for various actions. For example, the United States did look to the UN for support in its initial decision to go to war against Afghanistan following the attacks of 9/11. However, the decision to go to war against Iraq seriously divided the countries when it did not get UN approval.

After reaching consensus to insist on Iraqi disarmament and send back UN weapon inspectors, the Security Council split on whether to authorize force against Iraq—the United States and Britain voted in favor; France, Russia, and

China against. After France threatened to veto a UN resolution authorizing war, a U.S.-British coalition toppled the Iraqi government without explicit UN backing. UN Secretary-General Kofi Annan later called the war "illegal."[17]

This example illustrates some of the limits of IGOs, especially when there is a conflict between the goals of the nation-state and those of the organization. In this example, the United States took action in defiance of the will of the UN. Yet the UN continues to exist with the United States as a member.

We will now turn to nongovernmental organizations, other nonstate actors that also play a role in the international system. What makes these especially unique, however, is that none of them is made up of nation-states, although what each does affects nation-states and, in fact, the entire international system.

NONGOVERNMENTAL ORGANIZATIONS (NGOS)

The prominence and role of nongovernmental organizations have grown as they have become recognized by other legitimate actors within the international system, such as nation-states and other IGOs, such as the UN. Some transnational movements have grown up around very positive and progressive ideas, such as protecting the environment or human rights. Some coalesce around specific ideological causes, such as population control/family planning or immigration. What these social movements have in common is the desire to bring about change in international law or policy, or within an individual nation-state. And often they seek legal and legitimate ways to bring pressure to bear on numerous governments and the international system in order to achieve their goals without resorting to acts of violence.

Groups that are dedicated to cleaning up the environment (such as the Sierra Club) or human rights (such as Amnesty International) are examples of such NGOs that bring together people from different nation-states to work for or advocate for a larger global good. NGOs can also serve economic needs (such as chambers of commerce) or business-related functions (such as the International Air Transport Association [IATA], which coordinates airlines worldwide). Among the things that make NGOs especially difficult to define or characterize is that they vary quite a bit in terms of mission, size, membership, and resources.

Because they are not tied to any individual nation-state but cross state borders, NGOs are also in a unique position to effect change at the international level. Generally, they do not advocate for any single state's position but for issues pertaining to a group of people or for a broad idea. And as the world has become smaller and more globalized, technology has enabled them to spread their message quite broadly and to appeal to a larger group of people.

What does all this tell us? If you google "NGO," you will get almost forty million entries. And if you further subdivide these, you can get a good idea of the range and extent of these organizations. The point is that NGOs exist to advocate for almost any cause and purpose, and these transcend political borders. Further, NGOs can play an important role in influencing policy in the international system.

For example, when the UN organized the various conferences on women,[18] it included participation by NGOs representing women. In fact, the website for the UN Division for the Advancement of Women (DAW) states explicitly,

> The active participation of NGOs is a critical element. . . . NGOs have been influential in shaping the current global policy framework on women's empowerment and gender equality—the Beijing Declaration and Platform for Action. They continue to play an important role in holding international and national leaders accountable for the commitments they made in the Platform for Action.[19]

In this case, NGOs based in various countries around the world came together to contribute to an international agenda that promoted and recognized the role of women under the auspices of the UN. And there are many other such examples.

The United Nations has a website

> for our global NGO community (Non-governmental organizations associated with the United Nations). Its aim is to help promote collaborations between NGOs throughout the world, so that together we can more effectively partner with the United Nations and each other to create a more peaceful, just, equitable and sustainable world for this and future generations.[20]

In other words, there is a network linking UN-recognized NGOs to facilitate their collaboration.

One statistic notes that in 2009 there were approximately twenty-eight thousand documented NGOs worldwide. Furthermore, the "socially constructed image of NGOs widely accepted throughout the world is highly positive—humanitarian movements dedicated to improving the human condition rather than seeking to benefit themselves at the expense of others."[21] This positive image has been reinforced by the public and also by the response of NGOs to natural disasters, such as the earthquake in Haiti in January 2010 or the earthquake and tsunami in Japan in March 2011. Where countries were seen as lagging in their responses, it was international NGOs such as the International Red Cross and Doctors Without Borders that were the first to respond.

In many ways, NGOs play an important and otherwise unfilled role in international relations. But this also makes them vulnerable and makes them targets in situations of conflict. For example, one of the first buildings to be bombed in Sarajevo, Bosnia, in 1992 at the start of that war was the building housing the International Federation of the Red Cross (IFRC), which was identified by its flag.[22] Attacking that building was important symbolically because it was identified so strongly with the international community, and the bombing sent a message internationally about the gravity of the conflict. That destruction aside, the IFRC and its associated organizations continued their work in Bosnia during the war and after, including taking on the task of clearing land mines that had been planted during the war.

Here we can ask another important question, and that is, who would take on these tasks if NGOs did not step up? For example, clearing land mines is tedious and expensive work that most militaries are reluctant or unable to do. And yet because land mines are so inexpensive to make and plant, they have become a weapon used in many civil conflicts. The International Campaign to Ban Landmines (ICBL), another NGO, was awarded a Nobel Peace Prize for its work in trying to enact an international treaty banning land mines. The Treaty to Ban Land Mines entered into force in March 1999, but thirty-five states, including the United States, have not yet signed. The ICBL also estimates that as of 2015, more than seventy states were still affected by land mines, primarily as a result of civil wars, and 6,460 people were hurt or killed by a land mine in 2015.[23] This NGO continues to work for the elimination of land mines and expanding the list of countries that are signatories. It serves as an example of an NGO that advocates for a cause that affects many countries and the people within them, which the countries are unwilling or unable to address themselves.

Those NGOs that advocate for a particular policy position, such as family planning, are seen as more controversial because of the stand that they take.

While few would argue with the need to help a country or a people who have suffered because of an event not of their making, to advocate for the distribution of contraceptive devices flies in the face of some religious or cultural tenets or traditions. In those cases, the NGO often does not get the same level or type of support.

Here we get into the dangers of *cultural imperialism* as well: the imposition of one set of cultural norms on another country or group. While those in the developed West might advocate for the use of condoms for family planning purposes as a way to reduce the poverty rate of a country, ensure freedom for women from unwanted pregnancy, and reduce the rate of HIV/AIDS, some in the target countries might see this as the West imposing its cultural norms on another group. Thus, what one NGO might advocate as a positive policy option for a host of reasons might elicit a negative response for cultural or social reasons.

Like the IGOs noted above, different theoretical traditions respond in different ways to NGOs and the roles that they play. Realists would question the validity of such organizations as playing any legitimate role internationally. Since they believe that power is tied to and derived from the nation-state, NGOs by definition do not and cannot play a role as independent actors. Any power that they might have internationally has to be granted to them by the nation-state.

Here we can also see the divergence among theoretical perspectives. Liberals, in contrast to realists, would see the growing role of NGOs as indicative of changes in the international system. They would argue that NGOs represent different perspectives and points of view and that they actually help facilitate cooperation and collective action around policies that are designed to further the greater good. Thus, they would argue, NGOs play a unique role in coalescing support for policies such as improving the environment or protecting the rights of children worldwide. Constructivists too would see the emergence of NGOs as indicative of changes in the structure of international relations that can ultimately alter the policies of nation-states.

Feminists especially see the importance of NGOs, which emerged beyond the constraints of formal political channels and therefore can be far more receptive to the inclusion of women and to addressing the needs of women. In fact, "women have a long history of nongovernmental political engagement at the international level. In the nineteenth century, women began to organize internationally over a broad range of issues such as antislavery, temperance, peace, and women's suffrage."[24] Clearly, women saw that they could play a role in influencing policy decisions, even if they could not yet vote. But it also is important to note that many of these women's movements were driven by generally elite women from the northern developed countries such as the UK and the United States. This, in turn, seemed to set a precedent "that international women's movements have tended to reflect the priorities of those in Western liberal states; this has given rise to legitimate claims from women in the South that their concerns have been ignored or misunderstood."[25]

Nonetheless, the international agenda for all women took an important step forward in the 1970s with the declaration of the UN Decade for Women and the subsequent women's conferences held under UN auspices. At these various conferences,

> there was an increasing recognition of the multiple experiences of women depending on their class, race and nationality; feminist concerns with difference and cautions about universalism were articulated by the activist community. A wide variety of issues was raised, including women's participation in informal labor markets, environmental issues, and violence against women.[26]

The point here is that the emergence and growing roles of NGOs internationally have made it possible to put policy issues on the international agenda that nation-states have had to address in a serious way. This is one example of the ways in which nonstate actors, in this case NGOs, can affect the behavior of nation-states and the international system.

TERRORISM: A CHALLENGE TO THE INTERNATIONAL SYSTEM

Thus far, we have looked at international organizations of various types that have been recognized as an ongoing and legitimate part of the international system. We are now going to turn our attention to a very different type of nonstate actor: terrorist groups. Terrorist groups, such as ISIS and al-Qaeda, are among the nonstate actors that have gotten a lot of attention, especially in the wake of 9/11. But various other events, including bombings in the city of Mumbai, India, London, Madrid, and other European capitals, and more recently the use of trucks to mow down civilians in London, Nice, and Berlin, are examples of the types of events that have drawn attention to terrorist groups as nonstate actors that have had a significant impact on nation-states and the international system.

A Historical Perspective on Terrorism

In looking at terrorism, it is important to note that it is not a new phenomenon; examples of what could be called terrorist acts can be documented going back to ancient Rome. "Historically, the vast majority of terrorism of traditional societies has been religiously inspired; indeed, terrorists often claimed they were carrying out the will of God. These historical examples are a good reminder that religiously inspired terrorism—a major contemporary concern—is certainly not new."[27] However, what should also be remembered is that terrorism is not confined to religious extremism. In fact, it is often called the weapon of the weak due to its use by groups with political agendas that could not get access to the political system or by groups that felt they had no other way of making their views known beyond resorting to acts of terrorism.

In fact, it was often the state that used tactics we have come to think of as terrorist in order to keep their citizens in check. For example, the "knock at the door" in Nazi Germany or Stalin's Russia was a way to remind people of the power of the state and of the fact that they needed to behave. The idea of purges, which Stalin engaged in as a way to control the population, can be seen as acts of state-sponsored terror. So the idea of the use of violence (either real or perceived) was often sufficient to get the citizens to comply with the desires of the government.

It was in the nineteenth century that individuals started to take advantage of many of the same types of arbitrary actions that the government used to keep citizens in line. The emergence of this type of *political terrorism* can be defined as

> the deliberate use or threat of violence against noncombatants, calculated to instill fear, alarm, and ultimately a feeling of helplessness in an audience beyond the immediate victims. Because perpetrators of terrorism often strike symbolic targets in a horrific manner, the psychological impact of an attack can exceed the physical damage. A mixture of drama and dread, terrorism is not senseless violence; it is a *premeditated political strategy* that threatens people with a coming danger that seems ubiquitous, unavoidable, and unpredictable. (emphasis added)[28]

That is, terrorism is a tactic that is specifically used to strike fear into innocent civilians and thereby threaten the stability of the state, which ultimately will pressure political decision makers to bring about the ends desired by the terrorists. Or it can be used to recruit more like-minded individuals into their ranks to work against the state.

Terrorism can be used to support or change the status quo. And as noted above, it can be used by states as well as nonstate actors. But it is the latter that we have come to think of when we think of terrorism—usually groups that want to change the status quo, bring attention to their cause, change the political leader or even the political system, and so on. It is also important to remember that terrorism can be and has been used by groups on both the left and right wings of the political spectrum, by secular as well as religious groups—but all resort to the same sorts of tactics in order to achieve their goals.

Terrorism can have an important impact on the policies of the nation by focusing primarily on the people *within* the nation. Thus, terrorist actions do not necessarily result in the desired outcome because the government gives in to the demands of the terrorists. Rather, what is more likely is that the terrorist actions have an impact on the people, who then bring pressure to bear on the government to change its policies or who might even rise up against the government, including joining the terrorist group in the hope of bringing about change.

Many of the tactics of political terrorism came into prominence in the nineteenth century in Europe and North America, at a time when the very nature of the state was changing. The Industrial Revolution and the growth of science and technology contributed to some important advances for the world at that time. But along with those came the growth of cities as the base for the new industries, and with that, laborers necessary to do the work in those industries. The UK is one of the classic examples of this movement from rural areas to the industrial cities. But the United States, France, and to a lesser extent the other countries in Europe gradually went through similar transitions. While many people grew rich, especially those who owned the factories, many others became poor, and the urban areas gave rise to slums and poverty. It was out of this disconnect between those who owned the means of production and those who worked in them that Karl Marx and other communist theoreticians talked about the need for the workers to rise up, as noted in chapter 2.[29]

In *The Communist Manifesto*, Marx, writing with Friedrich Engels, declared, "The proletarians have nothing to lose but their chains. They have a world to win. Working Men of All Countries, Unite!"[30] This became a rallying cry for rebellion against the state. This call gave rise to a group known as *anarchists*, who took it upon themselves to wage war against the emerging order. But it is also important to note that they waged their attacks primarily against the officials of the government, not innocent civilians.

The United States was a victim of this type of terrorist attack allegedly perpetrated by anarchists in the 1920 bombing of the J. P. Morgan Bank headquarters in New York. More than thirty people were killed and scores were injured in this bombing. While the bombers were never caught, a message was found in a mailbox of a building nearby signed "American Anarchist Fighters." This bombing coincided with a period in which the United States was already focused inward, and this incident provided further reason to enact legislation that limited immigration, as well as repression against "undesirables" such as communists. In many ways, this presaged what we saw following the terrorist attacks of 9/11.[31]

After World War I and into the years preceding and following World War II, the nature of terrorism started to change. Often the goals of the new terrorist groups were tied to issues of self-determination and the desire to create a new and independent state using military force if necessary. During the Cold War, this often took on an ideological edge, contributing to the growth of "revolutionary movements," whose goal was to overthrow the existing dominant order. Often these terrorist groups had their roots in what they saw as their nationalist mission to bring to the country a different form of government most consistent with the goals of the peoples of that nation. And these groups also felt that the only way they could get their ideas across and make their point was to root it in acts of violence.

Terrorist acts were also committed in the name of nationalism in which the groups felt they had to act in support of the peoples of their nation and against the state, even if that meant killing innocent civilians. In their viewpoint, no one could truly be innocent. For example, nationalism became part of the rallying cry for the Irish Republican Army (IRA) and its acts of violence directed against the British and the Union supporters in Northern Ireland. In this case, they were hoping that the campaign of violence would result in the British forces leaving Northern Ireland so that Northern Ireland could become free of British rule. Clearly this did not happen, and the IRA's campaign of terror turned many people away from the cause they were advocating. Eventually the IRA leadership and the majority of people within the IRA concluded that they would be more successful negotiating for their goals rather than continuing their campaign of violence. Gerry Adams, who was involved with the IRA, served as a member of the Irish Parliament for Sinn Fein, the political arm of the IRA.

Terrorism was part of the landscape of the Israeli-Palestinian issue from the time of the Balfour Declaration in 1917 and the mandate that would lead ultimately to the creation of the state of Israel in 1948; and, perhaps surprisingly, it can be attributed to both sides. Prior to the formal creation of Israel in 1948, various Jewish organizations that were Zionist and nationalistic embarked on a series of terrorist acts directed against Palestinians but also against the British who were still in the region. One of the most notorious of those was the bombing of a wing of the King David Hotel in Jerusalem in 1946, resulting in ninety-one deaths and more than forty injured. But this act contributed to pressure on the British to leave, ultimately leading to the recognition of Israel as a Jewish state.[32]

On the Palestinian side, we see the growth of the Palestine Liberation Organization (PLO), which advocated for a Palestinian state and the concomitant destruction of Israel. The first of the PLO attacks came in the early 1960s; later attacks included the murder of Israeli athletes in the 1972 Munich Olympics and the massacre of civilians at the Rome and Vienna airports in 1985. Like the IRA, the PLO eventually moderated its tactics from acts of violence to pursuing its goals through political means, and the organization itself went from being a terrorist group to a governing political party that actually now negotiates with the government of Israel. However, in the case of both the PLO and the IRA, there are many who have not forgotten their acts of violence and continue to question their legitimacy.

Terrorism as a Political Tool

Why is terrorism effective? The fact that terrorism is so arbitrary means that everyone is potentially a target and a victim. Terrorism often does not target the military or the government, but innocent civilians. It is able to amplify the impact it has because by targeting people in what otherwise would be normal settings—a market, a bus going to school or work, an airplane—it makes it clear that anyone is potentially vulnerable, which has a psychological effect on a far larger population than just those who were affected by the attack. Furthermore, increasingly terrorist acts are being committed by women as well as men, which changes the dynamics as well as the perception of terrorism and who is a terrorist.

If terrorism is a weapon of the weak, it has been used more effectively in a world that has gotten smaller and that has come to rely more heavily on technology. One of the dangers of a globalized world is that borders are harder to control, so people can move easily and quickly across them, enter another country, and settle there, potentially waiting years before mounting an attack. Along with the movement of people comes the ease with which arms and explosives of various types can cross borders, making it easier to arm terrorists or criminals and resulting in untold amounts of damage in lives and property. And as we saw with the events of 9/11, any terrorist who is intent on inflicting damage can find a means to do so, even to the extent of using commercial aircraft as a weapon of destruction designed to inflict terror.

Clearly the United States has seen firsthand the impact of terrorism and why it poses such a challenge to the international system. Now that terrorist attacks are covered by the media and coverage is so instantaneous, they unfold in real time, making them all the more frightening to any observer. For example, as soon as the 9/11 attacks were reported, we could all watch the second plane crash into the World Trade Center *in real time*. Virtually no one could be untouched by the scenes of death and destruction in Manhattan, but the imagery also brought home the important lesson that potentially everyone is vulnerable—no one is immune to terrorist attacks.

We started this chapter by talking about new challenges to the international system. While terrorism has been around for a long time, for many of the reasons noted above it has become even more of a challenge to the international system. Furthermore, as a nonstate transnational actor, it can cross borders and affect many people in many states, thereby making it even more difficult for any nation or group of nations to formulate a response or even a strategy to fight it. The ongoing multinational fight against ISIS is a case in point.

Women as Terrorists

With the growth of terrorism as a political tool, the concept of what a terrorist looks like has changed. The proliferation of women as terrorists has made it even more difficult for states to identify who is a terrorist. Women as terrorists—whether as suicide bombers, snipers, leaders of a rebellious guerilla group, and so on—runs counter to the commonly held perception of women as peacemakers and women as peaceful. Women have always been engaged as spies and even terrorists, since it is often easier for them to move through society without attracting the attention a man would. And with the increase in civil wars and wars of national liberation since the end of the Cold War, women have become more prominent. The "Black Tiger" Tamil women fighting for a state against the Sinhalese in Sri Lanka, the "Black Widows" who fought in Chechnya, and the women who made up the Palestinian "army of roses" are but a few of the cases in which women have been prominent as terrorists and even suicide bombers.

In many ways, the role of women as terrorists emerged prominently in the 1960s and 1970s with the proliferation of terrorist groups in general. Although the "typical terrorist" was male, "several of the most active left-wing terrorist groups during this period had a strong female presence"[33]—for example, Ulrike Meinhof of the Baader-Meinhof group in Germany; Leila Khaled, who was actively involved with the Popular Front for the Liberation of Palestine (PFLP); and Fusako Shigenobu, founder and leader of the Japanese Red Army. But in giving these examples, it is also important to note that

> from modern terrorism's beginnings, women have tended to be more active as leaders and members of groups that have worked to *overturn* traditional values, rather than those seeking to restore old ones—stated another way, they have been less likely to play an active role in right-wing groups that idealize the past and incorporate sexism into the political ideologies. (emphasis added)[34]

It should also be noted that the emergence of these women as leaders of these left-leaning organizations coincided with the advance of the women's movement (second-wave feminism), a basic premise of which was to advocate the philosophy that women should not be bound to traditional "women's roles" and that both women and men would benefit from situations of equality. That means that both men and women could—and did—engage in acts of terrorism.

In looking at terrorism and terrorist groups and the role that they play in the international system, they "are more willing than states are to violate the norms of the international system because, unlike states, they do not have a stake in that system."[35] In fact, from a traditional levels-of-analysis perspective, it is questionable where terrorist groups even fit within the system. Yet the impact that they have on that system cannot be debated.

Cyberterrorism: A New Threat to International Security

As Internet technology has become ubiquitous, so have the dangers associated with the ease of access to that technology. This became especially apparent during the U.S. 2016 presidential election, when Democratic National Committee computers were hacked into. More and more information started to leak out to the public, including private e-mails of John Podesta, candidate Hillary Clinton's campaign manager. While these leaks had political implications for the outcome of the election, what became even more troubling was the subsequent revelation that Russia was likely behind the release of much of that information and, in fact, had been hacking into the U.S. election system for the specific purpose of disrupting the elections and calling into question the legitimacy of the electoral process. This then led to congressional investigations about the role that Russia played in the election, investigations that are under way as we write this. These investigations are likely to be lengthy as well as comprehensive as members on both sides of the aisle have raised concerns about the sanctity of the U.S. electoral process in the face of cyberthreats.

Further, it was not just the United States that was subjected to this type of data breach. Having been alerted to this possibility, during the French presidential election process in May 2017, then-candidate Macron employed a host of countermeasures to protect his information and to minimize the dangers that this type of breach could have on the French elections. The government of Russia has denied any involvement in the attacks in both the United States and France and has claimed that if there were such breaches coming from that country, they were not initiated by the government. But given the increasingly hostile relations between Russia and the countries of the West, many doubt their claims. Or, if the government of Russia was not directly involved and the hacks were coming from private sources as has been claimed, the government did not interfere with such hack attacks and might in fact have encouraged them.

These revelations and the subsequent investigations they engendered come on the heels of a global hack attack in May 2017 when thousands of computers were infected with malicious software known as WannaCry. This particular attack was tied to ransomware, or the demand by the hackers that individuals, companies, or even countries pay the ransom demanded or risk losing their data that had been captured by the hackers. In Great Britain, parts of the National Health Service came to a grinding halt as computers were taken over and held hostage to the ransom demands. Nonemergency surgeries and a significant number of outpatient appointments were canceled because of the inability to access patient records online. Countless organizations have been hit by this latest attack. Japanese companies Hitachi and Nissan Motor both acknowledged being hacked but also reiterated their unwillingness to pay a ransom.

This vast array of cyberattacks has raised to the international system the myriad dangers faced with the increased reliance on technology. Because data and technology cross borders, and because hackers can be individuals or countries (North Korea and Russia are two recent examples), the only way to combat this threat will be for countries to work together. While individual countries have created organizations to try to address the problem, and some multilateral organizations such as NATO and the EU have started to do so as well, it is clear that will not be enough. Rather, there will need to be a major multilateral cooperative effort to address the issue, something that will not be easy.

Increasingly, countries themselves are engaging in acts of cyberterrorism as another security measure. A study commissioned by the European Parliament in 2009 titled "Cyber Security and Politically, Socially and Religiously Motivated Cyber Attacks" notes that "at the level of states and governments, it is clear that in some quarters the Internet is becoming viewed as a battlefield where conflict can be won or lost."[36] For example, a series of cyberattacks directed against Iran's nuclear program in 2012 originated in the United States and Israel. Iran had been on high alert for such attacks since the revelation of an invasion by the cyberworm called Stuxnet in 2010. The Stuxnet invasion caused Iran's uranium enrichment centrifuges to spin out of control and self-destruct, thereby slowing that country's progress on its nuclear energy program.[37]

Evidence suggests that North Korea recently has been involved with a major ransomware attack directed especially against China, one of its few allies. In May 2017, the press reported that North Korea may have links to a ransomware attack that destroyed more than two hundred thousand computers globally and hit forty thousand institutions in China, crippling computers at universities, major businesses, and local governments and adding a potentially dangerous new element to a relationship that has increasingly tested Chinese leaders. Interestingly, China's response to this attack has been muted.[38]

Clearly, all countries and international organizations such as NATO and the EU are aware of this growing threat and trying to establish policies to deal with it proactively rather than waiting for an attack to occur. On the other hand, it is also clear that attacks have already occurred and that the goal is really to try to minimize their impact, increase the possibility of detecting them, and find ways to avoid them or protect from them in the future. With the latest set of hacks—both the WannaCry ransomware and the potential threats posed to democratic elections by hacks coming from Russia—this issue has come to the top of the international agenda. But in trying to address ways to prevent such attacks, countries also have to balance security with the need to protect individual freedoms.

It should also be remembered that in addition to the dangers posed by cyberterrorism, Internet technology can be used as a force for good. For example, information about the uprisings associated with what has become known as the Arab Spring was spread using social media. We will discuss this aspect of technology below in the section on the role of the media.

MULTINATIONAL CORPORATIONS (MNCS)

Thus far, we have been talking about various transnational actors that have had an impact on the international system. Some, such as terrorist groups, exist outside the law, and their goal is to make their point by inflicting fear and terror through the arbitrary act of violence, either threatened or real. We also talked about other groups like NGOs that have social or political issues in common and transcend traditional state boundaries, which work to influence the international policy agenda.

What we are going to look briefly at now are multinational corporations, which are corporations or businesses based or headquartered in one country (the *home* country) that produce goods or services and conduct operations in two or more other countries (the *host* countries), and they can create both opportunities and problems for each. MNCs are chartered within one country and technically therefore function under the laws of the home country; however, when they operate in other countries, they are subject to the laws of that country. The resulting confusion surrounding jurisdiction and legalities also complicates the situation for MNCs and the people who work for them.

One of the major changes regarding MNCs has been their origin or home countries, which in many ways is also representative of the changes in global power. Initially, most MNCs were housed in the United States, Japan, and parts of Europe. But more recently, we have seen that change with the emergence of companies based in China, for example, and other parts of Asia. Hence, MNCs are no longer the purview of the developed world of the North, nor can all blame for the behavior of MNCs be placed on just those countries.

As we begin this discussion, it is important to remember that MNCs are not a new phenomenon but existed in earlier cycles of globalization, although on a different scale. For example, the Dutch East India Company was a critical force behind the exploration and colonization in the earlier era of globalization.[39] That company, based in the Netherlands, helped fund exploration to other parts of the world, looking for spices and other valuables. Those colonies then became the bases for their activities, which brought wealth back to the company, its investors, and the home country.

In many ways, that is analogous to the growth of MNCs that we see today, albeit on a larger scale. The growth of technology and globalization has made it easier for companies to be based in one country, have factories or the means of production in a number of others, and then sell their products in still other countries. Thus, MNCs have grown in size, scope, and power with the globalization of the international economy, especially since World War II, and changing technology, which makes it cheaper and easier to produce goods virtually anywhere.

MNCs have a great deal of power within the international system because of their size and the amount of money they command. According to data compiled in 2015 by the World Bank, if we look at countries and corporations in terms of revenue, Wal-Mart Stores ranked tenth, with three major Chinese companies ranked in positions fourteen through sixteen, following Spain, Australia, and the Netherlands.[40] Thirty of the top one hundred countries and corporations by size of economy and revenue are countries, and the other seventy are MNCs. This wealth, as well as global reach, has made MNCs both hated and loved. Advocates for liberal free trade see such corporations as playing an active and important role in the international economic system. They can spur economic investment and improvement, often transmit ideas, move money to different places through their markets, and, by ensuring competition, actually lower prices. This perspective moves beyond a world defined by states to one driven by economics and economic

BOX 5.3

TOP 100 COUNTRIES AND CORPORATIONS BY ECONOMIC STRENGTH (AS OF 2015)

	Country/Corporation	Revenue (US$, bns.)
1	United States	3,251
2	China	2,426
3	Germany	1,515
4	Japan	1,439
5	France	1,253
6	United Kingdom	1,101
7	Italy	876
8	Brazil	631
9	Canada	585
10	WAL-MART	482
11	Spain	474
12	Australia	426
13	Netherlands	337
14	STATE GRID	330
15	CHINA NATIONAL PETROLEUM	299
16	SINOPEC GROUP	294
17	South Korea	291
18	ROYAL DUTCH SHELL	272
19	Mexico	260
20	Sweden	251
21	EXXONMOBIL	246
22	VOLKSWAGEN	237
23	TOYOTA MOTOR	237
24	India	236
25	APPLE	234
26	Belgium	227

	Country/Corporation	Revenue (US$, bns.)
27	BP	226
28	Switzerland	222
29	Norway	220
30	Russia	216
31	BERKSHIRE HATHAWAY	211
32	Venezuela	203
33	Saudi Arabia	193
34	MCKESSON	192
35	Austria	189
36	SAMSUNG ELECTRONICS	177
37	Turkey	175
38	GLENCORE	170
39	INDUSTRIAL & COMMERCIAL BANK OF CHINA	167
40	DAIMLER	166
41	Denmark	162
42	UNITEDHEALTH GROUP	157
43	CVS HEALTH	153
44	EXOR GROUP	153
45	GENERAL MOTORS	152
46	FORD MOTOR	150
47	CHINA CONSTRUCTION BANK	148
48	AT&T	147
49	TOTAL	143
50	Argentina	143
51	HON HAI PRECISION INDUSTRY CO.	141
52	GENERAL ELECTRIC	140
53	CHINA STATE CONSTRUCTION ENGINEERING	140
54	AMERISOURCEBERGEN	136
55	AGRICULTURAL BANK OF CHINA	133
56	VERIZON	132

	Country/Corporation	Revenue (US$, bns.)
57	Finland	131
58	CHEVRON	131
59	E.ON	129
60	AXA	129
61	Indonesia	123
62	ALLIANZ	123
63	BANK OF CHINA	122
64	HONDA MOTOR	122
65	JOAN POST HOLDINGS	119
66	COSTCO	116
67	BNP PARIBAS	112
68	FANNIE MAE	110
69	PING AN INSURANCE	110
70	United Arab Emirates	110
71	KRONER	110
72	SOCIETE GENERALE	108
73	AMAZON.COM	107
74	CHINA MOBILE COMMUNICATIONS	107
75	SAIC MOTOR	107
76	WALGREENS BOOTS ALLIANCE	103
77	HP	103
78	ASSICURAZIONI GENERALI	103
79	CARDINAL HEALTH	103
80	BMW	102
81	EXPRESS SCRIPTS HOLDING	102
82	NISSAN MOTOR	102
83	CHINA LIFE INSURANCE	101
84	J.P. MORAN CHASE	101
85	GAZPROM	99
86	CHINA RAILWAY ENGINEERING	99

	Country/Corporation	Revenue (US$, bns.)
87	PETROBRAS	97
88	TRAFIGURA	97
89	NIPPON TELEGRAPH & TELEPHONE	96
90	BOEING	96
91	CHINA RAILWAY CONSTRUCTION	96
92	MICROSOFT	94
93	BANK OF AMERICA CORP.	93
94	ENI	93
95	NESTLÉ	92
96	WELLS FARGO	90
97	Portugal	90
98	HSBC HOLDINGS	89
99	HOME DEPOT	89
100	CITIGROUP	88

Source: https://blogs.worldbank.org/publicsphere/world-s-top-100-economies
-31-countries-69-corporationsas.

competition. Clearly, MNCs prosper in a stable international environment characterized by free and open trade and investment.

In contrast, however, MNCs are also the target of much hostility, as they are seen as taking jobs away from people at home, exploiting labor, and producing shoddy products. Some of the nationalistic rhetoric of the 2016 U.S. presidential election, "Make America Great Again," was directed at corporations that were said to be moving jobs out of the United States as well as at immigrants who were accused of taking American jobs here at home. The reality is, however, that the United States lost manufacturing jobs not necessarily to other countries but because of increased technology and automation that makes U.S. companies more productive and also more competitive. Nonetheless, MNCs, and especially the specter of "outsourcing," make for an easy target, especially in an election campaign.[41]

In the poorer, less developed countries, MNCs are perceived as subverting the sovereignty of the state, since the corporations have more money—and often more economic and political power—than the state appears to have. On the other hand, they create jobs in the poorer countries, often in areas where economic options are otherwise limited. This also means that the government is often dependent on the corporation.

In the first of a series of Pulitzer Prize–winning articles about Wal-Mart published in November 2003 in the *Los Angeles Times*, the authors wrote,

> Wal-Mart's decisions influence wages and working conditions across a wide swath of the world economy, from the shopping centers of Las Vegas to the factories of Honduras and South Asia. Its business is so vital to developing countries that some send emissaries to the corporate headquarters in Bentonville, Ark., *almost as if Wal-Mart were a sovereign nation*. (emphasis added)[42]

The second article in the series, which focuses on the impact on the countries in which Wal-Mart has factories, also illustrates well this symbiotic relationship between corporation and government:

> The company's size and obsession with shaving costs have made it a global economic force. Its decisions affect wages, working conditions and manufacturing practices—even the price of a yard of denim—around the world. . . . To cut costs, Honduran factories have reduced payrolls and become more efficient. The country produces the same amount of clothing as it did three years ago, but with 20% fewer workers, said Henry Fransen, director of the Honduran Apparel Manufacturers Assn., which represents nearly 200 export factories.
>
> "We're earning less and producing more," he said with a laugh, "following the Wal-Mart philosophy."
>
> That's harsh medicine for a developing country. The clothing industry is one of the few sources of decent jobs for unskilled workers in this nation of 6 million. Many of those jobs depend on Wal-Mart.[43]

Another criticism leveled at MNCs—and the Wal-Mart example illustrates this quite well—is that the MNCs not only control the wages of the labor force but can also alter the wage structure, which has implications for the social structure of the country. Women who might have previously participated in agriculture or creation of traditional arts and crafts turn to working in the factories, often under deplorable conditions, because of the salaries that they get. And in some countries, children are also hired to work in those factories.

> U.S. retailers began making their way to Bangladesh in the 1980s. They found a large population of poor, young women willing to work from dawn to dusk for a few pennies an hour.... Many factories lacked ventilation and fire escapes. Labor activists estimated in the mid-1990s that as many as 50,000 Bangladeshi children were sewing apparel for companies such as Wal-Mart and Kmart Corp.[44]

On the other hand, the wages are good in relative terms, and the work is steady. For some, it's their only source of income.[45]

MNCs are often the focus of much of what is seen as bad in the area of globalization, but the reality is that the role of MNCs is complex as well as controversial. To some, MNCs are agents of their home national governments, which give MNCs clear national identities. Or, put another way, the image of the MNC and the country become intertwined. The Wal-Mart example is a case in point: Wal-Mart is equated with the United States. This, in turn, has contributed to the undermining of the "soft power" of the United States; when a major U.S. corporation is seen as exploiting the people or infringing on the rights of others or taking wealth out of the country, the United States is blamed, rightly or not. Some actually make the argument the other way— that is, that states exist as agents of corporations, and that state intervention is therefore specifically used to enhance the well-being of the corporation. We made this point in chapter 4 with reference to the "military-industrial complex." That fear remains and ties the United States and its foreign and security policy more firmly to corporations.[46]

As the role and wealth of MNCs have grown, so has their prominence in the international system, which has also made them a target for much of the hatred tied to globalization. For one thing, as wealth and power appear to be more concentrated, the larger MNCs seem to become even more powerful. Their global reach and power have enabled them to be involved in the internal affairs of nations—they are not only international nonstate actors, but they try to or actually do influence policies within nations. For example, MNCs actively lobby for the passage of legislation that will be to their advantage, such as on trade, tax policies, and so on. MNCs can also serve as instruments of a nation's foreign policy, which further blurs the boundaries between corporations and their interests and nations' foreign policies.

Another thing that makes MNCs so difficult to deal with in the study of IR is the fact that, as nonstate actors, they really do not fall clearly within any theoretical perspective. But we do know that they have an influence on nation-states and even international relations. In looking at the roles that they play and who is affected by their actions, Marxist and feminist theorists can actually be of some help. The Marxists would look at the relationship between the corporation and the workers, especially those who are often exploited in order to ensure that the corporation makes as much profit as possible. Here we have an unequal relationship between those who have the power, the corporations, and those who work for the corporation, often at low wages and in poor conditions—that is, the workers. There is clearly a tension that exists between these two groups, although in some ways, both benefit. The Marxists would also advise us to look at the relationships between the corporation and the various nation-states, as this also provides some important information in understanding their roles. What nations are the corporations based in, and where do they actually do their work (extracting oil, manufacturing clothing, and so on)? Are the nation-states equal, or do we see an unequal relationship between the countries? What does each country get from the relationship that enables the relationship to continue? This, too, should provide some insight into our understanding of the way international relations works, especially when there are asymmetrical relationships.

In order to truly understand the role of MNCs, the feminists would once again ask us to reflect with gender-sensitive lenses. When we do so, we can see that often corporations can only prosper because of the exploitation of women's labor. This is a point made in the articles about Wal-Mart, but it is also echoed in the feminist IR literature. However, as Tickner also reminds us in her brief analysis of women and the global economy, there are some cases where women are being empowered through their ability to work, which comes at the expense of men.[47] So not only do we need to look at and understand the role of MNCs through gender-sensitive lenses, but we also have to remove our cultural blinders and assumptions so that we can get a more balanced perspective on who is affected, who benefits (including the consumer), and the costs.

In this section, we wanted to raise a number of issues about MNCs and also to illustrate the complexity and ambiguities of the roles that they play in the international system today. MNCs will not go away. Rather, the challenge for the members of the international system is how best to deal with them.

THE ROLE OF THE MEDIA

The media has taken on a new role in contemporary politics. While it is not an actor per se in the same way that MNCs or terrorist groups are, the important role that the media plays in influencing the perceptions of individuals and those in the government cannot be underestimated. The concept of "the media" has a number of component pieces. The most traditional is the print media, specifically newspapers, which had been the major way "the people" learned what was happening. The role of print media started to change as early as 1898 and the Spanish-American War when William Randolph Hearst used his *New York Journal* to incite "war fever" to get the American public to rally behind the idea of war with Spain. This marked an important transition in the role of the media specifically to influence public opinion and also policy.[48]

Following the Second World War, as more people got televisions, the nightly news augmented and in some cases replaced newspapers as the major source of world news. The Vietnam War was brought into American homes nightly, along with pictures of body bags and battles. Walter Cronkite, the anchor for *CBS Evening News*, who had the moniker "the most trusted man in America," swayed public opinion when he concluded his broadcast on February 27, 1968, with a three-minute commentary ending with the following: "To say we are mired in stalemate seems the only realistic yet unsatisfactory conclusion."[49] At a time prior to 24/7 cable news and the advent of "talking heads," it was a radical step for a news anchor to offer his own commentary. Following that broadcast, President Lyndon Johnson "turned to his press secretary, George Christian, and famously said, 'If I've lost Cronkite, I've lost the country.'"[50]

The next major step in the coverage of international news, especially wars, can be seen with the first Persian Gulf War, which was a true product of new technology both within the military and the media. The ongoing coverage of the attacks and the live coverage of what was happening in Iraq and Kuwait led to what has become known as "the CNN effect."[51] Now the American public was able to watch the progress of the war in real time. It was not a large leap to the next step, which was the "embedding" of journalists and reporters with military units during the wars in Iraq and Afghanistan that followed during the administration of George W. Bush. This allowed for true first-person reporting on the ground.

The advent of Internet technology and the growth of cable news giants who broadcast 24/7 made the world even smaller but also changed the public's expectations about news. It is now possible to tune in to those broadcasts and find people who see the world as you do, thereby reinforcing your own worldview. No longer is it necessary to rely on impartial and dispassionate reports and reporters; now you can find those whom you can count on to tell you what you want to hear. This reached a fever pitch during the 2016 presidential election when candidate Trump disavowed news he did not like or that did not support him or his positions as "fake news." Then shortly after the president's inauguration, when the size of the crowd watching was under discussion, presidential adviser Kellyanne Conway, when asked about this, defended then press secretary Sean Spicer's claim that this was "the largest audience to ever witness an inauguration" by saying that Spicer had offered "alternative facts." *Meet the Press* host Chuck Todd responded by stating that "alternative facts aren't facts, they are falsehood," an assertion that was also debated by Conway.[52] This explains why the American public is growing increasingly skeptical about the media.

The ongoing attacks by President Trump against the media, especially the mainstream press (e.g., "fake news"), is increasingly seen as unhealthy by the American public and as getting in the way of Americans' access to important political information. Furthermore, this belief is shared across party lines.[53] According to recent polls, rather than swaying the public about the lack of veracity of mainstream news, the barrage of attacks against the media has served to harden positions about the importance of such news outlets, at least for now.

The Role of Social Media

The growth of social media has enabled diverse groups of people to communicate, come together, and even rise up against perceived tyrannical governments, as we saw in a range of countries during the Arab Spring in 2011. But it has also contributed to the growth of sites like Twitter, used by current U.S. president Trump as a way to not only get his message directly to the American public but also to make policy in a most unconventional way. While his supporters like the fact that social media can get a president's message to "the people" unfiltered by press secretaries or other intermediaries, it has also caused great consternation to the policy-making community within the United States, as well as to other countries. Even Fox News, among the president's strongest supporters, notes that "the problem with Trump's tweeting is not only that it bolsters his 'enemies' in the media; it also saps enthusiasm and airtime for his very real accomplishments."[54] Basically, it has served to circumvent the traditional decision-making processes, leading to questions about what really is a new policy direction.

The use of social media, whether Facebook, Twitter, Instagram, etc., has clearly made the exchange of information and ideas readily available. As noted above, in some cases, it has been a force for social and political change. However, there are no "fact checks" here, nor any other way of ensuring that the information transmitted is real or accurate, thereby making it even more important for any "news" to be read critically.

SUMMARY

In this chapter, we looked at the actors that exist outside the traditional levels-of-analysis framework but that have an important impact on the international system nonetheless. Because they do not fit neatly within the levels of analysis does not mean that we need to throw out that organizational framework or assume it is useless and out of date. It continues to serve as an important organizing principle in international relations. However, what we also need to be aware of is the fact that it is no longer as complete a model as it was when Kenneth Waltz put the idea forward in 1954 and then as it was developed further by J. David Singer in 1960. The world has changed a lot since then, while the levels-of-analysis approach really hasn't adapted. In fact, as we recognize the existence of other actors, we can modify the model a bit to take them into account, specifically by addressing the impact of each of these nonstate actors on the various levels, including the international system as a whole. Doing so will allow us to have a more complete picture of international relations in general and the actors within it specifically.

FURTHER READINGS

These additional readings are worth exploring and elaborate on some of the points raised in this chapter. This list is not meant to be exhaustive but only illustrative.

Goldman, Abigail, Nancy Cleeland, et al. "The Wal-Mart Effect." *Los Angeles Times*, November 23, 24, and 25, 2003. http://www.latimes.com/la-walmart-sg-storygallery.html.

Snow, Donald. Chapter 8, "Globalization and Terms of International Trade: The Case of the WTO and NAFTA"; chapter 10, "International Efforts to Promote Well-Being and Development: The Tragic Case of the South"; and chapter 11, "Population Movement: The Contrasting U.S. and European Experiences." In *Cases in International Relations: Principles and Applications*, 7th ed. (Lanham, MD: Rowman & Littlefield, 2018).

UN Division for the Advancement of Women. "Non-Governmental Organizations (NGOs)." http://www.unwomen.org/en/csw/ngo-participation.

NOTES

1. See John Lewis Gaddis, "The Long Peace: Elements of Stability in the Postwar International System," *International Security* 10, no. 4 (Spring 1986): 99–142.

2. CIA, *World Factbook*, "India," updated July 19, 2017, https://www.cia.gov/library/publications/the-world-factbook/geos/in.html.

3. Reginald DesRoches et al., "Overview of the 2010 Haiti Earthquake," https://escweb.wr.usgs.gov/share/mooney/142.pdf.

4. "About the IMF," http://www.imf.org/en/About.

5. Paul Viotti and Mark V. Kauppi, *International Relations and World Politics: Security, Economy, Identity*, 4th ed. (Upper Saddle River, NJ: Pearson Prentice Hall, 2009), 215.

6. Euan McKirdy, "UNHCR Report: More Displaced Now than after WWII," CNN, June 20, 2016, http://www.cnn.com/2016/06/20/world/unhcr-displaced-peoples-report.

7. McKirdy, "UNHCR Report."

8. See Joyce P. Kaufman, "The US Perspective on NATO under Trump: Lessons of the Past and Prospects for the Future," *International Affairs* 93, no. 2 (March 2017): 251–66.

9. "About ISAF: History," http://www.isaf.nato.int/history.html.

10. Mary Ann Tetrault and Ronnie D. Lipschutz, *Global Politics as if People Mattered* (Lanham, MD: Rowman & Littlefield, 2005), 172.

11. Although it is somewhat dated, the documentary *Life and Debt*, about the impact of such policies on the country of Jamaica, makes these points very clearly. *Life and Debt* (2001), directed by Stephanie Black, summary at http://www.lifeanddebt.org.

12. J. Ann Tickner, *Gender in International Relations: Feminist Perspectives on Achieving Global Security* (New York: Columbia University Press, 1992), 78.

13. OAS, "Who We Are," http://www.oas.org/en/about/who_we_are.asp.

14. See, for example, J. Ann Tickner, *Gendering World Politics: Issues and Approaches in the Post–Cold War Era* (New York: Columbia University Press, 2001). Also see V. Spike Peterson and Anne Sisson Runyan, *Global Gender Issues*, 2nd ed. (Boulder, CO: Westview Press, 1999).

15. BBC News, "France Ends Four-Decade NATO Rift," March 12, 2009, http://news.bbc.co.uk/2/hi/7937666.stm.

16. BBC News, "France Ends Four-Decade NATO Rift."

17. Joshua S. Goldstein and Jon C. Pevehouse, *Principles of International Relations* (New York: Pearson Longman, 2009), 59. There are a number of excellent books that detail the U.S. decision to go into Iraq despite UN and international reservations. See, for example, Thomas Ricks, *Fiasco: The American Military Adventure in Iraq* (New York: Penguin, 2006); Todd S. Purdum, *A Time of Our Choosing: America's War in Iraq* (New York: Henry Holt, 2003); and Richard N. Haass, *War of Necessity, War of Choice: A Memoir of Two Iraq Wars* (New York: Simon & Schuster, 2009).

18. The Commission on the Status of Women has been responsible for organizing and following up the world conferences on women in Mexico (1975), Copenhagen (1980), Nairobi (1985), and Beijing (1995). There was also a special session of the General Assembly on women held in June 2000 to follow up on Beijing. One of the things that marked the Beijing conference was the number of NGOs related to the status of women that attended.

19. UN Division for the Advancement of Women, "NGO Participation," http://www.unwomen.org/en/csw/ngo-participation.

20. "NGO Global Network," http://www.ngo.org/index3.htm.

21. Charles W. Kegley with Shannon L. Blanton, *World Politics: Trend and Transformation*, 12th ed. (Belmont, CA: Wadsworth Cengage Learning, 2009), 190–91.

22. This was told to me at an interview with members of the IFRC delegation in Sarajevo in September 2000.

23. For more information, see International Campaign to Ban Landmines website, http://www.icbl.org/en-gb/home.aspx.

24. Tickner, *Gendering World Politics*, 117.

25. Tickner, *Gendering World Politics*, 117.

26. Tickner, *Gendering World Politics*, 117–18.

27. Viotti and Kauppi, *International Relations and World Politics*, 257.

28. Kegley, *World Politics*, 387.

29. See Karl Marx and Friedrich Engels, *The Communist Manifesto*. There are countless editions of this readily available. It is also available online at http://www.marxistsfr.org/archive/marx/works/download/manifest.pdf.

30. Marx and Engels, *The Communist Manifesto*.

31. See Beverly Gage, *The Day Wall Street Exploded: A Story of America in Its First Age of Terror* (New York: Oxford University Press, 2009).

32. For more context on this event, see "The Palestine Mandate and the Birth of the State of Israel," in William L. Cleveland, *A History of the Modern Middle East*, 2nd ed. (Boulder, CO: Westview Press, 2000), 233–66.

33. Cindy D. Ness, "In the Name of the Cause: Women's Work in Secular and Religious Terrorism," in *Female Terrorism and Militancy: Agency, Utility, and Organization*, ed. Cindy D. Ness (New York: Routledge, 2008), 13.

34. Ness, "In the Name of the Cause," 13.

35. Goldstein and Pevehouse, *Principles of International Relations*, 141.

36. Paul Cornish, "Cybersecurity and Politically, Socially and Religiously Motivated Cyber Attacks" (report prepared for the European Parliament's Committee on Foreign Affairs, February 2009), 3, http://www.europarl.europa.eu/meet docs/2004_2009/documents/dv/sede090209wsstudy_/SEDE090209wsstudy_en.pdf.

37. See Rick Gladstone, "Iran Suggests Attacks on Computer Systems Came from U.S. and Israel," *New York Times*, December 25, 2012, http://www.nytimes .com/2012/12/26/world/middleeast/iran-says-hackers-targeted-power-plant-and -culture-ministry.html.

38. Paul Mozur and Jane Perlez, "China Is Reluctant to Blame North Korea, Its Ally, for Cyberattack," *New York Times*, May 12, 2017, https://www.nytimes .com/2017/05/17/world/asia/china-north-korea-ransomware.html.

39. For an excellent and straightforward explanation about the various stages of globalization, see Robert B. Marks, *The Origins of the Modern World*, 3rd ed. (Lanham, MD: Rowman & Littlefield, 2015).

40. World Bank, "The World's Top 100 Economies: 31 Countries; 69 Corporations," September 20, 2016, https://blogs.worldbank.org/publicsphere/world-s-top -100-economies-31-countries-69-corporations.

41. For a cogent explanation of some of the reasons for the loss of American jobs and the impact of technology, see Wolfgang Lehmacher, "Don't Blame China for Taking U.S. Jobs," *Fortune*, November 8, 2016, http://fortune.com/2016/11/08/china -automation-jobs.

42. Abigail Goldman and Nancy Cleeland, "The Wal-Mart Effect: An Empire Built on Bargains Remakes the Working World," *Los Angeles Times*, November 23, 2003. The series is available online at http://www.latimes.com/la-walmart-sg-storygallery .html. It is important to note that I have used Wal-Mart as an example in part because of the insights offered in this series of articles. I take no position on Wal-Mart.

43. Nancy Cleeland, Evelyn Iritani, and Tyler Marshall, "The Wal-Mart Effect: Scouring the Globe to Give Shoppers an $8.63 Polo Shirt," *Los Angeles Times*, November 24, 2003.

44. Cleeland, Iritani, and Marshall, "Scouring the Globe."

45. For another perspective on this "feminization of labor," see V. Spike Peterson and Anne Sisson Runyan, "Gendered Divisions of Violence, Labor, and Resources," in *Global Gender Issues*, 2nd ed. (Boulder, CO: Westview Press, 1999), 113–62.

46. This concern has been exacerbated with the suggestion that the Trump administration is looking at the possibility of bringing in more private contractors to augment

the U.S. military forces currently serving in Afghanistan. While this idea has been floated by the administration and is allegedly included in an Afghanistan policy review undertaken by the Department of Defense and National Security Council, there is also a great deal of opposition to it. For one argument against, see "The War in Afghanistan Needs a Change in Tactics. Privatizing the Military Isn't the Answer," editorial, *Los Angeles Times*, July 20, 2017, http://www.latimes.com/opinion/editorials/la-ed-trump-afghanistan-20170729-story.html.

47. Tickner, *Gendering World Politics*, 83.

48. For more information on the role of William Randolph Hearst and how he helped incite war fever, see Joyce P. Kaufman, *A Concise History of U.S. Foreign Policy*, 4th ed. (Lanham, MD: Rowman & Littlefield, 2017), 41–44.

49. Walter Cronkite, "We Are Mired in Stalemate," broadcast February 27, 1968, https://facultystaff.richmond.edu/~ebolt/history398/cronkite_1968.html. It can also be seen at various postings on YouTube.

50. Quoted in "Final Words: Cronkite's Vietnam Commentary," NPR, *All Things Considered*, July 18, 2009, http://www.npr.org/templates/story/story.php?storyId=106775685.

51. In 1995, Andrew Kohut and Robert Toth of the Pew Center for People and the Press issued a report that stated, "Until a generation ago, elites were probably the only Americans interested in foreign news. . . . Today, much broader and less sophisticated U.S. audiences are exposed to the world, but because most Americans lack much knowledge about international affairs, they can be easily stirred to demand action by dramatic stories that they read and that they see." What they are describing is what we have come to know as "the CNN effect." Andrew Kohut and Robert C. Toth, "A Content Analysis: International News Coverage Fits Public's Ameri-Centric Mood," http://www.people-press.org/files/ legacy-pdf/19951031.pdf.

52. Eric Bradner, "Conway: Trump White House Offered 'Alternative Facts' on Crowd Size," CNN Politics, January 23, 2017, http://www.cnn.com/2017/01/22/politics/kellyanne-conway-alternative-facts/index.html.

53. "Belief That the Relationship between Trump and the Press is Unhealthy and Problematic Is Widely Shared," Pew Research Center, Journalism and Media, April 3, 2017, http://www.journalism.org/2017/04/04/most-say-tensions-between-trump-administration-and-news-media-hinder-access-to-political-news/pj_2017-04-04_trump-media-relationship_0-02.

54. Liz Peek, "Trump's Tweets Only Boost His Foes—The President Is Getting in the Way of His Own Agenda," Fox News, July 3, 2017, http://www.foxnews.com/opinion/2017/07/03/trumps-tweets-boost-his-foes-president-is-getting-in-way-his-own-agenda.html.

6

Pulling It All Together

INTRODUCTION TO THE CASES

In chapter 1, we introduced some basic concepts and ideas that are necessary for you to understand if you are going to master the study of international relations. Many of these concepts and theories were formulated to simplify a complex reality so that you can hold parts of it constant in order to focus on one piece at a time. Doing this is clearly an artificial construct, as we know that the various components of the international system—from the international system level to the nation-states within it, the cultures and societies of the nation-states, and the individuals who make decisions and respond to those decisions—all exist and act together, not in discrete parts. But imposing these artificial boundaries also makes it possible to look at and answer a range of questions that would seem to be too big and difficult to address otherwise.

We also started the discussion by noting the impact of globalization on the international system and various components of it. Like it or not, globalization is here to stay. Therefore, what we need to do is to be able to understand the impact of globalization on the international system and what that means for anyone who studies international relations.

In chapters 2 through 5, we then went through the levels of analysis and focused on some of the big questions in IR: What do we mean by war and peace? Why do nations go to war? Why do some nation-states hold together and others fall apart, some peacefully and others violently? We even looked at the role that individuals play in influencing international relations. In doing all this, we also examined the various theories that were designed to help us describe what happened and explain why certain events occurred or why nation-states behave as they do.

As noted earlier, the nature of the nation-state system, which has defined international relations since the Treaty of Westphalia, is changing. For example, since the end of the Cold War nation-states have been characterized by patterns of both integration and disintegration in a way that we have not seen since the current international system came into being. Nation-states are further challenged by a scarcity of necessary resources, such as oil and water, which also has changed the pattern of international relations. We don't know yet whether this will lead to more conflict or cooperation. But no doubt it will require nation-states to rethink their relationships with other countries and nonstate actors.

The nature of power is changing as well. The major economic and military powers of Europe and the United States have become more integrated. The emergence of other democratic and capitalist countries made for even more integration. Yet these same countries are also vying for resources, such as fossil fuels. And countries have different understandings of how to meet that resource need in ways that will not destroy the environment. In short, the very nature of international relations and the international system is changing and no doubt will continue to change as priories shift and relationships are reordered.

In this chapter, we are going to try to pull all these ideas together in some way. What follows are four different cases. In three of them, we are going to look at some current international issues that affect virtually all members of the international system from the most micro (the individual) to the most macro (the system as a whole). The fourth case focuses on China, an important and increasingly powerful nation-state. China's rising power, its economic strength, and especially its relationship to the United States but also to the countries of Latin America and Africa as well as other countries in Asia, make it an important case to study. Its changing attitude toward the environment and its emergence as a leader on that issue also adds a different dimension to the understanding of the role of that country.

We are not going to presume to provide answers in any of these cases. Rather, what we are going to do is outline a number of issues that the international system is grappling with at the present time. In order to reflect some of the changes in the current international political reality, in the three issue cases (environment, movement of people, and women's rights), we are going to stay away from the traditional "hard power" issues of military security and focus more on some of the other things that are plaguing the international system. This is not meant to discount or minimize the impact or importance of these issues—quite the contrary. As illustrated by events in the Middle East, with a civil war in Syria and the threat from a possibly nuclear Iran, and a North Korea that has been asserting its military strength, these issues that we think of as "security" are an ongoing part of international relations. However, a lot of attention has been given to these issues. Far less attention is devoted to issues of human security or the assurance that all people have their basic human needs met.

For years the international community has struggled to agree upon standards for environmental protection. But all too often the concern to protect the environment seems to be in conflict with the goal of development and industrialization. While countries might support the importance of a clean environment, they don't want to enact any policy that will hurt their economic growth. Although the international community was able to reach an important agreement on climate change in Paris, which technically went into force in November 2016, one of President Trump's first actions upon taking office was to remove the United States from that agreement. As one of the major actors behind creating this agreement, this put the United States out of the mainstream and alienated its allies. It also shifted leadership for this issue from the United States to China, which has been aggressive in fighting its own environmental issues as well as global issues.

Immigration and the movement of people is another issue that we need to think about. Although it has been a factor for centuries—think of the pilgrims who left England to come to America in search of political and religious freedom—it has become a more prominent part of the international agenda relatively recently. A globalized world has made it easier for people to leave one country for another in search of economic opportunity. But it has also contributed to a growth of nationalism and nativist sentiments. These were exacerbated during the 2016 presidential election in the United States when candidate Trump spoke disparagingly of immigrants from Mexico and of the need to curb immigration by Muslims. Similar sentiments have contributed to race riots in France and the emergence of nationalist candidates in France, the Netherlands, and other European countries. This growth of anti-immigrant feeling has been coming at a time when there has been an out-pouring of refugees from parts of the Middle East and Africa seeking to escape war or environmental catastrophes, thereby pitting nationalists against immigrants and refugees in a number of countries.

Similarly, while countries might support the importance of basic human rights for all in theory, they also want to ensure that they—not the international system—determine what is best for their own people. And the case of women's rights not only puts forward issues pertaining to women, but it also raises questions about the difference between having the international community accept resolutions or treaties and the realities of implementing them.

China is a nation-state that has experienced great change in a relatively short period of time, going from a so-called developing country to a major economic as well as military power. That has put it into a unique position that can be seen especially in its relationship to the United States, one that might be described as "frenemies" to use a colloquialism. The U.S. withdrawal from the Paris Climate Change Agreement and the Trans-Pacific Partnership (TPP) has empowered China to come forward and take the leadership role that would have been attributed to the United States. China and the United States have a relationship of tension regarding China's role in the South China Sea. Yet the two countries are interdependent economically. Further, the United States looks to China to help control the situation with North Korea, China's client state. This complicated set of relationships as well as the changing role China is playing internationally make it a fascinating case study of applied international relations.

As you go through the cases, your task will be to try to find ways to address these issues given what you know about international relations and the actors who make up the international system. These cases represent only a brief starting point. There are many other cases you could explore, and I would encourage you to try to do that. What are some other prominent issues? How would you develop those into a case, and what does exploring that particular case tell you about international relations? And, as you explore the cases included here plus any others that might interest you, how do the lessons of the cases contribute to your understanding of international relations today?

CASE 1: ENVIRONMENTAL PROTECTION AS A COMMON GOOD

Protecting the environment is one of the areas that falls under the heading of "common good" in that it is something that affects all countries and peoples; environmental degradation knows no national boundaries. Countries can assume that it is not only in their national interest but in the interest of all nations to ensure that the quality of the environment is protected, and that it is incumbent upon them to work together to achieve this goal; this is a position that the liberal theorists would take. Or countries can take the "free rider" position and assume that other countries will take the lead and that they do not have to spend the money or invest resources in this policy area since others will do it for them—and they will benefit anyway. In that regard, consistent with the more realist position, each nation-state would ask whether and how it is in their best interest to work on improving the environment and what will happen if they don't.

According to a Pew poll conducted in 2017, people around the world view global climate change as one of the leading global threats. Of polls done in eighteen countries, on the whole, climate change ranks only slightly behind ISIS as the major security threat.[1] This suggests that this issue is one that reaches to the society and individuals, which should send an important message to decision makers about policy priorities.

Countries are facing a number of severe environmental issues that have implications for each of them and for the world. Issues of deforestation, access to clean and safe water, and the contribution of pollution and greenhouse gas emissions to global warming are among the issues that transcend borders. The April 2010 oil spill in the Gulf of Mexico caused by an explosion at the British Petroleum (BP) *Deepwater Horizon* oil rig has shown that environmental issues can be caused by or attributed to corporate negligence, as well as national neglect or ignorance. However, the international system has few means available to make corporations take responsibility for any problems they cause. This illustrates clearly some of the problems caused by the reach of MNCs.

If environmental issues are to be addressed, countries will need to work together. But can they?

Background of the Issue

The Kyoto Protocol to the United Nations Framework Convention on Climate Change (known as the Kyoto Protocol) was adopted in 1997 and was set to expire in 2012. The Kyoto Protocol is linked to the UN Framework Convention on Climate Change (UNFCCC) and

> sets binding targets for 37 industrialized countries and the European community for reducing greenhouse gas emissions (GHG). . . . The major distinction between the Protocol and the Convention is that while the convention *encouraged* industrialized countries to stabilize GHG emissions, the Protocol *commits* them to do so. (emphasis in original)[2]

To ensure that the goals associated with protecting the environment that grew from the Kyoto Protocol were met, subsequent meetings were scheduled annually to bring the international community together for further discussion and negotiation. In general, the goal of these various international meetings was to frame follow-up agreements to move forward issues surrounding climate change.

While 184 countries ratified the protocol, many of its terms were controversial. For example, the agreement places a heavier burden on the developed versus the developing countries, a point that both sets of countries had problems with. The developed countries felt that this unfairly punished them, while the developing countries, which included India and China, wanted international assistance that would allow them to develop economically *and* provide assistance in helping them do so in an environmentally friendly way. At a time when India and China are among the fastest-growing economies in the world, labeling them "developing" countries underscores another of the problems that can be identified quickly when looking at this issue. Specifically, what really constitutes a developed or industrialized country versus a developing one?

Despite some of these flaws, the Kyoto Protocol was seen as an important first step toward reducing global emissions. In addition, it provided a framework for the next steps that the international community needed to take in controlling greenhouse gas emissions.

Countries know that it would be virtually impossible to try to tackle all the environmental issues—greenhouse gas emissions, deforestation, ensuring biodiversity, promoting principles of sustainable development—at the same time. Therefore, one of the goals of the subsequent Copenhagen meeting of 2009 that was to build on Kyoto was to frame an agreement that would set priorities and guide countries' policies into the future.

In November 2009, prior to the start of meetings in Copenhagen, many were optimistic when China announced its plan to reduce significantly its greenhouse gas emissions over the next decade. This was a departure from China's position to that point, and other countries saw it as a positive step. Despite the initial optimism, reaching an agreement proved to be difficult. An accord finally was reached on the last day, brokered in part by U.S. president Barack Obama, assisted by the BRIC countries China, India, Brazil, and South Africa. While the accord fell short of what some environmentalists hoped for, it accomplished the objective of getting countries to commit to keeping the maximum temperature rise to below two degrees Celsius. But, as UN official Yvo de Boer also noted, "the challenge now is to turn what is agreed into something that is legally binding in Mexico one year from now."[3]

That became the starting point for the conference in Cancún, Mexico, held late in 2010. Copenhagen "produced a lot of ill will and an 'accord' put together by only a small subset of nations. . . . In Cancun the ill-will faded and large chunks of that accord were at last translated into the official UN process."[4] Given the history of the meetings to that point, countries went into the Cancún summit in November 2010 with low expectations. Nonetheless, the Cancún Agreements provide emission mitigation targets and actions for approximately eighty countries, including Brazil, one of the world's largest greenhouse gas emitters. By agreeing to cut its greenhouse gas emissions, Brazil was aligning itself with the EU, South Korea, and other countries that had similarly adopted emissions targets.

One of the other areas that made the agreement reached at the Cancún meeting unique is that it was able to identify and build upon areas of common concern between the developing and developed countries. Among these was a pledge to create a Green Climate Fund of $100 billion a year to go from the countries of the North (the developed countries) to those of the South (developing) to help pay for emissions cuts and climate adaptation by 2020. This helped minimize one of the major problems of reaching an agreement, which was how to pay for it. As noted by one article, the challenge was that "all of these now need to be turned from paper agreements into practical ones."[5]

Despite the successes, the agreement failed in other ways. The text did not address proposals on agriculture, a major greenhouse gas emitter equal to deforestation. The pledges made are not strong enough to really hold down climate change to an increase of two degrees Celsius, as some had hoped. Some claim that such specific targets will not be applied as long as some countries (notably the United States and China) object. And there is a danger that if that is treated as a make-or-break issue, then agreement will never be possible.

International experts were not optimistic going into the next set of talks in Durban, South Africa, in December 2011, as the developed countries (especially Japan, Russia, and Canada) had already indicated that they did not want to take on any additional legally binding responsibilities to cut their greenhouse gas emissions. Of the developed countries, only the Europeans, who are responsible for about 13 percent of global emissions, agreed to consider being part of another round of cuts. And while the developing countries, including China and India, had already promised to cut the energy or carbon intensity of their economies, they refused to turn their pledges of commitment into legally binding pacts. "Their main concern is for their economies to grow rapidly, not least to help deal with the fallout of warming."[6] So part of the challenge that countries faced going into Durban and beyond was a very different set of needs and expectations.

The conference in Durban resulted in some agreement on the need to work toward a new global treaty and to make progress on the Green Climate Fund. Progress on the more contentious issue, a formal treaty, was made possible only after Brazil came up with wording all could agree upon, specifically that "the new deal is not to be 'legally binding.' It will, instead, be 'a protocol, another legal instrument or an agreed outcome with legal force.'"[7] The new protocol begins the process of replacing the Kyoto agreement "with something that treats all countries—including the economic powerhouses China, India and Brazil—equally." The expiration date and additional specifics are to be negotiated in the future. The Green Climate Fund "would help mobilize a promised $100 billion a year in public and private financing by 2020 to assist developing countries in adapting to climate change and converting to clean energy sources."[8] But questions about implementing the fund remain to be determined.

In November–December 2012, countries met in Doha, Qatar, for the annual UN climate change negotiations. Among the few accomplishments at this meeting was the agreement from the wealthier developed countries to provide funding in aid to those primarily developing countries that are most affected by climate change, thereby building on the idea of the Green Climate Fund. Looking forward to the 2013 Warsaw meetings and the 2014 meetings held in Lima, countries hoped to progress toward finalizing a legally binding agreement to be concluded and signed by 2015 in Paris if the myriad issues pertaining to protecting the environment really are to be addressed.

The Paris Climate Change Agreement

The United Nations' Intergovernmental Panel on Climate Change (IPCC) identified a target goal of keeping temperatures from rising more than two degrees Celsius compared to preindustrial levels, which will require a world-wide reduction in greenhouse gas emissions. In Paris in November 2015, 195 countries agreed on the goal of limiting the increase in average global temperature and also that individually they will pursue a goal of zero net emissions—that is, removing as much greenhouse gas from the atmosphere as added to it—by the second half of the twenty-first century. One hundred eighty-seven countries have pledged to make "intended nationally deter-mined contributions" (INDCs), which are lodged with the secretariat of the UN Framework Convention on Climate Change (UNFCCC). While there was virtually universal praise for the agreement, the INDCs are not strong enough to ensure that the goals are reached. Talks are already scheduled to take place in 2018 as a target for countries to reexamine their own goals and to set new targets if necessary.

"The climate issue is rising on the international agenda, due to the growing scientific, industry and government consensus that extreme weather events (2011 floods in Thailand; droughts in India, US, and Africa; unprecedented Arctic sea ice melting; typhoons and hurricanes in US, Southeast Asia) are outside regular climatic fluctuations and in line with the Intergovernmental Panel on Climate Change's predictions."[9] And, more recently, we have seen drought and extreme heat in India, parts of the United States, and Europe; unprecedented Arctic sea ice melting; and typhoons and hurricanes in the United States and Southeast Asia, just to name a few of the apparent climatic anomalies. Even generally conservative bodies, such as the World Bank, have issued reports warning of the potential impact of climate change. Clearly, this is seen as an international issue that affects all countries, and where the risks will continue to grow if they are not checked.

In 2012, the World Bank issued a climate change report titled "Turn Down the Heat: Why a 4° Warmer World Must Be Avoided." The report warns that "we're on track for a 4°C warmer world marked by extreme heat-waves, declining global food stocks, loss of ecosystems and biodiversity, and life-threatening sea level rise."[10] It also warns that the adverse effects of climate change work disproportionately against the world's poorest regions and could undermine any economic development gains they might have made. This report was released ahead of the IPCC's 2013–2014 comprehensive study, both of which played an important role in the climate change discussions that took place in Lima. Both studies come to the same conclusion: not only is the earth's temperature warming, but the reasons for climate change can be attributed to human action, and deliberate decisions should be made that could stop or even reverse the pattern. But doing so will require important policy changes.

In 2014, the IPCC issued its fifth assessment report on climate change as well as a summary specifically directed at policy makers. It reiterates what has been known for many years: the climate has been warming (as has the temperature of the oceans) because of human activity. According to the IPCC report, "each of the last three decades has been successively warmer at the Earth's surface than any preceding decade since 1850. The period from 1983 to 2012 was *likely* the warmest 30-year period of the last 1400 years in the Northern Hemisphere, where such assessment is possible" (emphasis in original).[11] During the period between 1992 and the present, the Greenland and Antarctic ice sheets have been melting, which has implications for the level of the oceans as well as for the various land and sea animals that depend on the ice sheets. The temperature of the oceans is rising, as are the sea levels, threatening low-lying areas. The extent of water evaporation from the oceans because of the change in the earth's temperature has altered climatic patterns in other ways. Although the overall average rainfall globally might not be very different, the patterns of rain and snowfall have changed considerably, leading to drought in some areas and flooding in others. Some places have experienced record warm temperatures while others are suffering from bone-chilling cold. These factors have had an impact on crops and food production, which have affected the poorer and less developed countries most dramatically.

Countries are facing a number of severe environmental issues that have implications for the world. It is apparent that if there really is to be progress made on these important environmental issues, countries need to move beyond generalities to the specifics of implementation. This makes clear one of the challenges of trying to address an international agreement: reaching an agreement is only one part of the process; implementing it is another issue.

The accord that was agreed upon in Paris had been in process for nine years and required every country to take some action. Although the agreement itself will not solve the problem of global warming, it will cut global greenhouse gas emissions as a step toward holding off an increase of two degrees Celsius, the point at which scientists have predicted devastating consequences. The deal also "could be viewed as a signal to global financial and energy markets, triggering a fundamental shift away from investment in coal, oil and gas as primary energy sources toward zero-carbon energy sources like wind, solar and nuclear power."[12]

The success of the agreement still depends on global peer pressure and the actions of governments in the future. A core requirement of the agreement is that every nation take part and put forth plans as to how they would cut their own carbon emissions by 2030. If enacted, those plans alone should cut emissions by half the levels required to hold off the worst effects of global warming. However, while every country is required to put forward a plan, there is no legally binding requirement dictating how or how much countries should cut emissions. What the Paris Agreement did build in is the requirement that countries ratchet up the stringency of their climate change policies in the future. Further, countries will be required to reconvene every five years with updated plans. The next meeting will be in 2020, with preliminary talks to be held in 2018.

Another way in which the agreement holds countries accountable is that it requires them to publicly report every five years, starting in 2023, the progress they are making in cutting emissions relative to their plans, and they will be legally required to monitor and report on their emissions levels and reductions using a universal accounting system. This hybrid system was designed to meet political realities. While the individual countries' plans are voluntary, the legal requirements regarding monitoring and reporting as well as publicly releasing updated plans are ways to hold countries accountable through global peer pressure. This, of course, will depend on who the future leaders are and their own attitudes toward climate change.

Early in June 2017, President Trump announced that the United States would withdraw from the Paris Agreement, claiming that the pact "imposed wildly unfair environmental standards on American businesses and workers."[13]

In addition, he said that he wanted to negotiate a better deal for the United States. However, the decision only served to isolate the United States from the rest of the world on this issue, especially its major allies. At the G20 meeting that followed Trump's announcement, although the world leaders "acknowledged" Trump's decision, they also agreed to move forward collectively, albeit without the United States, to combat climate change, and they signed a detailed policy outline of the ways in which their countries could move forward toward meeting their environmental goals.[14]

In addition to environmental issues that are the result of national policies such as those mentioned above, other environmental challenges are the result of conflict or of corporate irresponsibility. On April 20, 2010, an explosion aboard the *Deepwater Horizon*, a drilling rig working on a well for the oil company BP one mile below the surface of the Gulf of Mexico, led to the largest oil spill in American history. It took three months to cap the well, allowing more than five million gallons of oil to pour into the Gulf, affecting more than 1,300 miles of shoreline from Texas to Florida. The full and lasting extent of the damage to the environment, including sea and animal life, the marshlands of Louisiana, and the coastline of the Gulf continues to be felt. That does not even take into account the human toll on the people whose livelihood depends on the Gulf of Mexico in some way. A study done in 2016, six years after the explosion, documented some of the environmental damage that resulted.[15] A presidential panel convened to study the accident called it "a preventable one, caused by a series of failures and blunders by the companies involved in drilling the well and the government regulators assigned to police them."[16]

As you can see in this case on the need for global cooperation on environmental issues, corporate irresponsibility, interstate and intrastate conflict, and poor policy decisions are among some of the many man-made reasons for the ongoing depletion of the environment. All of these have different causes and different environmental impacts, which makes it even harder to determine how to solve the problems or even address them.

Analysis of the Case

What this case illustrates is the fact that tied to the issue of sustainable development is the need for countries to develop in an environmentally safe way. This requires that countries do whatever they can to develop cleaner energy technology and fuels and simultaneously find ways to limit harmful

CO_2 emissions that are associated with global climate change. But it will also require countries to work together and compromise, not only in reaching an agreement but in ensuring that the agreement reached will be implemented.

The challenge posed by environmental issues gets to the heart of some of the issues raised pertaining to international relations. Environmental issues are difficult to address because they do not respect international borders. Thus, what happens in one country has a direct impact on other countries beyond its borders. Furthermore, countries and the people who live within them ideally would like to have a clean and safe environment. But how much is that worth if it comes at the expense of economic growth and development? Do all countries put the same value on ensuring a clean environment? If not, then the starting point alone is one of conflicting perspectives and priorities, which makes it even more difficult to come to a satisfactory outcome.

From a realist perspective, each country will only pursue those policies that are in its own best interest. From a liberal theoretical perspective, however, cooperating and moving toward achieving a climate change agreement will benefit all countries, the people who live in those countries, and the international system as a whole. Therefore, it would make sense to cooperate in order to achieve a common good. To the radical or Marxist theoretical perspective, the dilemma is really about who controls the resources and, therefore, can make the decisions. The constructivists would look at this case as an example of changing international norms and the ways in which they affect the discourse of international relations. And each of these would assign a different priority to the environment as a policy issue.

But let's say we could move beyond the differences stemming from theoretical perspectives and countries could negotiate an international agreement, as they did in Paris. Implementing that agreement pertains to a different set of issues that would have to be confronted stemming from differences in perspective. The developed countries would want to ensure that they are not burdened unfairly, either with the costs of implementing the agreement or in terms of the specifics of the agreement, which could impose more stringent requirements on them than on other countries. The developing countries, on the other hand, want to be able to industrialize and progress economically without feeling like they are impeded by an agreement. Thus, another way to look at the problem at the nation-state level is to look at what happens when what is in the best interest of the nation-state conflicts with the greater good or with the interests of the international system.

If we look within the nations, we see the issue still another way. For example, the people within a country want to know that they have access to potable water, that the air they breathe is clean, and that the government will ensure that they have these basic necessities. These qualities are tied to their basic security and well-being. But in some countries, they also want to make sure that they have land to plant the crops necessary to feed their own families and perhaps provide a little extra to trade. If that means clearing part of the rain forest, can the government forbid them to do so?

This case also points out clearly the impact that MNCs can have as well as questions about who regulates and monitors them. In the case of the *Deepwater Horizon* oil spill, the drilling rig was actually owned by Transocean Ltd., a Swiss company, and leased to BP, which operated the well. The rig and well were operating in the Gulf of Mexico under a lease granted by the U.S. government. In November 2012, BP agreed to plead guilty "to felony manslaughter, environmental crimes and obstruction of Congress and pay a record $4 billion in criminal fines and penalties for its conduct leading to the 2010 *Deepwater Horizon* disaster that killed 11 people and caused the largest environmental disaster in U.S. history." The $4 billion "is the single largest criminal resolution in the history of the United States and constitutes a major achievement toward fulfilling a promise that the Justice Department made nearly two years ago to respond to the consequences of this epic environmental disaster and seek justice on behalf of its victims."[17] A settlement reached in January 2013 with the U.S. Justice Department resolved Transocean's role and required that company to pay $1 billion in civil penalties and $400 million in criminal penalties and to plead guilty to violating the Clean Water Act, according to a press release from the U.S. Department of Justice.[18]

Ultimately, it is up to the government to negotiate any international agreement and to determine whether to abide by it or abrogate it, as the United States has recently done. International agreements are between countries. But as this case illustrates, what about corporations?

The greater good versus the good of the individual nation—who wins?

CASE 2: THE MOVEMENT OF PEOPLE IN A GLOBALIZED WORLD

Globalization has changed how countries interact in a number of ways. One of those is in the movement of people, where individuals travel to different countries either legally or illegally, in search of economic opportunity, to escape a conflict, to seek asylum from political persecution, and even to find food or water because of severe environmental crisis. At a time when many countries are struggling to find workers to fill the lowest-paid and unskilled jobs, often these same countries are finding a void at the upper ranks as well. Individual countries have different labor needs; in a global economy that is increasingly interdependent, it seems only logical that countries look to one another to augment their own labor/workers.

The open borders that often come with the creation and growth of free-trade zones have made the migration of workers from country to country, legally and illegally, even easier. But not all who flee one country for another do so for economic reasons, although ultimately they will need a way to ensure their livelihood in their new country. At a time of economic recession, many countries resent the influx of immigrants, who often make demands on the system (education, health care, etc.) and who are perceived as taking jobs away from the native born. This creates further divisions within the social structure of the country.

In the United States, the issue of illegal immigration has become a political "hot button," especially in the states of the Southwest that border Mexico. During the presidential campaign of 2016, then-candidate Trump talked about the need to build a wall between the United States and Mexico (which he claimed Mexico would pay for) in order to stem the tide of migration from Mexico into the United States. Yet statistics now show that there is more movement *from* the United States *to* Mexico than the other way around.[19]

In the Middle East, the protracted civil war in Syria has contributed to a surge of émigrés fleeing the violence by crossing the borders into Jordan or Turkey and ultimately into other countries. This has caused strains on all the countries affected. And sub-Saharan Africa has seen the movement of people who are fleeing current crises not only of war, but also of drought and famine. For example, the UN High Commissioner for Refugees (UNHCR) has estimated that hundreds of thousands have fled the violence and drought in the African country of Mali, and "with more than one million Somali refugees in the East and Horn of Africa and some 1.36 million internally displaced persons (IDPs) in Somalia, the country remains at the center of one of the worst humanitarian crises UNHCR has faced."[20] In Europe, the arrest of immigrants accused of acts of terrorism has conflated the issue of immigration with terrorism. In short, the movement of people is a problem that affects virtually every part of the world, developed and developing, rural and urban.

In thinking about this issue, it is important to note that not all immigrants are terrorists, nor are all terrorists immigrants who seek to gain entry into a country for illegal and destructive reasons. Yet at a time when they already feel threatened, many immigrants (especially those from the Middle East, who look different and are often Muslim) resettling in places like Europe or the United States seem to be a symbol, as well as being easily identifiable.

Many countries want to do all they can to make sure that the needs of their own citizens are met at a time of budgetary constraints, which often means cracking down on immigration. Yet some countries, peoples, and NGOs also feel that all would benefit if an international agreement could be reached as to how best to monitor the movement of people and to guarantee protection to all migrants and immigrants, whether legal or illegal. Countries know that this will be a challenge but also that if they can come up with an agreement, it could be a classic "win-win" situation.

Given the range of issues involved as well as perspectives, this is a difficult task.

Background of the Issue

Globalization is a fact of twenty-first-century life. As we saw in chapter 1, in reality, the process of globalization began with the early years of exploration in the sixteenth century, when the original patterns of trade between and among countries were established. Along with that came the sale of human beings (slaves) who were bought and sold to provide the labor needed to ensure the economic benefit of the colonial power. What has made the globalization of the twentieth and twenty-first centuries different, however, is the growth of technology that can move people, goods, and ideas farther and faster than ever before.

In a world in which people can move freely and cross borders relatively easily, it is not unusual for people to leave one country and move to another in search of economic opportunity. Many move between countries for legitimate reasons, such as the quest for better economic opportunity than they would have at home. However, the cases that seem to attract the most attention are those involving the movement of people for illegal or illicit reasons such as terrorism or human trafficking. These are often unskilled and uneducated people, who are willing to do whatever they have to do in order to leave one country and migrate to another in search of economic opportunities. Because they enter a country illegally, they can also be exploited and forced to work for very little, knowing that they have few legal options. Many of these cases are widely reported, as are the harrowing tales of what many of these émigrés have had to do in order to be able to leave one country and enter another.

Still other people leave one country to flee conflict or to escape persecution of some kind. Refugee camps have grown up in areas bordering war-torn states to shelter those people who hope to avoid war, but they often find that their new situation is almost as bleak. International organizations like the UN and NGOs often work with people in the camps to provide food, shelter, and basic health care, but that makes the refugees dependent on these organizations rather than offering them an alternative way of life.

It is often the people who are the poorest and most desperate who become the victims of the trade in and sale of human beings, and they often take the greatest risk in trying to escape. Newspapers in the United States and Europe seem to have an increasing number of stories about migrants trying to flee their home country to enter another country illegally who are found dead or close to death. Some of these are illegal immigrants who are being sent from one country to another to enter into a life of servitude. Others, however, choose to leave voluntarily, often paying thousands of dollars to smugglers to take them into another country safely. These immigrants are desperate to escape their plight at home and to find opportunity in another (and developed) country. Those who are able to escape safely can become success stories, sending hundreds or even thousands of dollars home to the families they left behind, which in turn encourages others to try the same thing.

However, the amount sent home in remittances can vary significantly. For example, the World Bank has found that remittances sent from migrants in one country to another hit a high of about $414 billion in 2008, with $316 billion of that sent to developing countries. Like many other things, the global economic crisis has had an impact on remittances, which are estimated to have declined 2.4 percent in 2016 following a 1 percent drop the previous year; India, which is the largest recipient of such remittances, decreased by 8.9 percent. This decrease can be attributed to a number of factors, and the pattern also varies by region. Thus some areas have been affected more dramatically than others.[21]

At a meeting of the general assembly in September 2010, the director general of the International Organization for Migration noted that "migrant remittances—the money sent home by migrants—helps reduce poverty by providing families in countries of origin with additional, often vital, income."[22] He also noted that the "increased feminization of migration— women migrating independently, or, as the 'breadwinner,'" can promote gender equality and empower women; nearly half of the world's migrants today are women. And through diaspora communities, migrants can develop ties that can aid their home country as well as their adopted country.[23]

In 2010, the UN secretary general, in prepared remarks delivered to a global forum on migration and development was prescient when he noted,

> Rising unemployment among natives and international migrants has spurred discrimination. *The politics of xenophobia is on the rise.* For millions of international migrants, life has become more treacherous. . . . Migration is more likely to benefit all stakeholders when it is safe, legal and orderly. Yet these opportunities for regular migration have diminished. (emphasis added)[24]

Economic recession clearly has fostered the growth of anti-immigrant feeling in the United States and parts of Europe, which has made life more dangerous for migrants and immigrants. This sentiment can be seen clearly in the rhetoric of the 2016 presidential election in the United States and the 2017 elections in France and the Netherlands. In the first case, then-candidate Trump not only talked about building a wall between the United States and Mexico but also about imposing a ban on Muslims entering this country, allegedly to protect the country from terrorists. As early as 2015, Trump was talking about closing mosques and/or creating a database of Muslims in the United States. And following the attacks in San Bernardino, California, in December 2015, he escalated the anti-Muslim rhetoric and his campaign issued the following statement: "Donald J. Trump is calling for a total and complete shutdown of Muslims entering the United States until our country's representatives can figure out what is going on." He continued these attacks throughout the campaign, often stating simply that "I think Islam hates us."[25] These comments were embodied in the administration's policy decision to impose a travel ban on people entering the country from six majority-Muslim countries initially in March 2017, which was challenged in the courts. Limiting all immigration to the United States was one of the important planks in candidate Trump's platform, a point he reiterated at various campaign-style rallies during the first year of his presidency.

In contrast, this nationalist anti-immigrant theme was repudiated in elections held in the Netherlands in March 2017 when conservative prime minister Mark Rutte defeated ultranationalist Geert Wilders. This was seen as a victory for the pro-European factions and a significant defeat for the nationalist anti-immigrant factions. Wilder's election manifesto "included pledges to close borders to immigrants from Muslim nations, shutter mosques and ban the Koran, as well as to take the Netherlands out of the European Union."[26] Although his party did gain a small number of seats in the election, it was not as much as he had hoped for, and his sharp decline in the polls seemed to be vindication that the Dutch people were turning away from his message. The European leaders, including Emmanuel Macron of France, who would also face an anti-immigrant nationalist opponent in Marine Le Pen, and Angela Merkel of Germany both expressed their delight at the results.[27]

The presidential election in France in June 2017 was another repudiation of nationalist anti-immigrant values. Emmanuel Macron, a young and relatively untested politician, was able to defeat the ultranationalist party of Marine Le Pen to become president of France. His victory was further solidified in subsequent weeks when his party won a majority of seats in the Parliament, thereby assuring that Macron will have the ability to govern. Many read this election not only as a repudiation of Le Pen but also of Donald Trump, and the election became a further affirmation of a united Europe that could move forward without the United States and even without the UK following Brexit.

Much of the anti-immigrant rhetoric, especially in Europe, has been driven by an influx of refugees into virtually all the countries. There is no doubt that the Second World War was a time of trauma and disruption for the international community. An estimated sixty million people were displaced by that war, including all those who chose to flee Nazi Germany and its territories.[28] Yet the Office of the United Nations High Commissioner for Refugees reports that "the number of displaced people is [currently] at its highest ever—surpassing even post–World War II numbers, when the world was struggling to come to terms with the most devastating event in history. The total at the end of 2015 reached 65.3 million—or one out of every 113 people on Earth, according to the United Nations High Commissioner for Refugees (UNHCR).

The number represents a 5.8 million increase on the year before."[29] And that number has only increased since 2015. According to a UNHCR report released in June 2016, at that time, about 1 percent of the world's population was either "an asylum-seeker, internally displaced or a refugee."[30] Yet neither individual countries nor the international system as a whole is equipped to deal with this situation.

The civil war in Syria has raised the issue of refugees, migrants, and asylum seekers to the top of the international agenda. It is estimated that more than 5 million people have fled Syria by May 2017, with approximately 6.3 million more displaced within the country.[31] In addition to finding housing for the millions who have fled to other countries, they need other services on the ground, such as food and water as well as protection from abuse. The lack of housing, clean water, and sanitation in many refugee camps has also contributed to the spread of disease within the camps, exacerbated because children are not getting vaccinated, which could also help ensure their health. Many have fled to neighboring countries such as Turkey and Jordan, while others are moving on, seeking refuge in countries in Europe, but some have gone as far as Brazil and South Korea. Within Europe, Germany has been the most welcoming country, and other countries in Western Europe have been willing to take in refugees as well. However, countries in Eastern Europe generally have not been; for example, Hungary put up barbed-wire fences and built walls to keep refugees out. A poll in the Czech Republic showed that 70 percent of the population was opposed to taking in any refugees at all. And Slovakia has indicated that if it had to accept refugees, it would prefer that they not be Muslim. This echoes fears raised especially by right-wing politicians and members of various nationalist groups that the refugees are just seeking the generous social welfare benefits that many of the countries have. And contributing to the anti-refugee/anti-Muslim sentiment is fear of terrorism, especially in the wake of the attacks in Paris in November 2015, San Bernardino in December 2015, Brussels in March 2016, and Istanbul in June 2016, all perpetrated by refugees who happened to be Muslim.[32] What is often overlooked is the fact that many of these terrorists are "homegrown" rather than refugees who entered a country specifically for the purpose of inflicting harm. Many argue that the British vote to exit the EU in June 2016 was a direct reaction to the influx of refugees, and certainly it was a factor in the French presidential elections.

With the environmental impact caused by global warming, a new class of refugees has emerged, what might be called "environmental refugees." These are people who are fleeing the impact of environmental disasters, such as rising sea levels that threaten low-lying and island nations, drought, and flooding. The inability to sustain themselves because of changing environmental conditions has also caused people to flee either within their country or to another country.

The anti-immigrant sentiment is creating fear of a different kind than the terrorists do. While the terrorist attacks have made people in the major cities edgy, many also fear the backlash that will contribute to the growth of anti-immigrant sentiment. Such sentiment is becoming more acute as thousands of migrants struggle to reach Europe's shores.

Germany has done more than other countries in the EU to address the situation. It takes in more than 40 percent of all the EU's refugees. Facing mounting pressure to deal with the situation, in September 2015 Angela Merkel made the unilateral decision to suspend European asylum rules and to allow tens of thousands of refugees stranded in Hungary to enter Germany via Austria. She also indicated that "the right to asylum has no upper limit,"[33] a point disputed by the generally apolitical president of Germany. But the numbers are dramatic. More than 200,000 migrants are believed to have arrived in Germany in September 2015 alone. Estimates for the year range from 450,000 to almost one million. Local authorities are struggling to find housing for the refugees, especially as they faced the winter, and Germany's resources are being stretched. Cities such as Hamburg are taking empty office buildings to house refugees, and other cities are expected to do the same.[34]

The anti-immigrant fervor has been fueled even more in Europe and the United States with the conflation of immigration and terrorism, which has contributed to this anti-immigrant feeling. A spate of killings loosely labeled "terrorist" attacks has contributed to this fear. The 2016 Bastille Day attack in Nice, France, was perpetrated by a Tunisian man living in France. Although ISIS claimed responsibility, there was no evidence that the lone perpetrator was linked to that terrorist group.[35] An attack in Manchester, England, in June 2017 killed twenty-two people and injured more than one hundred others as concertgoers were leaving an Ariana Grande concert. Although the suicide attack was carried out by a British-born man who allegedly had expressed views that he was supporting terrorism, there was no evidence of that prior to the attack. The attacks in San Bernardino, California, in December 2015 were carried out by a husband-and-wife team—he was born in Illinois and she in Pakistan—who had met initially online and physically in Saudi Arabia. The FBI has concluded that they were "self-radicalized," meaning that they "were inspired by terrorist groups, officials said, but did not receive financial support from any foreign or domestic organizations." Basically, they were "homegrown terrorists."[36] There are any number of similar cases of "lone wolf" attacks against civilians designed to instill fear, which is one of the hallmarks of terrorism, but perpetrated by people who were born in that country, as opposed to those who emigrated to a country specifically for that purpose. However, as many of them are Muslim and have ties to Middle East countries associated with terrorism or instability at the very least, they contribute to fears of immigrants in general and Muslims in particular.

Despite the passage of laws in the West, in Europe, and in the United States to try to stop the flood of illegal immigrants and to encourage sound migration policies, governments readily agree that it is extremely costly as well as very difficult to try to enforce them. As long as there is hope for a better life, people will continue to try to move from one country to another that promises them more. While in some cases this might mask people who migrate specifically for illegal purposes, it appears that the majority do not have malevolent intentions.

It is apparent that no country acting alone can address all the aspects of the issues outlined here, which clearly cross borders and national boundaries. Not only do immigrants deal with the international system as a whole because they cross borders, but they have an impact on the politics, cultures, and societies within countries—both the countries these émigrés flee from and the ones they go to. Thus, the issue crosses multiple levels of analysis, which makes it even more difficult to sort out and address.

Analysis of the Case

Like the environment, the movement of people is an issue that transcends national borders, affects many if not all countries in some way, and has been exacerbated by the globalization of the late twentieth and twenty-first centuries. It is also an issue that can be seen at all levels of analysis, which makes arriving at any solution especially difficult. The focus here, though, must start at the individual level, because it is individuals who make the decision to leave one country and settle in another. Thus, in many ways, this becomes the starting point for understanding this issue. Who are these people and why do they choose to leave one country for another? What do they hope to find? Are they leaving legally or illegally, and conversely, what are their intentions regarding the host country in which they will be settling? These are all questions that must be asked at the individual level, which helps give this issue a very human dimension, more so than many other issues in international relations.

Continuing through the levels of analysis, we can then ask about the impact that these immigrants, migrants, or refugees have on the culture and society of their adopted state. Do they blend into an already dominant culture, or will they have an influence on it in some ways? Are they joining an already established national group within the larger nation-state (for example, the North Africans in Paris or Indians and Pakistanis in London), or will they be "outsiders" who will be expected to assimilate into the dominant culture? Will they become part of the educated workforce in their new country, even if that comes at the expense of their home country? What will they contribute in general, culturally, economically, socially, politically? And, of course, how does their departure affect what happens/happened at home? And these questions do not take into account those who resettle in another country specifically with the goal of causing harm in some way.

Implicit in the impact that immigrants have on the society and culture, as noted above, is the impact on the political system. People who come to another country and see this move as a permanent one often want to become citizens and make a contribution politically, if just to vote so that their voices can be heard. But an émigré population can have a marked impact on the political priorities of the adopted country. That was certainly the case with Cuban émigrés who fled to the United States and have had an influence on U.S. policy toward Cuba. Different countries have different expectations and criteria for citizenship, and these too are political decisions sometimes specifically designed to limit that access. While some countries welcome immigrants, especially educated ones, that does not necessarily mean that they want them to have a say in how the country is run.

Furthermore, as we have seen in the last elections in the United States, the Netherlands, and France, the presence of an immigrant population and the visibility that has accompanied them has contributed to anti-immigrant and nationalist sentiments that can also affect the outcome of a political race. So the mere presence of this group can have an impact on the political system of a country.

And of course, at the nation-state and international levels, the movement of peoples is a by-product of other decisions, whether benign or positive ones (such as accelerating free trade) or more insidious ones (such as conflicts). States will guard their own sovereignty and do not want to have the international system imposing regulations on them. They want to be able to determine who can and should enter their country. However, the growing integration of countries makes that more challenging. For example, the Schengen Agreement signed in 1985 between five member countries of the then European Economic Community to gradually abolish checks at their common border has become part of EU law, establishing a borderless zone among all the EU countries.[37] And the issue of immigration has directly affected relations between the United States and neighboring Mexico.

Finally, nonstate actors come into play in this case in a number of ways. Clearly, terrorist groups can take advantage of a globalized world to move people from one country to another specifically for the purpose of inflicting death and destruction. But putting those aside, other nonstate actors are also factors here, both as advocates for immigrants but also as interest groups advocating to limit immigration. The UN is a major player in this area, through its High Commissioner for Refugees and other specialized agencies. In this case, the UN is in a unique position to look at the international system as a whole and make determinations about issues pertaining to the movement of peoples.

From the different theoretical perspectives, the movement of peoples gets to the heart of their understandings of the nation-state and its role in international politics. The very notion of the movement of people from one state to another raises issues about sovereignty, the sanctity of the state, and state security so central to the realist perspective. But it can be approached from other theoretical perspectives as well. Something like the Schengen Agreement that exists among the EU countries can be understood by drawing on the liberal perspective and the idea that the movement of peoples across borders is really an issue of cooperation and not conflict or an infringement on sovereignty. Constructivists might ask what impact immigration has on the structure and policies of the new country, as well as on the country that they left. They could easily explore the issues of understanding national identity and what changing national identities then might mean for the state as well as the people within it. Even the Marxists could contribute to this discussion by asking in what ways economic development has contributed to immigration as the trend toward capitalism has changed the working relationships within a country, thereby contributing to movement from one country to another. And, of course, the feminists would ask us to look at the people themselves to see who has been affected, in what ways, and why.

In many ways, the issue and approaches to it fit more comfortably into the theoretical perspectives that focus on the individual, such as the liberal, Marxist, and feminist perspectives. But as noted above, depending on the way in which you frame the question you are asking about the issue, any of the theoretical perspectives could provide some insight into our understanding of it. What we are really asking in this case is this: If the movement of peoples has become a fact of globalization, how can we best account for it and understand where it fits within traditional international relations—or does it?

CASE 3: WOMEN'S RIGHTS AS HUMAN RIGHTS

In 1975, the UN held the First World Conference on Women in Mexico. This became a catalyst for drafting any number of resolutions that pertained specifically to the rights and roles of women, both within countries and also internationally. Part of the impetus for the conference and the subsequent passage of a number of resolutions was the growing international attention paid to violations against women. Some of those were the result of cultural practices, but some were due to conflict and to the fact that women were being used as weapons of war. With little international law behind them and with few ways to implement the laws that were in place, the UN took the lead in starting to recognize the role that women can and do play, and also to ensure that there are international guarantees in place to protect women.

The Convention on the Elimination of All Forms of Discrimination against Women (CEDAW) was passed in 1979, and it is seen by many as the international bill of rights for women. Since then, UN Security Council Resolution 1325 on Women, Peace, and Security[38] was passed in October 2000, followed by Resolution 1820, Eliminating Violence against Women and Girls[39] in June 2008. Resolution 1325 was passed following the Fourth World Conference on Women, held in Beijing in 1995, and stressed the importance of the full participation of women in the political process if peace and security in any country is to be assured. It also highlighted the need to increase women's role in decision making pertaining to conflict prevention and resolution and the need for postwar reconstruction. Resolution 1820 was passed by the Security Council to demand

> the "immediate and complete cessation by all parties to armed conflict of all acts of sexual violence against civilians," [and] expressing its deep concern that, despite repeated condemnation, violence and sexual abuse of women and children trapped in war zones was not only continuing, but, in some cases, had become so widespread and systematic as to "reach appalling levels of brutality."[40]

Capping a daylong ministerial-level meeting on women, peace, and security, the fifteen-member Security Council unanimously adopted Resolution 1820 (2008), which noted that "rape and other forms of sexual violence can constitute war crimes, crimes against humanity or a constitutive act with respect to genocide." It also affirmed the council's intention, when establishing and renewing state-specific sanction regimes, to consider imposing "targeted and graduated" measures against warring factions who committed rape and other forms of violence against women and girls. While most nations applaud and support the goals of these resolutions, there are virtually no mechanisms in place to enforce them.

Once the resolutions are passed and become part of the canon of international law, one of the challenges facing the international system is to determine how to implement those resolutions that are in place to protect civilians, especially women and girls.

Background of the Issue

When the United Nations was created, of the original fifty-one member states, "only 30 allowed women equal voting rights with men or permitted them to hold public office." However, the Charter of the UN refers to the "equal rights of men and women" and declared the UN's "faith in fundamental human rights" and "the dignity and worth of the human person."[41] These phrases suggested that working for the rights of women would be a critical part of the mission of this IGO and that the weight of the UN would ensure compliance by all countries.

> During the first three decades, the work of the United Nations on behalf of women focused primarily on the codification of women's legal and civil rights,

and the gathering of data on the status of women around the world. With time, however, it became increasingly apparent that laws, in and of themselves, were not enough to ensure the equal rights of women.[42]

Rather, the UN realized that there would have to be significant specific efforts made if there was to be true equality for women worldwide.

To begin to address this issue, the UN convened conferences specifically to develop strategies and action plans for the advancement of women. The First World Conference on Women was held in Mexico City in 1975 to coincide with International Women's Year. This was observed "to remind the international community that discrimination against women continued to be a persistent problem in much of the world."[43] The General Assembly also launched the United Nations Decade for Women (1976–1985) to open a broader dialogue on equality for women. At the first conference and each of the three subsequent ones, key objectives and a plan of action were set that would define the work of the UN on behalf of women.

Three critical objectives were set for the 1975 Mexico City conference: "1) full gender equality and the elimination of gender discrimination; 2) the integration and full participation of women in development; and 3) an increased contribution by women in the strengthening of world peace."[44] The conference adopted a World Action Plan that set guidelines for governments and the international community to follow in order to pursue the key objectives. It also set minimum targets to be met by 1980 "that focused on securing equal access for women to resources such as education, employment opportunities, political participation, health services, nutrition and family planning."[45]

One of the things that made the Mexico City conference unique was that women played a key role in shaping the discussions. Including the official delegations and a parallel NGO forum, approximately four thousand participants attended. Many of the official delegations were headed by women.

From the beginning, though, women were far from unified in their perspective on what should happen. For example, women from the Eastern bloc "were most interested in issues of peace, while women from the West emphasized equality and those from the developing world placed a priority on development."[46] In other words, the divisions among the women attending reflected their own national, political, economic, and social perspectives and experiences. Nonetheless, the conference was deemed a success because of its ability to set in motion a process that would unite women and the international system behind set goals that would benefit all women.

Within the UN framework, in addition to the Division for the Advancement of Women, the International Research and Training Institute for Women and the United Nations Development Fund for Women (UNIFEM) were also created. Then in 1979, the General Assembly adopted the Convention on the Elimination of All Forms of Discrimination against Women (CEDAW), which requires states to report regularly on steps they have taken to remove obstacles they face in implementing the terms of the convention. "By 2006, 182 states— over 90 percent of UN's membership—had ratified it. Many countries, including Uganda, South Africa, Brazil and Australia, have incorporated CEDAW provisions into their constitutions and national legislation."[47]

The second conference on women met in 1980 in Copenhagen specifically to review progress that had been made on the action plan. Despite the strides made since 1975, the Copenhagen conference "recognized that signs of disparity were beginning to emerge between rights secured and women's ability to exercise these rights." To address these, this conference identified three broad areas that would require focused action if the goals identified in Mexico City were ever to be achieved. These three areas were "equal access to education, employment opportunities and adequate health care services."[48]

Deliberations at the Copenhagen conference identified various factors that have kept women from achieving full rights. These included lack of involvement of men (decision makers) in improving women's roles and a shortage of women decision makers; lack of political will; lack of recognition of women's contributions and attention to women's needs; insufficient services, such as child care, that would help and support women; lack of financial resources; and lack of awareness on the part of women about opportunities. The Copenhagen Program of Action called for a set of measures that would address these factors in order to promote the status of women.

"The movement for gender equality had gained true global recognition as the third world conference on women, The World Conference to Review and Appraise the Achievements of the United Nations Decade for Women: Equality, Development and Peace, was convened in Nairobi in 1985."[49] The conference itself, combined with the parallel NGO forum, was seen as "the birth of global feminism" for the way it united women under the goals of equality, development, and peace. While this was seen as a positive development, the conference also brought to light how little had actually changed regarding improvements in the status of women. In general, women in the developing world had seen only marginal improvement at best. This suggested that most of the objectives identified earlier had not been met.

The conference developed and adopted the "Nairobi Forward-Looking Strategies to the Year 2000" as a blueprint for the future of women to the end of the century. "The Forward-looking Strategies for the Advancement of Women during the Period from 1986 to the Year 2000 set forth in the present document present concrete measures to overcome the obstacles to the Decade's goals and objectives for the advancement of women." The document explicitly recognizes the failures to that point, attributed in part to the economic crises affecting the developing nations that have impeded their ability to implement programs in support of women. And it was explicit in recognizing that full participation for women was essential to the development of all states:

> The role of women in development is directly related to the goal of comprehensive social and economic development and is fundamental to the development of all societies. Development means total development, including development in the political, economic, social, cultural and other dimensions of human life, as well as the development of the economic and other material resources and the physical, moral, intellectual and cultural growth of human beings.[50]

After identifying the obstacles to achieving the goals, the document then identified basic categories for achieving equality at the national level, although it was left up to individual governments to set their own priorities. First, "political commitment to establish, modify, expand or enforce a comprehensive legal base for the equality of women and men and on the basis of human dignity must be strengthened." This in turn would require legislation. Other categories were (2) social and cultural changes that would lead to equal access to education and training for all people; (3) along with legislation to improve the status of women, the need for educating the public and, if necessary, altering some of the social and cultural norms that worked against the advancement of women; (4) ongoing research about and collecting data to track the changing status of women within each country; and (5) fostering the equality of women in political participation and decision making at all levels of government by identifying and implementing strategies to enhance access for women. The document lists countless others, as well as identifying the obstacles to achieving these goals.[51] In effect, the document that grew from the conference asserted that all issues are women's issues and that society in general would benefit from an expanded role for women that could be achieved with true equality. From a levels-of-analysis perspective, the document provided a blueprint for what could and should be done at each level in order to achieve the stated goals.

By 1995, when the Fourth World Conference on Women was convened in Beijing, there was a renewed commitment to the empowerment of women globally. The conference adopted the Beijing Declaration and Platform for Action, which was an agenda for women's empowerment. It outlined twelve critical areas concerning women's lives: poverty, education and training, health care, violence against women, armed conflict, unequal access to resources (the economy), power and decision-making structures, the need for mechanisms to promote women effectively, a guarantee of human rights for women, access to means of communication and media, environmental concerns, and discrimination against female children.[52]

The Beijing Conference, therefore, allowed women to come together to raise a range of issues that affected them, and it gave governments the opportunity to commit to including a gender dimension to their institutions, policies, planning, and decision making. In endorsing this program for action, the UN General Assembly called upon all states, international organizations, and NGOs to begin to implement the recommendations in order to further the goals pertaining to equality for women.

UN Resolution 1325 grew in part out of the attention that the Beijing Platform for Action gave to armed conflict. In 1995 when the Beijing Conference was held, there was growing international attention given to the ethnic and civil conflicts that had emerged in the wake of the Cold War; the war in the Balkans, with its ethnic cleansing and the public attention given to women as refugees and as weapons of war, made apparent the concerns regarding the impact of conflict on women and children. Hence, the UN Security Council, in passing Resolution 1325, recognized both the impact of war on women and also the contributions that women could play in conflict resolution and in building sustainable peace. As a result, the Security Council affirmed

the important role of women in the prevention and resolution of conflicts and
in peace-building and stressing the importance of their equal participation and
full involvement in all efforts for the maintenance and promotion of peace and
security, and the need to increase their role in decision making with regard to
conflict prevention and resolution.[53]

However, even though it was unanimously adopted by the Security Council,
Resolution 1325 is virtually impossible to implement.

In further recognition of the impact of conflict on women, in 2008 the Security Council also passed Resolution 1820 against sexual violence in conflict.
Resolution 1820 builds on Resolution 1325 in that it reaffirms

the important role of women in the prevention and resolution of conflicts and
in peacebuilding, and stressing the importance of their equal participation and
full involvement in all efforts for the maintenance and promotion of peace and
security, and the need to increase their role in decision-making with regard to
conflict prevention and resolution.[54]

This resolution makes it clear that violence against women during conflict is
a war crime and that ultimately states are responsible for the behavior of their
citizens and for ensuring that such behavior does not occur. However, as was
the case with Resolution 1325, there really is no implementation or enforcement mechanism.

Despite the many conferences on women and the recognition of the roles
that women can and should play in resolving conflicts and in ensuring the
creation of a postconflict society that is safe for all people, the reality is that
women have not made progress in many of the areas identified. Furthermore,
the proliferation of ethnic conflicts has shown that women still suffer greatly
from the impact of conflicts and that they remain excluded from the decision
making that is central to the rebuilding of a conflict-torn society.

The resolutions that were passed made important political statements
about the treatment and role of women. However, they also made it clear
that ultimately it is the nation-state that is responsible for the behavior of its
citizens—to ensure that women and children are protected during wartime,
but even in peace to ensure that women have a say in the political processes
of the state and to set their own priorities. But they also note that eventually

there will need to be social and cultural changes within the nation-state if the role and responsibilities of women are ever to change significantly.

As noted in chapter 5, further attention was given to women by the UN first in the Millennium Development Goals (MDGs) and then in the succeeding Sustainable Development Goals (SDGs). Adopted by world leaders in 2000, the Millennium Development Goals were designed to ensure that all people benefit from "development." While helping women is inherent in all the goals, Goal 3, "Promote Gender Equality and Empower Women," is explicit in its call to action on behalf of women worldwide. One of the underlying principles of this goal is to "eliminate gender disparity in primary and secondary education, preferably by 2005, and in all levels of education, no later than 2015."[55] In addition to ensuring greater access to education for women and girls, this goal also addresses the need to increase the number of women employed in areas outside of agriculture, and also increasing the number and percentage of women who participate in government.

The successor Sustainable Development Goals that were adopted in 2015 and entered into force in January 2016 ask countries to go further than was outlined in the MDGs by working to end poverty and promoting prosperity for all while also protecting the planet. Thus these seventeen goals recognize that "ending poverty must go hand-in-hand with strategies that build economic growth and addresses a range of social needs including education, health, social protection, and job opportunities, while tackling climate change and environmental protection."[56] As was the case with the MDGs, addressing the needs of women and girls is implicit in virtually every goal; however, Goal 5 is explicit: Achieve gender equality and empower all women and girls. And it is also explicit that "gender equality is not only a fundamental human right, but a necessary foundation for a peaceful, prosperous and sustainable world."[57]

Like the other resolutions adopted by the UN specifically to enhance the role of women, the Sustainable Development Goals certainly stress the importance of gender equality starting with access to education. However, like the other resolutions addressed above, implementing the goals depends on countries, not all of which have the political will to see these goals through.

Thus, while women's rights as human rights have been a focus of international attention, there are no assurances that they will be achieved as long as they depend on individual countries, political systems, and decision makers to implement them.

Analysis of the Case

As we begin the analysis of this case, it is important to remember that it is not just a "women's issue," but the broader issue really is about basic human rights, which is a value that many states espouse and which pertains to human security writ large. In this case, though, we see the important role played by the UN (an IGO) and various NGOs in moving forward the issues pertaining to women. We also see the problems/challenges inherent in such an approach. Clearly, despite the support of the international system in passing these various resolutions, ultimately the impact will be limited unless or until nation-states take up the cause and make changes consistent with the implementation of the points made in these resolutions.

This points to a very important failing in the international system, especially pertaining to international law: the absence of any enforcement mechanism. It also reinforces the realist position that ultimately it will be up to individual nation-states to make policy determinations in their own best interest, and that they will conform to the dictates of international law when it suits them to do so. Clearly, this flies in the face of both the liberal and constructivist perspectives, both of which would advocate for cooperation in this issue, which reinforces an important value or norm. Liberals would see women's rights as an issue of human security that *should* be on the international agenda. Similarly, constructivists would draw attention to this norm as a way to influence and/or change both individual and state behavior. And the feminist theorists would support the importance of recognizing women and the role that they can and do play as actors in the international system.

This case also points out the relationships that exist among the various levels of analysis. Here we have an issue that was agreed upon by nation-states acting within an IGO and facilitated by NGOs, which ultimately would have an impact on groups of people within the state and would result in changes to the political, social, and cultural components of the state.

In this case, what we need to ask ourselves is what impact Resolutions 1325 and 1820 have actually had. The short answer is, not much beyond raising awareness of the issue. Since the passage of Resolution 1325, conflicts have continued to be resolved with little or no involvement by women. Similarly, since the passage of Resolution 1820, there have been numerous examples of civil conflict in which women and children were violated despite the protections that 1820 was supposed to offer. And in a globalized world with the media ubiquitous, the international community cannot say that they were unaware of the problems.

The feminist theorists would ask us to think about who makes the decisions and who has been affected by the decisions. These questions are especially relevant at a time when there seems to be a proliferation of civil conflicts, many of which have resulted in the displacement of civilians, especially women and children. And many of these conflicts have also changed the nature of warfare, where what might have previously been the protected domain of the home, which is generally seen as women's space, has become part of the battlefield. Suicide attacks do not distinguish between civilians and combatants as their victims, nor do pilotless drones. What had been private space has become public, as the battle lines have become blurred.

Perhaps an even more important question to think about at this point is, what happens after war ends? How is it possible for a society to rebuild and knit itself back together, unless all people, including women, are part of the peacemaking and peace-building processes? In many ways, it is questions like these that Resolutions 1325 and 1820 were designed to address. But implementing them requires decision makers to comply with the terms.

CASE 4: CHINA, REGIONAL OR GLOBAL HEGEMON?

Writing in 2001, realist thinker John Mearsheimer was prescient when he wrote about China. At that time, he wrote that "China is the key to understanding the future distribution of power in Northeast Asia."[58] And then he posited what would happen if (when) China's economy continues to grow and the country modernizes, both of which have since happened. He wrote at the time that

> we would expect China to attempt to dominate Japan and Korea, as well as other regional actors, by building military forces that are so powerful that other states would not dare challenge it. We would also expect China to develop its own version of the Monroe Doctrine, directed at the United States. Just as the United States made it clear to distant great powers that they were not allowed to meddle in the Western Hemisphere, China will make it clear that American interference in Asia is unacceptable.
>
> . . . it is hard to see how the United States could prevent China from becoming a peer contributor. Moreover, China would likely be a more formidable superpower than the United States in the ensuing global competition between them.[59]

As Mearsheimer predicted, China's rise as a major regional, if not global, power is perhaps one of the major challenges to security in the region for any number of reasons including raising questions about the power balance in the Pacific. China is highly integrated into the global economy in general, and the U.S. economy in particular, which to a large extent constrains the policy options available to the United States. On the one hand, a sound argument can be made that China's integration into and role in the world economy suggest that it is unlikely to engage in any armed conflict that would disturb that balance. On the other hand, though, China's recent actions in Asia, especially in the South China Sea, have resulted in tensions between China and the United States and its allies in the region, including South Korea, Japan, and the Philippines, but they also lead to the question of whether China's continued ascendency can remain peaceful.

Interestingly, China is one of the countries that has been especially helpful in dealing with the issue of climate change, taking a major role in the resolution of the Paris Agreement, and also regarding North Korea because of its unique relationship with that country. At a time when tensions between the United States and North Korea have been escalating, both sides have been looking to China to serve as intermediary and to help ratchet things down.

The cooperation on some pressing international issues can be balanced by China's aggressive behavior in the South China Sea. Like many other countries, China is trying to understand the United States and what its policies might be in the Trump administration. In fact, shortly after the election in 2016 a Foreign Ministry spokeswoman said, "China like every other country is closely watching the policy direction the US is going to take. Cooperation is the only right choice for both sides."[60] There is little doubt that this was directed especially to Trump's comments made during the campaign about China's role as a "currency manipulator" and its unfair trade practices. At that time, Trump also threatened to impose high tariffs, which would likely elicit a harsh response from China, which is buying aircraft from Boeing as well as farm exports from "red states" in the Midwest. China's concerns have been heightened by a number of Trump's appointments, especially that of Peter Navarro to head a newly created national Trade Council; Navarro has argued that "China's accession to the World Trade Organization in 2001 halved American economic growth and cost it 70,000 American jobs,"[61] claims that China, and other economists, have said are groundless and which have drawn a harsh response from China. At a time when tensions between the United States and China have been running high because of security issues, trade tensions will only make them worse.

Those tensions were exacerbated when Trump took a phone call from Taiwan's President Tsai Ing-wen shortly after his election in what was considered a major breach of U.S. policy regarding China. Further inciting confusion, Trump also said that he would meet with President Tsai should she be in the United States after he takes office. Although officials associated with Trump have indicated that there are no plans to alter the long-standing one-China policy, Chinese officials remain very concerned, especially given the unpredictable nature of the president of the United States.

Clearly China is in a unique position internationally, which it is willing to exploit for its own national interest.

Background of the Issue

Concerns about China's intentions in the region were echoed by Pacific countries at the Shangri La Dialogue in June 2016, a meeting of the defense ministers and ranking military officers of twenty-eight Asia-Pacific states. Initiated in 2002 by the International Institute for Strategic Studies (IISS), an independent think tank based in London, this meeting has become one of the most important arenas for discussion of security issues in the region. At that meeting, Admiral Sun Jianguo, deputy chief of the Chinese military's Joint Staff Department, "dismissed what he characterized as U.S. interference in Asian security issues, and rebuffed accusations that Beijing risked isolating itself through its assertive behavior and expansive claims in the South China Sea. 'We were not isolated in the past, we are not isolated now, and we will not be isolated in the future,' Adm. Sun said. . . . Instead, he criticized other countries for retaining a 'Cold War mentality' when dealing with China, saying they may only 'end up isolating themselves.'"[62]

According to published reports, Sun and other members of the Chinese delegation spent a great deal of time at the conference repeating China's territorial claims in the South China Sea. Some felt that their response was provoked by then–Defense Secretary Ashton Carter's comments that China was erecting a "Great Wall of self-isolation," while others thought that the bluster was designed for the domestic Chinese audience. And the comments made by Sun and others in the Chinese delegation did nothing to reassure other Pacific countries, such as South Korea and Japan, who are already suspicious of Chinese intentions in the region.[63] Sun's comments are consistent with the tone and substance of comments made by China's President Xi Jinping, who continues to promote "the Chinese dream."

China has been unapologetic in its expansion beyond Asia. In 2015, Xi Jinping visited more countries than President Barack Obama (fourteen against eleven for Obama), and he made his first trip to the Middle East early in 2016. He started in Saudi Arabia and then went on to Egypt and Iran; no Chinese president had been to the region since 2009.[64] While China certainly does not want to be embroiled in the conflicts in that region, it also has a big stake in what goes on there. China is the world's largest oil importer, getting more than half its crude oil from the Middle East. The "new Silk Road" linking China and Europe, made possible because of Chinese-funded infrastructure, runs across the Middle East. The visit was carefully designed to have Xi visit both Saudi Arabia and Iran at a time when tensions are high between the two countries, thereby reinforcing China's desired image as a "non-interfering champion of peace."[65]

Xi's desire to create a new Silk Road and the glory for China that went with it are born from the image of the "Pax Sinica," a time when "Chinese luxury items were coveted across the globe and the Silk Road was a conduit for diplomacy and economic expansion."[66] China's desire to create the new Silk Road has led China to invest in building a high-speed rail network linking the Greek port of Piraeus, the country's largest, to Hungary and eventually Germany. It is funding the creation of a highway in Pakistan as well. "In the first five months of this year [2016], more than half of China's overseas contracts were signed with nations along the Silk Road—a first in the country's modern history."[67] In June 2016, Xi visited Serbia and Poland, making deals for other projects in each country. Then Russia's President Putin paid a visit to China, and the two leaders promised to link infrastructure plans with the new Silk Road. In addition, finance ministers from about sixty countries held the first meeting in Beijing of the Asian Infrastructure Investment Bank (AIIB) created specifically to finance many of these projects.[68] China clearly is positioning itself to be a major economic and trade powerhouse globally, a position that it will exploit still further with the United States' exit from the Trans-Pacific Partnership (TPP).

The creation of this new Silk Road with China as a major player is an important goal to Xi, who sees this as a critical part of expanding China's commercial interests and soft power internationally. It is also consistent with the view that China faces a self-proclaimed "period of strategic opportunity," in which it sees a relatively benign security environment that China can use to achieve its aim of strengthening its global power without causing conflict.[69] It also fits with Xi's "Chinese dream" of recreating China's great past.

Another aspect of this plan that cannot be underestimated is that it poses a challenge to the United States and its thinking about world trade, which divides the world into two major trading blocs, a Trans-Atlantic and a Trans-Pacific one, and puts the United States in the center of each. However, China's vision creates Asia and Europe as a single space with ongoing trade between and among the countries, and in that vision it is China that is the focal point.[70] That represents another area of potential conflict with the United States.

It is also important to remember that China has been developing ties with countries in Africa, some of which, like Kenya, are part of the new Silk Road, and also in Latin America. In November 2016, Xi embarked on his third trip to that region since 2013 with a number of trade deals. Here, too, we see Xi's vision of China as the focal point of international trade and development as indicated by the change in China's trade patterns with Latin America. For example, in 2016 China bought a 23 percent stake in a Brazilian energy utility for about $1.8 billion. A Brazilian construction company signed a deal with China Communication and Construction Company International to build a port in Brazil's northeast state of Maranhão, and a Chinese investment company bought a controlling stake in an asset management company in São Paulo.[71] China has been focusing on four Latin American countries, all of which have left-leaning governments: Venezuela, Brazil, Argentina, and Ecuador, but it has been emphasizing its relationship with the business-friendly governments of Brazil and Argentina. It has also been establishing more bilateral free-trade agreements with countries in the region.

China sees an opportunity with the death of the TPP. Specifically, "China is hoping to use a meeting in Peru of 21 Pacific Rim economies to boost the prospects of its TPP-alternative, the Regional Comprehensive Economic Partnership, which includes India and Japan, but not the United States."[72] For China, these relationships are about far more than trade but are about developing a "strategic partnership" that would counterbalance U.S. interests in Latin America, much as China sees the United States as staking a claim with its allies in East and Southeast Asia. This also potentially puts the United States and China on a collision course in still another region.

Ties between the United States and China have been difficult, to say the least. In June 2013, President Obama invited then-new President Xi Jinping to an informal summit. This meeting was seen as a critical one, coming early in Xi's presidency. Billed as an "informal" summit (no neckties), the two men were scheduled to spend two days at an estate in Rancho Mirage, California. Obama was said to be encouraged by Xi's willingness to tackle tough economic reforms, and Xi indicated his willingness to work with the United States on climate change issues, a priority for Obama, and on bringing North Korea in line. Since that meeting, China has given numerous signals that it will not only chart its own course but would do so even if it alienates other countries, including the United States. Much of this became very clear in spring 2015 when China began dredging on some of the reefs in the South China Sea that it has claimed. This island-building effort in order to create more military bases in the area is not necessarily new, as other countries have attempted to do this as well, albeit on a much smaller scale. In addition to the scale of the project, the pace has been threatening to other countries in the region. Recently published high-resolution satellite imagery has documented China's rapid buildup of installations that have military uses.[73] Although China's ambassador to the United States said that his country would act "with restraint" in the South China Sea, he also noted that the country had to defend its own interests. At its meeting in April 2015, the twenty-eight nations of the Association of Southeast Asian Nations (ASEAN) issued a strongly worded statement calling the island-building effort "a potential threat to 'peace, security and stability.'" And during a meeting in Washington with Japan's Prime Minister Shinzo Abe, President Obama expressed "concern" at what the Chinese were doing and accused them of "flexing their muscles."[74]

The future direction of China will depend to a large extent on Xi Jinping—formally appointed state president in March 2013 and reappointed at the Communist Party Congress in October 2017—and his relationship with Donald Trump. To many China watchers, what was especially telling was the focus of the annual National People's Congress (NPC), which was held in March 2016. At the opening session, Prime Minister Li Keqiang announced that China had met all of the economic targets that it had set five years ago for completion by this year. Another senior official told reporters that China would not suffer a "hard landing," in spite of declining economic growth and an increase in the budget deficit.[75] In his talk, Prime Minister Li announced a target range of between 6.5 percent and 7 percent growth, which is modest by China's standards but still very respectable. Attaining this will require various stimulus measures, which Li hinted about. However, the longer term is more problematic because of a "complicated and challenging international environment" and declining global trade.[76]

Under Xi's predecessor, Hu Jintao, the middle class grew, and with it came a relatively stable economic situation in the country. This same middle class, which now has access to information through the Internet, is also the basis for dissent. Where social media has enabled the government to monitor public opinion and identify potential problems before they become real threats to the Party, it has also spurred the development of NGOs, a more vibrant civil society, and groups that have found a way to unite in dissent. Coupled with this has been demographic changes; plunging birth rates and an aging population have caused other sorts of social and political issues for the government. While Xi has tried to present himself as a reformer, his crackdown on dissent belies that image.

One area in which China has made progress is the environment. One of the main points Li made at the NPC in March 2015 that really resonated both domestically and internationally was the government's pledge to control smog and other forms of pollution. This has been a problem not only in China but for neighboring countries as well that are affected by the bad air. The Chinese government has started to crack down on polluters, enacting environmental measures that include closing offending industries such as mills, factories, and quarries. Even small family-owned businesses are not immune to air pollution restrictions or the punishments if they don't comply. Cleaning up the air, especially in the capital city of Beijing, has become a political priority. "Chinese leaders have been embarrassed by the damage caused to China's international image by the city's relentlessly grey skies. They worry that the smog could fuel dissatisfaction with the government and undermine stability in the capital, as well as affect their own and their families' health."[77] The neighboring province of Hebei has been blamed for much of the smog in Beijing; since the start of 2013, it has been reported that Hebei has closed down eighteen thousand state-run factories, the focus of much of Prime Minister Li's attacks.

In September 2015, the government announced plans to launch a national carbon-trading scheme in 2017 aimed at reducing greenhouse gas emissions. China was also a critical player in securing the climate change deal in Paris in 2015. And on March 5, 2016, China announced that its new five-year plan "would include a target to cap annual energy consumption at a tough-sounding 5 billion tons of coal equivalent by 2020, up from 4.3 billion now."[78] This is consistent with China's slowing GDP rates, which will help it achieve these targets. In addition, statistics show that China's CO_2 emissions have already started to fall as the country continues to increase its reliance on renewable energy sources, such as solar and wind. China already invests more in these than the United States and Japan combined.[79] "China believes its security might be threatened if it becomes overly dependent on imported fossil fuels, and it wants to reduce the smog created by coal-burning because it is causing public anger and many premature deaths. Between 2010 and 2014, non-fossil fuel energy generation capacity increased by 73 percent."[80]

The real question that many are asking is where does China see its own position in the world at this point? A number of years ago, a senior colonel argued that "China should regain its position as the most powerful nation in the world, a position it had held a thousand years before its humiliation."[81] Henry Kissinger, writing in his own book, suggests that this view reflects "at least some portion of China's institutional structure."[82] It is also clear, however, that China's aggressive foreign policy stance has caused concern for a number of countries. Asia in general, and China in particular, are playing an ever more important role in current international politics and economics. As one of five permanent members on the UN Security Council, China is able to wield even more power internationally. This can be seen not only with its stance regarding the South China Sea, but also in the major role it has been playing regarding North Korea and Iran and, more recently, Syria. China is a model for developing countries that also hope to be able to wield power and influence internationally. Yet, as a number of recent events have pointed out, there are some serious issues and challenges that lie just below the surface.

The first face-to-face meeting between Xi and Trump took place in April 2017 at Trump's club, Mar-a-Largo, in Florida. Despite all the campaign rhetoric about China being a currency manipulator and tough talk about trade, all reports were that the meetings went quite well. In fact, the two countries announced their plans to continue the high-level strategic dialogue initially started during the administration of George W. Bush. Subsequent to that in-person meeting, the two leaders have spoken by phone periodically, specifically about the rising tensions caused by North Korea and its ongoing missile tests. As North Korea's major and perhaps only ally, China is in a unique position to help ease tensions on the Korean Peninsula. In their phone calls, Xi has urged Trump to show restraint regarding North Korea, an admonition made in response to Trump's hostile tweets about North Korea. Xi realizes that he is in a unique position to mediate between the United States and North Korea, but he also realizes that the stakes are high in case of failure.

Analysis of the Case

This case focused on China as a nation-state that potentially could shift the global balance of power. Each level of analysis, from the individual leader through the culture and society to the government and nation-state, must be involved if we are to truly understand not only China's place in the world today but also, perhaps more important, where it sees itself heading. Here, not only are Mearsheimer's speculations valuable but also those of Graham Allison, who more recently wrote about China's rise and what that might mean for the United States in particular and world politics in general. In fact, Allison asserts that "the world has never seen anything like the rapid tectonic shift in the global balance of power created by the rise of China."[83] And he explains the ways in which China has been able to use various economic instruments to achieve its geopolitical goals, which he refers to as "geoeconomics."[84] What is especially important has been the way in which China has been able to conduct its foreign policy because of its economic strength, which in turn has also allowed it to build its military.

How is all this possible? Again, here we have to start with decisions made by the individual leaders, most recently President Xi Jinping, who, since coming to office as president in 2013, was able to build on the base created by his predecessor into the China we see today. Where Xi has been especially effective, as Allison notes, is that as he and other leaders of the country have become unhappy with existing international economic institutions, such as the IMF and World Bank, they have been extremely effective at creating their own alternative ones. For example, when the United States refused to accommodate China's request for a larger share of votes at the World Bank, China created its own competing institution, the Asian Infrastructure Investment Bank (AIIB). In this case, we have the individual leader creating a new international organization that would allow China to have further economic advantages, something that the countries of the West had been doing for decades through the Bretton Woods institutions. This is all part of Xi's goal to make China great again. And just to be clear, that did not refer to making China a global superpower, but only to allowing China to regain its regional dominance.

We see changes at the level of culture and society that have encouraged the Chinese to support its leaders, even in the absence of political reform. For example, as the country developed and industrialized, it did so at the expense of the environment. But a more affluent and educated citizenry started to demand change. Over the past twenty-five years, NGOs have flourished "to convey the concerns of the people, participate in co-governance to address problems together with the government and the market, and deliver social services."[85] This marks a dramatic shift in the way the peoples' views are being expressed and heard on a range of issues, including the environment, food and water safety, and health issues, to name a few. However, China's NGOs cannot interfere with national security.

Xi serves as general secretary of the Communist Party of China and chairman of the Central Military Commission, as well as president of the People's Republic of China, and therefore his vision guides the direction of the government. So, in this case, there is a close correlation between the individual and the government, which normally would serve as distinct levels of analysis.

And of course what this case is really about is the way in which China's policy changes, directed by a strong leader and a compliant government, have enabled that nation-state to take its place on the world stage in a way that furthers its national interest.

Before we move on to the conclusion, there is one more point that needs to be made that makes this case especially salient. While there is little doubt that China is acting in its own self-interest to maximize power (realist thinking), it has also played a major role in facilitating international agreements, such as the Paris Climate Change Agreement, and also served as a mediator to help minimize conflict in the case of North Korea. One could argue that these are liberal, cooperative ventures. Clearly, they further China's interests, but they also have a beneficial impact internationally. And one could also argue that this would not have been possible had it not been for structural changes both nationally and internationally, as seen through the eyes of social constructivist theory.

LESSONS OF THE CASES: UNDERSTANDING INTERNATIONAL RELATIONS IN A GLOBALIZED WORLD

The purpose of these cases was not only to introduce you to some important global issues but to show you clearly how difficult it is to deal with them. When you started reading each of these issues, I am sure you already had your own point of view. After all, who could not be in favor of ensuring a clean environment? Issues pertaining to the movement of people can be more complicated, but you probably still had your own bias and perspective as you started. And who could not be for expanding the role of women internationally, especially if it would help stabilize a war-torn country and therefore minimize the risk of future violence? Finally, in the fourth case, it is logical to ask questions about China's intentions as well as its role in a world that seems to be changing rapidly. But as you can see from studying these cases, different theoretical perspectives make different assumptions about the role of the nation-state and the desired outcomes. And examining the cases from different levels of analysis will also lead you to draw very different conclusions.

As noted at the start of this chapter, the same type of analysis could be done for virtually any current international issue, whether it pertains to the traditional view of security or human security. Pick up a major newspaper any day, and you will see examples of these issues. The civil war in Syria: who is fighting, who is suffering, and what impact has it had on neighboring Turkey, not to mention the dangers should the war spread and envelop the region? A war of words between the United States and North Korea has also raised issues about the value of diplomacy versus the threatened use of military might. And the increasing tensions between those two countries has once again put China into a unique position to help mediate, thereby further strengthening its role internationally. A study on climate change scheduled to be released in fall 2017 illustrates clearly the conflict between politics and policy in the United States; however, that could also be true of virtually any (democratic) nation. These examples are drawn from the news of just a few days in August 2017, and any of them could be developed further into a case or issue to study that could help illustrate the reality of contemporary international relations.

So what do the cases we included here tell us about international relations in a globalized world? First, they remind us that there are many actors to consider, both within and outside the nation-state, which in turn makes it more difficult to arrive at easy or set answers about how to address current global issues. All of these actors can play a role in any policy decision or in implementing policy. Often they work at cross-purposes, which means that what might appear to be a sound policy decision does not get implemented. And, as we have also seen, in the international system without any form of global governance, implementing any decision is virtually impossible unless states want to do so.

Second, these cases show us how the borders between nation-states have broken down as countries have become more interdependent. It is not only the easy movement of people that is a result of these transparent borders. We also see increased trade patterns leading to economic interdependence, which in turn has broken down some of the old distinctions between the developed and developing countries and, along with that, has brought a changing understanding of which countries truly are powerful. But another aspect of this interdependence is the rapid flow of information. Media coverage is virtually instantaneous now, not only through the established media outlets like CNN, but also through cell phones and Twitter. As we saw in the revolutions that swept the Arab world in spring 2011, even repressive states have a difficult time controlling the flow of information.

Third, we learned that these global issues are raising important questions about the role of the nation-state as the central actor in international relations. Clearly, these cases illustrate the role of IGOs and NGOs in influencing policy, even in those cases where the policy requires or presumes a change in the political, cultural, and/or social levels within the nation-state. We can argue that the third case, the changing role of women, stresses the continued sovereignty of the nation-state, as the policy changes advocated by the UN resolutions would not/could not be implemented without state compliance. On the other hand, there are far more actors, both within and outside the state, who can bring pressure to ensure compliance. This is a relatively new concept and one that suggests rethinking the nature of the traditional approach to understanding the role of the nation-state as the primary actor.

Fourth, we learned that although there are flaws in the traditional levels-of-analysis approach to understanding international relations as envisioned when the approach was articulated decades ago, it still provides a framework that allows us to answer some important questions. By understanding the flaws or weaknesses in the approach, which should have become relatively apparent here, we can be better prepared to address them, thereby ensuring that we can arrive at a more complete picture of or answer to the questions or issues discussed. Furthermore, we have yet to arrive at a comprehensive theoretical framework to replace it as a starting point for analysis.

Fifth, we saw clearly how the different theoretical perspectives diverge in their understanding of issues, perspectives, and approaches to the international system and the actors within it. And as is the case with the levels-of-analysis approach (above), we can also identify more readily the weaknesses or failings in these approaches.

And sixth, we have seen how power relationships between and among nation-states can shift quickly. A change in policy by one nation can have an impact on the balance of power internationally, as we have seen with the shifting relationship between the United States and China.

We concluded chapter 1 by noting that "understanding IR in a globalized world also means going beyond the traditional state-centered approach that the field has often had. We need to be able to see the limits of that approach and to expand our understanding and definitions in order to incorporate the roles of nonstate actors."

As you have learned the fundamentals of IR and how to understand some of the questions inherent in this approach to political science, we hope that you will now be better able to pick up a newspaper and understand why a state did what it did and the ways in which others responded. You should now be able to understand more about the ongoing discussions of trade pacts and why they are important. You should be better able to analyze why war broke out within a country and how that conflict can be resolved in a way that can help ensure peace rather than future conflict.

Is this easy to do? No. But you should now have the tools to be able to do all this and more. And as you are doing this and arriving at your own answers to some of these fundamental questions, you should also be able to determine whether you are a realist in your thinking or a liberal, or whether you can formulate your own approach that will help you describe, explain, and perhaps even predict international relations in a globalized world.

FURTHER READINGS

Much of the information for these cases was drawn from UN documents, which present the best starting point for specific international agreements. The specific references are listed in the notes. The UN home page is http://www.un.org/en.

It is also possible and often wise to get the perspectives of a particular country or organization. For example, the European Union website (http://europa.eu/index_en.htm) provides an excellent starting point in understanding EU policies and the evolution of those policies.

For U.S. policies on many of these issues, a good starting point is the State Department website at http://www.state.gov. This includes U.S. policy regarding other countries and also U.S. policy on a range of international issues. Virtually every country has a similar resource that is easily accessed.

And the role of reputable mainstream newspapers, such as the *New York Times*, *Los Angeles Times*, *Washington Post*, and *Wall Street Journal*, cannot be minimized as sources for "real" facts.

NOTES

1. See Jacob Poushter and Dorothy Manevich, "Globally, People Point to ISIS and Climate Change as Leading Security Threats," Pew Research Center, August 1, 2017, http://www.pewglobal.org/2017/08/01/globally-people-point-to-isis-and-climate-change-as-leading-security-threats/?utm_source=Pew+Research+Center&utm_campaign=8a6ded1530-EMAIL_CAMPAIGN_2017_08_02&utm_medium=email&utm_term=0_3e953b9b70-8a6ded1530-399479813.

2. "Kyoto Protocol," http://unfcc.int/kyoto_protocol/items/2830.php.

3. United Nations Framework Convention on Climate Change, http://unfccc.int/2860.php.

4. "The Cancun Climate-Change Conference: A Sort of Progress," *The Economist*, December 18, 2010, 16.

5. "Climate-Change Diplomacy: Back from the Brink," *The Economist*, December 18, 2010, 121.

6. "Climate-Change Talks: Wilted Greenery," *The Economist*, December 3, 2011, 74.

7. "A Deal in Durban," *The Economist*, December 17, 2011, http://www.economist.com/node/21541806.

8. John M. Broder, "Climate Talks in Durban Yield Limited Agreement," *New York Times*, December 11, 2011, http://www.nytimes.com/2011/12/12/science/earth/countries-at-un-conference-agree-to-draft-new-emissions-treaty.html.

9. Thomas Kerr, "Outcomes from the Doha UN Climate Meeting: What You Need to Know for 2013," *Huffington Post*, March 4, 2013, http://www.huffingtonpost.com/thomas-kerr/outcomes-from-the-doha-un_b_2397134.html.

10. World Bank, "Climate Change Report Warns of Dramatically Warmer World This Century," November 2012, http://www.worldbank.org/en/news/feature/2012/11/18/Climate-change-report-warns-dramatically-warmer-world-this-century.

11. United Nations Intergovernmental Panel on Climate Change, "Climate Change 2014: Synthesis Report," 1, http://www.climate-service-center.de/imperia/md/video/csc/syr_ar5_spmcorr1.

12. Coral Davenport, "Nations Approve Landmark Climate Accord in Paris," *New York Times*, December 12, 2015, https://www.nytimes.com/2015/12/13/world/europe/climate-change-accord-paris.html.

13. Michael D. Shear, "Trump Will Withdraw U.S. from Paris Climate Agreement," *New York Times*, June 1, 2017, https://www.nytimes.com/2017/06/01/climate/trump-paris-climate-agreement.html.

14. Steve Erlanger, Alison Smale, Lisa Friedman, and Julie Hirschfeld Davis, "World Leaders Move Forward on Climate Change, without U.S." *New York Times*, July 8, 2017, https://www.nytimes.com/2017/07/08/world/europe/group-of-20-climate-change-agreement.html.

15. Charles K. Ebinger, "6 Years from the BP Deepwater Horizon Oil Spill: What We've Learned, and What We Shouldn't Misunderstand," Brookings Institution, April 20, 2016, https://www.brookings.edu/blog/planetpolicy/2016/04/20/6-years-from-the-bp-deepwater-horizon-oil-spill-what-weve-learned-and-what-we-shouldnt-misunderstand.

16. John M. Broder, "Blunders Abounded before Gulf Spill, Panel Says," *New York Times*, January 5, 2011, http://www.nytimes.com/2011/01/06/science/earth/06spill.html.

17. U.S. Department of Justice, "BP Exploration and Production Inc. Agrees to Plead Guilty to Felony Manslaughter, Environmental Crimes and Obstruction of Congress Surrounding Deepwater Horizon Incident," November 15, 2012, https://www.justice.gov/opa/pr/bp-exploration-and-production-inc-agrees-plead-guilty-felony-manslaughter-environmental.

18. U.S. Department of Justice, "Transocean Agrees to Plead Guilty to Environmental Crime and Enter Civil Settlement to Resolve U.S. Clean Water Act Penalty Claims from Deepwater Horizon Incident," January 3, 2013, https://www.justice.gov/opa/pr/transocean-agrees-plead-guilty-environmental-crime-and-enter-civil-settlement-resolve-us.

19. A Pew research poll published in 2015 showed that more Mexicans have been leaving the United States than coming into the country, a pattern that started in 2009.

This includes children who were born in the United States and who are American citizens. This change in migration patterns can be attributed to a number of reasons. But it is important to note that the trend predates the Trump administration. Ana Gonzalez-Barrera, "More Mexicans Leaving than Coming to the U.S." Pew Research Center, November 19, 2015, http://www.pewhispanic.org/2015/11/19/more-mexi cans-leaving-than-coming-to-the-u-s.

20. UN High Commissioner for Refugees, "2013 Country Operations Profile: Africa," http://www.unhcr.org/pages/4a02d7fd6.html.

21. See World Bank Group, "Migration and Remittances, Recent Developments and Outlook," April 2017, http://pubdocs.worldbank.org/en/992371492706371662/MigrationandDevelopmentBrief27.pdf.

22. Remarks by William Lacy Swing, director general, International Organization for Migration, September 22, 2010, General Assembly Hall, United Nations Head-quarters, New York, http://www.un.org/en/mdg/summit2010/debate/IOM_en.pdf.

23. Remarks by Swing, September 22, 2010, General Assembly Hall, United Na-tions Headquarters, New York, http://www.un.org/en/mdg/summit2010/debate/IOM_en.pdf.

24. UN Secretary General, "Message to Global Forum on Migration and Develop-ment," November 8, 2010, Puerto Vallarta, Mexico, http://www.un.org/esa/popula tion/migration/openingremarks-sg-puertovallarta.pdf.

25. This information comes from Jenna Johnson and Abigail Hauslohner, "'I Think Islam Hates Us': A Timeline of Trump's Comments about Islam and Muslims," *Washington Post*, May 20, 2017, https://www.washingtonpost.com/news/post-poli tics/wp/2017/05/20/i-think-islam-hates-us-a-timeline-of-trumps-comments-about -islam-and-muslims/?utm_term=.c2af10a926f1.

26. Chris Graham, "Who Won the Dutch Election and What Does It Mean for Geert Wilders and the Far-Right in the Netherlands and Europe?" *The Telegraph*, March 16, 2017, http://www.telegraph.co.uk/news/2017/03/16/won-dutch-election -does-mean-geert-wilders-far-right-netherlands.

27. See "Dutch Election: European Relief as Mainstream Triumphs," BBC News, March 16, 2017, http://www.bbc.com/news/world-europe-39297355.

28. Giada Zampano, Liam Moloney, Jovi Juan, "Migrant Crisis: A History of Displacement," *Wall Street Journal*, September 22, 2015, http://graphics.wsj.com/migrant-crisis-a-history-of-displacement.

29. Euan McKirdy, "UNHCR Report: More Displaced Now than after WWII," CNN, June 20, 2016, http://www.cnn.com/2016/06/20/world/unhcr-displaced-peo ples-report.

30. McKirdy, "UNHCR Report."

31. UNHCR, "Searching for Syria," updated May 30, 2017, http://www.unhcr.org/en-us/syria-emergency.html.

32. See "Europe's Challenge: Strangers in Strange Lands," *The Economist*, September 12, 2015, 24.

33. "Germany's Refugee Crisis: Merkel at Her Limit," *The Economist*, October 10, 2015, 51.

34. "Germany's Refugee Crisis," 51.

35. "Nice Truck Attack: French Police Arrest Eight More Suspects," *The Guardian*, September 20, 2016, https://www.theguardian.com/world/2016/sep/20/nice-truck-attack-french-police-arrest-eight-new-suspects.

36. Richard Winton, "A Year after the San Bernardino Terror Attacks, the FBI Is Still Struggling to Answer Key Questions," *Los Angeles Times*, December 1, 2016, http://www.latimes.com/local/lanow/la-me-san-bernardino-terror-probe-20161130-story.html.

37. For more background on this, see the "Schengen Agreement," https://www.schengenvisainfo.com/schengen-agreement.

38. UN Security Council Resolution 1325 on Women, Peace and Security, October 31, 2000, http://www.un.org/events/res_1325e.pdf.

39. UN Security Council Resolution 1820 on Eliminating Violence against Women and Girls, June 2008, http://www.securitycouncilreport.org/atf/cf/%7B65BFCF9B-6D27-4E9C-8CD3-CF6E4FF96FF9%7D/CAC%20S%20RES%201820.pdf.

40. UN Department of Public Information, "Security Council Demands Immediate and Complete Halt to Acts of Sexual Violence against Civilians in Conflict Zones," http://www.un.org/News/Press/docs/2008/sc9364.doc.htm.

41. United Nations, Division for the Advancement of Women, "The Four Global Women's Conferences, 1975–1995: Historical Perspective," http://www.un.org/womenwatch/daw/followup/session/presskit/hist.htm.

42. United Nations, Division for the Advancement of Women, "The Four Global Women's Conferences."

43. United Nations, Division for the Advancement of Women, "The Four Global Women's Conferences."

44. United Nations, Division for the Advancement of Women, "The Four Global Women's Conferences."

45. United Nations, Division for the Advancement of Women, "The Four Global Women's Conferences."

46. United Nations, Division for the Advancement of Women, "The Four Global Women's Conferences."

47. Sanam Naraghi Anderlini, *Women Building Peace: What They Do, Why It Matters* (Boulder, CO: Lynne Rienner, 2007), 14.

48. United Nations, Division for the Advancement of Women, "The Four Global Women's Conferences."

49. United Nations, Division for the Advancement of Women, "The Four Global Women's Conferences."

50. "Report of the World Conference to Review and Appraise the Achievements of the United Nations Decade for Women: Equality, Development and Peace," Nairobi, July 15–26, 1985, http://www.un.org/womenwatch/confer/nfls/Nairobi1985 report.txt.

51. See "Report of the World Conference to Review and Appraise the Achievements of the United Nations Decade for Women."

52. See Anderlini, *Women Building Peace*, 15; and United Nations, Division for the Advancement of Women, "The Four Global Women's Conferences."

53. UN Security Council Resolution 1325.

54. UN Security Council Resolution 1820.

55. United Nations, "Millennium Development Goals and Beyond 2015: Fact Sheet," http://www.un.org/millenniumgoals/pdf/Goal_3_fs.pdf.

56. United Nations, "The Sustainable Development Agenda," http://www.un.org/sustainabledevelopment/development-agenda.

57. United Nations, "Goal 5: Achieve Gender Equality and Empower All Women and Girls," http://www.un.org/sustainabledevelopment/gender-equality.

58. John Mearsheimer, *The Tragedy of Great Power Politics* (New York: Norton, 2001), 397.

59. Mearsheimer, *The Tragedy of Great Power Politics*, 401.

60. Quoted in Mark Magnier, "China Weighs Approach to Trump," *Wall Street Journal*, December 23, 2016, A8.

61. Magnier, "China Weighs Approach to Trump."

62. Chun Han Wang, "Maritime Spat Simmers as U.S., China Talk," *Wall Street Journal*, June 5, 2016, http://www.wsj.com/articles/u-s-china-trade-barbs-over-south-china-sea-at-shangri-la-dialogue-1465133442.

63. See Chun Han Wang, "Maritime Spat Simmers."

64. "China's Foreign Policy: Well-Wishing," *The Economist*, January 23, 2016, 38.

65. "China's Foreign Policy: Well-Wishing,"38.

66. "Foreign Policy: Our Bulldozers, Our Rules," *The Economist*, July 2, 2016, 37.

67. "Foreign Policy: Our Bulldozers, Our Rules,"37.

68. "Foreign Policy: Our Bulldozers, Our Rules,"37.

69. See Xu Jian, "Rethinking China's Period of Strategic Opportunity," China Institute of International Studies, May 24, 2014, http://www.ciis.org.cn/english/2014-05/28/content_6942258.htm.

70. See "Foreign Policy: Our Bulldozers, Our Rules,"38.

71. "Latin America and China: A Golden Opportunity," *The Economist*, November 19, 2016, 27.

72. "Latin America and China: A Golden Opportunity," 28.

73. "The South China Sea: Making Waves," *The Economist*, May 2, 2015, 37.

74. "The South China Sea: Making Waves,"37.

75. See "The National People's Congress: Unlucky for Some," *The Economist*, March 12, 2016, 42.

76. "The National People's Congress: Unlucky for Some,"42.

77. "Pollution: The Cost of Clean Air," *The Economist*, February 7, 2015, 41.

78. "Carbon Emissions: Aiming Low," *The Economist*, March 12, 2016, 43.

79. See "Carbon Emissions: Aiming Low,"44.

80. "Carbon Emissions: Aiming Low,"44.

81. "Chasing the Chinese Dream," *The Economist*, May 4, 2013, 25.

82. "Chasing the Chinese Dream," 25.

83. Graham Allison, *Destined for War: Can America and China Escape Thucydides's Trap?* (New York: Houghton Mifflin Harcourt, 2017), xvi.

84. Allison, *Destined for War*, 20.

85. Carolyn Hsu, Fang-Yu Chen, Jamie P. Horsley, and Rachel Stern, "The State of NGOs in China Today," Brookings Institution, December 15, 2016, https://www.brookings.edu/blog/up-front/2016/12/15/the-state-of-ngos-in-china-today.

Glossary of Key Terms

affective biases. The impact of emotions as they affect policy decisions that are made.

alliances. A union of two or more countries that agree to coordinate policy in order to achieve common goals, generally to ensure greater security.

anarchy. A situation in which the major actors in the international system are not subject to any rules or regulations and therefore behave solely in their own interests.

Arab Spring. A reference to the series of uprisings that swept many of the countries in the Middle East and North Africa in 2011.

balance of power. The assumption that conflict will be minimized and therefore peace maintained when military power is distributed roughly equally, thereby preventing any country from dominating.

bipolarity. The assumption that there are two major centers of power and that the power between them is roughly balanced. Most of the period of the Cold War was bipolar.

Brexit. The term given to the decision by the UK to exit the European Union following a national referendum in June 2016.

BRIC. An acronym for the countries of Brazil, Russia, India, and China, all of which have emerged as major international players. When they act together, as they have in a number of areas (along with South Africa, BRICS, and sometimes Nigeria), they can be a powerful bloc in the international system.

capabilities. Materials and resources that a country has relative to other countries and is willing to use in order to achieve its desired goals or ends.

CEDAW. The Convention on the Elimination of All Forms of Discrimination against Women (CEDAW) was passed in 1979, and it is seen by many as the international bill of rights for women.

civil war. Any armed conflict that takes place *within* the state. This might be due to ethnic, religious, nationalist, tribal, or other conflicts between and among different groups of people within the nation-state.

CNN effect. The expectation of ongoing media coverage, 24/7, of events such as conflicts.

coalition of the willing. As opposed to the more formal *alliance*, a group of countries that come together for a specific purpose. The term was widely used to describe the group of countries that joined together to fight Saddam Hussein in 1991 after Iraq's invasion of Kuwait.

cognitive biases. Systematic biases or distortions in thinking that affect policy decisions.

Cold War. The period that extended roughly from the end of World War II (1945) until the breakup of the Soviet Union in 1991, which was characterized by tension between the United States and its democratic allies in Western Europe and the Soviet Union and its client states in Eastern Europe. The Cold War was a period of political, economic, and military rivalry and competition between the two sides, each of which sought to balance the power of the other.

collective defense. Variant of the concept of collective security, but with the assumption that there will be alliances made up of nations that pool their power or capabilities in order to balance the power of other states or alliances.

collective security. A formal relationship of nation-states that hopes to keep peace by deterring any act of aggression with the knowledge of a collective military response.

common good. Something that affects all countries and peoples and does not know or respect borders. For example, ensuring a clean environment is a common good that requires countries to work together.

conflict. Disagreement over interests or desired outcomes that may be settled peacefully or lead to war.

conflict spiral. A situation often found during a crisis when decision makers overestimate the hostile intentions of the adversary while underestimating their own hostile intentions. The crisis situation exacerbates this interaction, which then contributes to an ongoing sense of crisis.

constructivist theory (also known as "social constructivists"). A major theoretical approach in international relations that assumes that states are critical players, but that their actions and behaviors are socially constructed or affected by the system(s) in which they operate. It assumes that states will act upon their own constructions of reality.

core interests. The values that tie directly to a country's security and are central to its national interest.

credibility. The perception of a country's willingness to use its resources to achieve its desired goals or ends.

cultural imperialism. The imposition of one set of global norms or values on another country or group.

cyberterrorism. The hacking of computers for the purpose of violating security, disrupting business or commerce, or for other illicit reasons.

democratic peace. The notion that democratic countries are more peaceful because they do not go to war against other democratic countries.

dependency theory. The idea that the poorer countries of the developing world (also known as the "third world") would remain tied to and dependent upon, as well as exploited by, the major developed countries.

developing countries. A category that is used by the World Bank to identify low-income countries, defined as those with a gross national income (GNI) per capita of $1,005 or less in 2016.

diplomacy. The formal process of interaction among the members of the international system, carried out by diplomats who are asked to implement a country's policy.

disintegration. The competing forces that result in the breakup of a country into other smaller entities that then seek statehood, either relatively peacefully (e.g., Czechoslovakia and the Soviet Union) or because of major armed conflict, as seen with the former Yugoslavia.

empire. An entity composed of many separate units, all of which are under the domination of one single power that asserts political and economic supremacy over the units, all of which accept that relationship. One of the goals of an empire is to perpetuate itself and to continue to expand its domain and therefore its wealth. All wealth and allegiance flow from the separate units to the central power, usually the emperor.

engagement. A foreign policy orientation that allows the country to be actively involved with a range of countries and with the members of the international system.

ethnic cleansing. The systematic extermination of one group by another (i.e., genocide), often with the approval and support of the state.

Eurocentric. Putting Europe at the center of the discussion or analysis.

European Union. A regional bloc of twenty-eight sovereign states that united first economically and then more broadly to create a common foreign and security policy.

euro zone. An economic and monetary union of seventeen of the EU countries that have agreed to adopt the euro as their common currency.

"fake news." The disavowal of news presented by the mainstream media with an alternative interpretation offered (also known as "alternative facts" or "alt facts").

feminist theoretical perspectives. A relatively recent approach which suggests that it is impossible to understand international relations without addressing the role that gender plays in making decisions. It asks who is affected by the decisions that are made and, more broadly, "Where are the women?"

foreign policy orientation. The particular type of foreign policy decision made by a country that should, theoretically, further its national interest. These include isolationism, unilateralism, neutrality and nonalignment, and active engagement.

free rider. The idea that since others will act to create a common good, it is not necessary for any individual actor to join in, since they will benefit from the work of the others at no cost to themselves or expenditure of resources.

gender-sensitive lenses. If we are to get a more complete picture of international relations, we need to refocus our questions and approaches specifically to include women in our analysis.

genocide. The systematic extermination of one group of people by another.

geoeconomics. The use of various economic instruments that will allow a country to achieve its geopolitical goals.

globalization. The assumption that all states and international actors interact and are interdependent in some way.

government. The entity within the nation-state that is responsible for ensuring the collective well-being and security of the state and the people within it.

groupthink. The tendency for members of a group to suppress dissent in order to arrive at a single decision.

"guns versus butter." The descriptor that suggests that a state can fund the military (guns) *or* the society (butter), but that often it is not possible to do both and that, therefore, there is a trade-off.

hard power. The use of a country's military power to influence events or the outcome of decisions.

hegemon. A state with the predominance of power, thereby enabling it to dominate political, economic, and/or political relations.

human security. A broad set of issues necessary to human survival such as protecting the environment, freedom from hunger, access to potable water, and so on.

integration. The merging of ideas and policies so that individual sovereign states start to blend into a unified whole. This can result in larger regional blocs, such as the European Union.

intergovernmental organizations (IGOs) (also known as "international organizations" [IOs]). Organizations that have nation-states as their members and represent regional groupings, such as the EU, or the international system, such as the UN. Some have been created for a specific purpose, such as the collective security of their members (NATO), while others are broader in scope. Within these organizations, nation-states work together to pursue common policies on behalf of the whole that are not seen as infringing upon the sovereignty of the individual nations.

International Monetary Fund (IMF). An organization of 188 countries that work together to help stabilize the international economic system. It was established in 1945 and grew from the Bretton Woods meetings, which brought representatives of forty-five countries together to arrive at a framework for international economic policies that would minimize the possibility of another Great Depression.

international political economy (IPE). The study of the intersection of politics and economics that focuses especially on the distribution of power and resources.

international relations. A field of study within political science that addresses the relationships between and among actors in the international system and the impact of decisions made by any one actor on another actor or other actors.

international system. The framework for international relations in which the system itself is composed of nation-states and nonstate actors that interact in some way and, in so doing, affect the behavior of one another.

ISIS. An extremist militant group known as Islamic State in Iraq and Syria. It is also known as ISIL (Islamic State of Iraq and the Levant) and by its Arabic name, Daesh.

isolationism. The foreign policy orientation that has a country turn inward and minimize political or military involvement with other countries.

just war doctrine. The moral criteria that states should use when going to war, in fighting a war, and in ending a war.

Kyoto Protocol. An international agreement negotiated in Kyoto, Japan, in 1997 that extended the UN Framework Convention on Climate Change and set targets for reducing greenhouse gas emissions.

legitimacy. The notion that political power ultimately rests with the people, who then accept the leader or government. Thus, political power is derived from "the consent of the governed."

levels of analysis. An approach to understanding international relations by breaking down the various actors who are involved with the making of international relations decisions and the impact of those decisions on the various actors.

liberal theory. A major theoretical approach to understanding international relations that grows from the confluence of economics and politics and believes that all states will benefit from the flourishing of free trade and the open exchange of ideas. It also assumes that countries will benefit from cooperating with one another and advocates pursuing policies that are in the "common good." This is also known as the pluralist approach.

"Long Peace." One of the ways in which the Cold War has been referred to, in part because of the relative stability that came with a bipolar balance-of-power system that ensured peace between the superpowers.

Marxism. Theory derived from Karl Marx and the assumption that there is an inherent conflict that exists within and across societies and even nations that pits the "have-nots" against the "haves." Marxist theory suggests that economic factors shape a country's relationships, with the richer oppressing the poorer. Inherent in this is the idea that those who are oppressed by the dominant (capitalist) economic system will rise up against it.

Millennium Development Goals (MDGs). Eight goals adopted by 191 member states in 2000 that commit national leaders to work to combat poverty, hunger, disease, illiteracy, environmental degradation, and discrimination against women, using 2015 as a target year for achievement of these goals.

monolithic actors. The assumption that states will behave as if they were one single entity rather than as many individuals and groups.

multinational corporations (MNCs). Major corporations or companies that are based in one country and do business of some kind in at least one other country.

multipolar system. A system in which there are a number of power centers with alliances shifting among them. This is perceived as the least stable type of system.

nation. A group of people with similar background, culture, ethnicity, and language who share common values.

national interest. A defined goal that furthers what is best for the country and guides that country's foreign policy decisions. States should be able to define what is in their national interest before they can act.

nationalism. Commitment to a central (national) identity or consciousness rather than loyalty to the ruler or the state. Hence, a situation where the primary loyalty of the group rests with the nation (the peoples and the group) at the expense of the state.

nation-state (also known as a "country"). A two-pronged concept that embodies the concepts of the *nation* and the *state*. A nation-state is made up of a group of individuals who live within a defined territory and under a single government. Together, they form a society that has certain values and beliefs in common. Generally referred to as a country. See **nation** and **state**.

negotiation. A dialogue or process of give-and-take on a particular issue that will result in an agreement that both or all sides can accept. This is an important tool of foreign policy used by allies as well as adversaries in the hope of reaching an agreement or arriving at common ground.

neutrality. The decision not to commit a country's military forces or engage in a military or security alliance with other countries. This orientation recognizes that the country has special status within the international system and that other countries should respect, and not infringe on, that neutrality.

nonaligned. A status designated during the Cold War, when some countries declared that they would not politically or militarily support either the Soviet Union or the United States.

nongovernmental organizations (NGOs). Organizations that operate across international borders whose members are individuals, rather than countries or nation-states. Often they try to influence policy or advocate for an issue that transcends international borders, such as the environment or human rights. Some NGOs also provide humanitarian and/or medical aid and assistance in the event of natural disaster or catastrophic events, such as earthquakes or tsunamis.

nonstate actor. An actor, entity, or group of any kind (e.g., terrorist group, MNC, or international organization) that is not a unique nation-state but plays a role in the international system and in international relations.

North American Free Trade Agreement (NAFTA). An agreement signed by the United States, Mexico, and Canada to create a trilateral trade bloc among the countries of North America. It went into effect in 1994.

North Atlantic Treaty Organization (NATO). A formal alliance created in 1949 to unite the United States with the democratic countries of Western Europe and Canada in order to deter a Soviet attack. The heart of the NATO treaty is Article 5, which states that an armed attack on any one member would be considered an armed attack against all, which embodies the notion of collective defense.

Paris Climate Change Agreement. Signed by 195 countries in Paris in November 2015, with a goal to limit the increase in the average global temperature to below two degrees Celsius above preindustrial levels and also that countries individually will pursue a goal of zero net emissions,

peace. A situation characterized by an absence of hostility and also by feelings of trust, a sense of security, and cooperation among peoples.

peace building. The actions that take place following the end of a conflict that contribute to strengthening and rebuilding the government structure and institutions in order to prevent conflict in the future.

peacekeeping. The efforts of third parties, such as the United Nations, to keep warring parties apart so that they do not continue to resort to hostilities. Peacekeeping forces may be inserted during the process of negotiating an end to a conflict. UN peacekeeping forces are often known as "blue helmets" because of their headgear.

peacemaking. The process of ending an armed conflict and resolving the issues that contributed to the conflict in the first place.

polycentric. An international system in which there are many national or regional centers of power.

power. The ability of one actor to influence another or to influence the outcome of events in order to achieve desired ends. Power is one of the central concepts in international relations.

proxy wars. During the Cold War, battles between the United States and the Soviet Union that were fought indirectly, through allies, rather than directly, thereby minimizing the risk of major nuclear confrontation.

"rally round the flag." A recognized phenomenon where a crisis galvanizes public support for the political leader.

rapprochement. Diplomatic term meaning a policy to reestablish a positive relationship.

rational actor. The assumption that an actor makes decisions based on a rational decision-making process.

rational decision making. The assumption that decisions will be made based on a logical process that allows for the assessment of choices, weighing of costs and benefits, and review of alternatives before arriving at a final decision that will further the actor's self-interest.

realist theory. One of the major approaches to understanding international relations, which assumes that states are the center of the international system and that all states will make decisions based on their national interest, which is defined by power.

Realpolitik. A German term that refers to foreign policy tied primarily to power and to maximizing power. It also refers to practical responses to specific political circumstances or events.

regime change. The expressed interest of one country to support the change of leadership in another country.

revolutionary movements. Seen primarily during the Cold War, the emergence of military movements whose goal was to overthrow the existing political order and replace it with a different one that was often more radical.

security. Ensuring the safety and protection of the people and the continuation of the state.

security dilemma. A situation in which one state improves its military capabilities in order to ensure its own security, but in so doing becomes a direct threat to another country, which responds with its own military buildup. The result is military buildup and feelings of insecurity and threat rather than protection.

self-determination. The desire for a people to be recognized as a nation that is able to govern itself. The belief that each group of people should be allowed to determine who is responsible for leading or governing them.

smart power. The ability to combine hard and soft power in order to influence policy.

soft power. Influencing others through cooperation or co-option by drawing on common values, ideals, and shared cultural norms.

sovereignty. Within any given territory, recognition of the government as the single legitimate authority. No external power has the right to intervene in actions that take place within national borders. The authority is derived from a monopoly over the legitimate use of force. The concept originates with the Treaty of Westphalia (Peace of Westphalia).

state. An entity with a defined border under the rule of a governmental structure that is accepted by the people within the border.

state-centric. The assumption that the nation-state or country is the primary or critical actor, thereby dismissing the roles of other (nonstate) actors.

stateless people. A group of people who seek to create their own state with defined borders and a government that is sovereign. They often have the trappings of statehood, including a governmental structure and a single dominant nation, but they do not see themselves as part of any existing state. The Palestinian people are one example of this group, as are the Kurds, who straddle a number of different countries.

structural adjustment programs (SAPs). Economic programs that impose specific spending restrictions on governments, especially pertaining to social welfare, health care, and education programs, while encouraging expenditures in other areas, such as for infrastructure, which should lead to economic growth.

structural violence. A situation in which violence and inequality are built into and are a part of the structure of a particular political system, which results in the unequal distribution of resources, opportunity, and power.

Sustainable Development Goals (SDGs). Successor to the Millennial Development Goals, the SDGs are a set of seventeen goals that were adopted in 2015 that would help end poverty and increase prosperity for all while also protecting the planet.

theory. A linked set of propositions or ideas that simplify reality in order to describe events that have occurred, explain why they happened, and predict what might happen in the future.

threat. The perception that a country, people, or way of life is under attack either by an external actor, a group, or even an idea within a country. A threat can be military, economic, political, or even cultural, such as when there is a perceived attack on values.

transnational actors. Another name for the broad group of nonstate actors that operate across national borders.

Trans-Pacific Partnership (TPP). A comprehensive trade agreement among twelve Pacific states signed in February 2016. In January 2017, U.S. president Donald Trump announced that the United States would withdraw from the agreement.

Treaty of Westphalia (Peace of Westphalia). Treaty of 1648 that ended the Thirty Years' War in Europe. The concepts of the modern nation-state and sovereignty have their origins in this document.

UNHCR. United Nations High Commissioner for Refugees, a UN organization created in 1950 specifically to deal with the number of people displaced by World War II. The UNHCR continues to address refugee crises around the world as they arise.

unilateralism. A foreign policy orientation that advocates a policy of political and military detachment but acknowledges the need to interact with other countries in a range of areas, such as economics and trade.

war. Acts of armed violence either within or across states involving two or more parties, designed to achieve a specific objective or outcome.

World Bank. Created as part of the Bretton Woods system (like the International Monetary Fund) and originally designed to help facilitate the rebuilding of Europe after World War II. It subsequently expanded to provide loans to developing countries and to promote foreign direct investment in those countries.

world systems theory. A theoretical perspective that claims that the world is divided not just into rich and poor and developed and less developed states, but into a core of strong and well-integrated states and a periphery of states that depend on a largely unskilled labor pool. The assumption is that the core group of nations exploits those at the periphery.

Index

Wilders, Geert, 243

Wilson, Woodrow, 31, 56–59, 92, 97–98

Wilsonian idealism, 57–59

women: citizenship of, 120n32; DDR process and, 116; democracy and, 137–38; essentialization of, 73, 74; IGOs and, 192; in IR and IR theory, 9, 13, 26, 54, 69–72; and marriage, 120n32; as migrants, 242; MNCs and labor conditions for, 214–15, 216; NGOs and, 196, 198–99; peace associated with, 70–74, 109, 110–11, 205; political roles of, 45–46, 167n15, 249; and public vs. private realms, 45–46, 73, 137–38; and Soviet disintegration, 155; as terrorists, 204–5; UN actions concerning, 181, 196, 221n18; war and, 9, 108–9, 120n32, 254–55. *See also* feminist theory; women's rights

Women in Black, 142

women's rights, as human rights, 228, 249–58

World Bank, 184–86, 233–34, 267

world systems theory, 68

World Trade Organization (WTO), 20

World War I, 91–92, 103

World War II, 92, 243

Xi Jinping, 261–67

Yanukovych, Viktor, 147–48

Youngs, Gillian, 36

Yugoslavia, 17, 84, 84–85, 149–50

Zakaria, Fareed, 82

About the Author

Joyce P. Kaufman is professor of political science and director of the Center for Engagement with Communities at Whittier College. She is the author of *A Concise History of U.S. Foreign Policy*, 4th ed. (2017) and *NATO and the Former Yugoslavia: Crisis, Conflict, and the Atlantic Alliance* (2002) and coeditor with Andrew M. Dorman of *The Future of Transatlantic Relations: Perceptions, Policy, and Practice* (2011) and *Providing for National Security: A Comparative Analysis* (2014). She is also the author of numerous articles and papers on U.S. foreign and security policy. With Kristen Williams, she is coauthor of *Challenging Gender Norms: Women and Political Activism in Times of Crisis* (2013), *Women and War: Gender Identity and Activism in Times of Conflict* (2010), and *Women, the State, and War: A Comparative Perspective on Citizenship and Nationalism* (2007) and coeditor of *Women, Gender Equality, and Post-Conflict Transformation* (2017). She holds a BA and MA in political science from New York University and a PhD from the University of Maryland.